Palisades.
Pure Romance.

Fiction that features credible characters and
entertaining plot lines, while continuing to uphold
strong Christian values. From high adventure
to tender stories of the heart, each Palisades
Romance is an undiluted story of love,
from beginning to end!

D1052676

A PALISADES HISTORICAL ROMANCE

STONEHAVEN

AMANDA MacLEAN

PALISADES

This is a work of fiction. The characters, incidents, and dialogues are products of the author's imagination and are not to be construed as real. Any resemblance to actual events or persons, living or dead, is entirely coincidental.

STONEHAVEN
published by Palisades
a part of the Questar publishing family

© 1995 by Amanda MacLean
International Standard Book Number: 0-88070-757-7

Cover illustration by George Angelini
Cover designed by David Carlson and Mona Weir-Daly
Edited by Paul Hawley

Printed in the United States of America

ALL RIGHTS RESERVED
No part of this publication may be reproduced, stored in a retrieval system, or transmitted, in any form or by any means—electronic, mechanical, photocopying, recording, or otherwise—without prior written permission.

For information:
QUESTAR PUBLISHERS, INC.
POST OFFICE BOX 1720
SISTERS, OREGON 97759

95 96 97 98 99 00 01 02 — 10 9 8 7 6 5 4 3 2 1

To Carolyn Coker

Your unfailing encouragement, infinite patience,
and extraordinary skill as fiction-writing midwife
brought to life this work, those preceding it,
and those that will follow.

Thank You.

In your unfailing love you will lead
the people you have redeemed.
In your strength you will guide them
to your holy dwelling.

You will bring them in and plant them
on the mountain of your inheritance—
the place, O LORD, you made for your dwelling,
the sanctuary, O LORD, your hands established.

Exodus 15:13, 17

Out of
the West

One

❧

New Mexico Province
Spring 1847

Sixteen-year-old Callie St. Clair rounded the bend above the arroyo, the wind flying through her red curls, as she urged Darley into a full gallop.

Moments earlier the bay mare had loped across the mountain meadow, away from Jeremiah and Sun Jones's cabin. Callie wanted a few minutes alone to enjoy the fresh smell of the mountain springtime and the warmth of the morning sunlight against her fair skin.

And so she urged the horse onward, lifting her face with eyes closed, not caring about the freckles she knew would soon grace her nose. Now that Callie lived in the mountains of New Mexico, instead of on Stonehaven, the Mississippi plantation of her childhood, she had inwardly declared she'd had enough of the vanities embraced by Southern belles, or former Southern belles. At least, that's what she told herself each day as she pulled on leather britches instead of a pretty gown and covered her feet with boots instead of dainty dancing slippers.

Callie had tried to keep the freckles from appearing by wearing her father's old felt field hat during the two-month trek west on the Santa Fe trail. But it hadn't helped. Afterward, the first time she examined her face in a looking glass, she had scowled at the new dusting of spots, then yanked the hat from atop her thicket of red curls and sailed it as far as she could.

It had been more than a month since her sister Juliana and Parker James had said their vows in front of a preacher, then left on their wedding trip to Santa Fe. Since that time, Callie had stayed with the trapper Jeremiah and his Mandan wife, Morning Sun, pitching in on their small farm. She had already helped Sun plant a kitchen garden by the light of a full moon. And now, following the Indian woman's instructions, each morning she gathered seedling plants and herbs from the meadow and nearby piñon forest for medicines and seasonings.

Callie nudged her heels into the bay's flanks, urging the mare to move even faster along the curving trail leading away from the meadow. With eyes closed, she tucked her head into the horse's neck, relishing the rhythm of movement and the thrill of Darley's surefooted speed.

After a few minutes, Callie felt rather than heard the pounding of other hooves on the trail. Just as she identified what she was hearing, she rounded a curve above a steep drop-off overlooking the arroyo.

Her eyes flew open. The rider of the other horse, which was a black whose mouth frothed from hard riding, shouted and reined his horse away from the bay.

The black reared backward, poised for a moment on its hind legs, screaming in protest.

Darley bolted sideways from the trail, tried to get up, stumbled, then half-slid, half-tumbled into the arroyo. Callie yelled words of surprise and anger at the stranger as she rolled from the horse.

For a moment after Darley hit the bottom of the arroyo, there was no sound but the bubbling of the creek a few feet away.

From her sprawling, prone position, Callie raised her head

and looked for the bay. Darley whinnied softly, and after a few tries on wobbly limbs, stood. Callie drew in a deep, shaky breath, did a quick assessment of her own limbs, then sat and dusted herself off.

"Are you all right?" The rider who had been on the black stood on the trail about fifty feet above her.

Am I all right? Callie muttered under her breath. *I just fell down a cliff and my horse is stuck at the bottom of an arroyo, and he wants to know if I'm all right?* She glared up the bank toward the rider, then stood and brushed more dust from her britches.

The man didn't wait for an answer but started down the steep incline toward her. Though at first she couldn't see his face, Callie could tell by his build and the way he moved that he was younger than she had first thought. He was dressed in city clothes, a well-cut dark coat and pants and fancy boots that were getting less fancy minute by dusty minute. His dress reminded her of the clothing men wore at Stonehaven. For the briefest moment she felt a pang of homesickness.

She smoothed her shirt and trousers the best she could, then with her fingers brushed her hair from her face as he slid the rest of the way down the bank.

Before she could say a word, the young man spoke. "Do you always ride with your eyes closed?"

"I thought you came down here to see if I was hurt—not to give me a lecture on riding."

"You're obviously not injured." His ice-blue eyes assessed her. "I could tell that from up there." He jerked his thumb toward the top of the arroyo.

"Well, then why did you bother—?"

He raised an eyebrow but said nothing.

"—bother coming down here, I mean, if you could see I hadn't been hurt."

"I came down to see about the horse," he muttered, then headed further down the incline to the place where Darley stood by the stream. He rubbed his hands gently over the mare's legs, neck, and back, speaking to her in a soft voice. Then, without a word to Callie, he led Darley by the reins, slowly, surely, up the incline.

The young man didn't look at Callie as he led Darley past her. He simply spoke to the mare in that same soothing voice, steadily moving her toward the trail.

Callie, growing more irritated by the moment, placed her hands on her hips, glaring at the stranger with each arrogant step he took away from her.

"Excuse me!" she finally yelled. "Where do you think you're going with my horse?"

The stranger didn't answer. He didn't even glance her direction.

She shouted at him again. "I said, where're you going with my horse?"

By now the man had reached the top of the arroyo. With Darley's reins still in hand, he turned and looked down the incline as if assessing some interesting creature in the wild. Then he turned, tied Darley's reins to a piñon branch, and remounted the black. Without a backward glance he nudged his horse to a gallop and rode down the trail.

"What do you think you're doing? Wait! Come back here!" Callie yelled, but the horse and its rider were out of shouting distance. His only answer was the billow of dust he left rising in the warm air. Darley whinnied softly as the sound of the black's hooves faded into the distance.

Callie pushed a strand of hair from her face, then studied her surroundings. Both sides of the arroyo fell in steep cuts to the stream below. Prickly brush abounded. Clumps of beavertail cactus covered much of the hill back up to the trail.

She looked at her palms; they were scraped and dirtied with drying blood. One pant leg had ripped when she tumbled off Darley, and she could see a deep purple welt rising on her shin. She poked at it, sniffling noisily as it began to throb with pain. The more she thought about the ruffian who'd done this to her, the more annoyed she became. How dare this insolent, arrogant, downright ill-mannered stranger run her off the trail? How dare he take care of her horse, then leave her injured at the bottom of the arroyo?

Callie began the arduous crawl upward through cactus and sagebrush. The day had warmed and she felt her face flush with heat and exhaustion as she dragged her injured leg through the dust. She finally reached the place where Darley was tethered and painfully swung herself into the saddle.

On the ride back to Sun and Jeremiah's meadow cabin, Callie tried to keep her mind off her injured limbs and pride by planning what she'd say to the insensitive boor if she ever saw him again.

Callie rode into the meadow an hour later, slid from Darley's saddle, hefted it astraddle the pasture fence, then led the horse to the tall grasses just beyond the cabin. Moments later she stormed through the doorway, delighted to find an audience—Sun and Jeremiah—sitting at the kitchen table across from the large stone fireplace in their cozy three-room cabin.

Sun looked up in surprise at Callie's abrupt entry. "What's happened, child?"

Callie felt tears of self-pity spring to her eyes. She stuck out her scraped and bleeding hands for them to see. They both frowned and murmured words of comfort. Jeremiah stood and stoked the fire in the nearby fireplace, then fetched warm water and a cloth to clean the wound.

Callie, now seated next to Sun, began her tale.

"I met this brute on the trail," she sniffed. "It was terrible. I've never seen such a barbarian. First his horse—a wild black creature—reared, forcing Darley to fall into the arroyo. I went over the side with her—"

Jeremiah was now dabbing at the abrasions on Callie's palm. She narrowed her eyes and flinched, though her tale went on uninterrupted. "We tumbled and rolled. I fell off, of course." She stood and demonstrated how she landed, lifted her pant leg and showed Sun the shin injury. Sun said she would make a warm herbal poultice that would take the swelling right down.

Callie sat at the table again and went on with her story. "Then—" she paused dramatically. "This rude stranger had the gall to ignore me completely."

"Didn't he ask if you were all right?" Jeremiah asked, incredulous.

"Well, yes, he did—but I could tell he wasn't sincere. He made his way into the arroyo. He didn't even look my direction." Callie sniffled again. "When he got to the creek at the bottom, he checked Darley to make sure she wasn't injured. The fact was, he checked her so thoroughly you would've thought the savage was a doctor."

Suddenly, Callie sensed the presence of someone behind her. Jeremiah and Morning Sun looked up, both smiling brightly at a place beyond Callie's shoulder and into the adjoining room.

The word *doctor* she'd just spoken, the image of the stranger examining the horse, and the expressions on Sun and Jeremiah's faces converged, telling Callie who was standing behind her.

Jeremiah spoke first, a not-so-subtle smile of knowing on his face. "Callie, there's someone we'd like you to meet."

Callie glanced at Morning Sun's face. It was alight with wonder and love as she gazed at the person standing behind Callie.

Groaning to herself and knowing full well what was coming, Callie took a deep breath.

"May we introduce our son, Jedediah?" Sun's voice was filled with pride as she looked at him. "Though he prefers to be called Hawk, his Mandan name."

Callie turned. Before her stood the stranger who'd run her off the trail. But she couldn't remember a word she'd planned to say.

She pushed back her chair and stood, dumbfounded, taking in everything about him, from his sun-streaked hair to his high-chiseled cheekbones and skin the color of the mesa sands. Then their eyes met, and his, the color of New Mexico skies, seemed to touch some hidden place inside her.

"I'm pleased to meet you," Hawk finally said. His expression held a secret merriment.

She tilted her chin and gave him what she hoped was a withering look.

Hawk didn't seem to notice and stuck out his hand. "I'm pleased to finally make your acquaintance," he repeated. "I've heard so much about you."

Callie ignored his gesture. "I can't shake hands with you. I've been injured." Her tone was cold.

His expression changed imperceptibly, though he continued to watch her.

She went on. "Some ill-mannered stranger ran me and my horse off the trail."

"Ill-mannered?" he repeated. "That's odd. I just met someone of that same description."

Callie ignored him. "The brute left me injured and suffering to fend for myself. Anything could have happened. It was, in my thinking, a hostile and unforgivable act."

"You strike me as the type who needs no one to fend for her—"

19

She glared at him speechless, because he was right.

"I've always felt"—Hawk went on, his handsome jaw cocked at an arrogant angle,—"that those people who blame others for their own mistakes should be left to find solutions for themselves."

Callie clenched her jaw, feeling her face redden. Suddenly she felt Sun's gentle touch on her arm and remembered that Hawk was her friend's son. Callie was a guest in this house, so she bit back the scathing words she was ready to spout. And she could see that Jeremiah had given Hawk a warning frown. He too fell silent.

"Come, let's sit down." Jeremiah nodded toward the table, and the three seated themselves while Sun fixed coffee.

Jeremiah began to question Hawk about his journey from St. Louis. And Sun asked about his mentor, Dr. Noble Jackson Hill. Hawk's expression softened as he turned to his parents and began to speak of his work with Dr. Hill as the physician prepared him for entrance to Harvard.

Callie watched Hawk as he spoke. How could this gentle-speaking, attentive man be the same insufferable boor she'd met on the trail? It had to be an act, she decided. And judging from Sun and Jeremiah's loving responses, they obviously didn't know their son's true nature.

Hawk seemed to sense her stare and, with a quizzical arch of one eyebrow, briefly held her gaze. Again Callie noticed the hidden amusement in his expression. But his look also held something else. Something indefinable. Something dangerously exciting and wonderful.

No, Callie told herself. She had to be wrong. Surely he couldn't fool her as he had Sun and Jeremiah.

Then Hawk smiled at her for the first time. It was as if she had suddenly stepped into a pool of liquid sunshine. The warmth of it filled her with a secret joy.

It no longer mattered that she had decided moments earlier never to forgive him for his behavior on the trail.

All that mattered was that Callie wanted to bask in the light of his smile forever.

Two

New Mexico Province
Winter 1848

I suppose you think the black is faster than Darley," seventeen-year-old Callie challenged, narrowing her eyes at Hawk, who rode beside her on the meadow trail. A light snow fell and Callie pulled the hood of her coat over her curls as she spoke. "Since that first day"—she had no doubt that he knew the time she referred to—"you've thought him the better mount. Probably because he wasn't the one to fall down the cliff when we collided."

Without acknowledgment or change in expression, Hawk kept his gaze straight ahead. For a moment Callie thought he hadn't heard her, then she saw a smile play at the corner of his mouth.

"I've never assumed the black was the better horse." Hawk's tone was sarcastic. He still didn't turn to look at her.

"But you think it. You just can't admit it." Callie took delight in disturbing Hawk's calm demeanor. In her opinion the young man was much too serious and arrogant.

Hawk let out an exasperated sigh and finally turned to meet her challenging gaze. Removing his hat, he brushed the snow from his hair. "You're determined to race me, aren't you, Callie

St. Clair?" The smile was gone. "You'd like to show me that a woman can outdo a man—whether it's in horse racing, house building, or reading Chaucer."

So he had noticed. Callie felt herself color. Since Hawk had arrived home for the winter holiday, Callie, pointedly making him aware she'd not forgiven him for their first encounter, took pleasure in ignoring him: lifting her chin loftily when he entered a room, reading while he described his studies with Dr. Hill, yawning when he related his travels.

But this past week had forced a change in her demeanor. She could no longer ignore Hawk: The two young people had been asked by Parker, Juliana, Sun, and Jeremiah to help them add a nursery onto their cabin.

Not to be outdone, Callie had turned to a different tactic: She matched Hawk's work nail for pounded nail. If he climbed a ladder to fill a hole between the logs, Callie climbed higher on hers. If he filled the spaces between three logs each hour, Callie filled four.

"I have no idea what you're talking about," she said with a sniff. "As if I'd bother trying to 'outdo' you." They rode in silence for a few minutes. They had come to an open place on the trail. Ahead stretched the snow-covered meadow. At the far end stood Sun and Jeremiah's cabin, and a short distance beyond, the tall fences of their corral.

Hawk reined the black to a stop and studied the scene for a moment. Then he cocked an eyebrow in Callie's direction.

She halted Darley and pulled the hood from her hair. Squinting, she measured the distance to the corral, figuring what Hawk had in mind. It was about a half mile. The snow fell faster now, nearly obscuring her visibility. "How many jumps?"

"We'll take all three fences."

Callie drew a deep breath, then grinned and nodded. Darley

could easily clear the obstacles. She'd done it dozens of times before, though not in the snow.

"All right. On three." Callie bent low in the saddle to reduce the wind resistance, setting her knees tight to Darley's back, holding the reins tight against the horse's neck. "I'm ready," she murmured, keeping her eyes on the farthest fence.

"One...two...*three!*" Hawk shouted, then kicked the black to a gallop.

Callie jabbed her heels into Darley's flanks and the horse responded with a powerful and fluid motion. Neck and neck, the two horses raced down the trail.

Hawk pulled away from Darley, first by one length, then by two.

Callie nudged Darley into a harder gallop. She was gaining on the black but couldn't overtake him.

Callie squinted into the rapidly flying snow. The wind stung her face; flakes stuck to her eyelashes. She kicked Darley again. The horse leapt forward. In a moment, she overtook the black.

Hawk spoke softly to his horse. *Indian words,* Callie thought. The black responded and again pulled ahead.

"Come on, girl," Callie whispered into Darley's ear. "Come on. You can do it. You can do it." But the black continued to pull away from Callie and her horse, his hooves kicking up chunks of snow that flew into Darley's path.

Callie pressed her heels harder into the horse's flanks. "Let's go, girl. Faster, girl! Faster." The distance closed between Darley and the black. Finally, they were side by side, galloping in unison. For a brief moment, Callie felt the beauty of the horses' mutual power and rhythm. Then gradually, Darley seemed to hit her stride and pulled ahead. A half length. A whole length. Then two.

Darley flew like the wind into the rapidly falling snow. She was breathing hard now and steam rose from her nostrils. Callie kept the pressure on her flanks, feeling beneath her the horse's power-filled gait. She didn't glance back to measure the distance between Darley and the black. She just kept her body bent low, her face close to Darley's neck, moving as one with the horse.

They neared the cabin, then passed it. Callie's eyes were nearly blinded with the cold sting of the snow.

The first fence loomed ahead. She could hear the black's pounding hooves closing in on them. Darley sprung into the air.

Hawk shouted to the black. He rose from the ground at the same instant Darley cleared the fence.

Side by side in parallel gait, the stallion and the mare raced to the second jump. Up and over. Hooves pounding, horses breathing hard, warm breaths showing in the frigid air.

Then the black, in a mighty burst of power, pulled ahead.

Callie urged Darley forward. "Faster, girl. Come on. Faster," she urged. But the stallion kept the lead.

The final jump rose ahead. The horses thundered toward it.

Callie sensed something was wrong just seconds before they reached the last fence.

The black seemed to break stride.

Callie squinted into what was now turning into a blizzard.

A movement to the side of the trail caught her attention. Then a rabbit in its snowy winter coat skittered in front of the black.

Callie gasped as Hawk's stallion whinnied and reared in terror. The horse slammed into the fence instead of jumping.

Hawk flew from his saddle. For a moment that seemed to last an eternity, he tumbled through the air, his limbs flailing wildly. Then he landed on his back on the other side of the jump. The black whinnied again and turned back toward the cabin, hooves pounding through the snow.

Quickly reining Darley to a halt, Callie dropped from her saddle. She scrambled over the fence, her heart pounding in fear.

Eyes closed, Hawk lay motionless, sprawled prone in the snow.

She knelt beside him. "Oh, no," Callie whispered. She tore her gloves from her hands and stroked his cold cheek with her fingers. "Oh, Hawk. I'm sorry." She felt under his jaw, searching for a pulse.

It was there. She drew a ragged and thankful breath. Though the rhythm was rapid and irregular, his heartbeat was stronger than she expected. Tears filled her eyes as she gazed at his face. "Oh, God," she whispered. "Please let him be all right."

Callie knew that she had to get him out of the snow, which was falling faster now than before. She couldn't carry him; she couldn't even lift him onto Darley's saddle. Besides, his injuries might worsen if she moved him. A cursory check told her that his limbs seemed to have survived the fall. But she worried that he might have broken his back or his neck.

The thought of such an injury brought fresh tears. What if Hawk died? It would be her fault. She had challenged him to the race. They both had been mad to attempt it in this snowstorm.

What would she do without him? Though she pretended annoyance at his every arrival, she lived for the day when the young man would again ride across the meadow, hair gleaming in the sun, bronzed face alight with life. And when he had finally come and his eyes met hers, something inside Callie leapt with secret pleasure.

She looked at him, lying still and pale in the snow. She would have to ride for help. Pulling her woolen cape from her shoulders, she gently covered his body and took his limp hand in hers. "Oh, Hawk. Please wake up," she whispered frantically. "I can't bear to leave you like this. Please, please...."

26

Suddenly, Hawk's cold fingers wrapped firmly around hers. The strength in them was not that of a dying man.

Callie's gaze flew to his. The blue eyes that met hers were filled with merriment.

She tried to pull her hand from his grasp, but he held it fast. "I'd like to hear the part again about how sorry you are," he said. He smiled slowly, brushing the snowflakes from his face with his other hand. He raised one eyebrow. "Or the words about not being able to bear to leave me." He chuckled. "I think those were my favorite."

This time Callie yanked her hand from his. "You've...you've been all right from the beginning? You...you heard everything I said?" she stammered, feeling her cheeks flame in embarrassment and anger. "Of all the low-down, liver-bellied, blackhearted..." She stood, backing away from him. "Hawk Jones, I will never forgive you for this."

"It seems you've spoken those words before."

"This time I mean it—you've gone too far." By now fresh tears were threatening. Callie choked them back, clinging to a shred of pride. She lifted her chin. "Someday you'll come begging my forgiveness for this spiteful act. But I'll not grant it. I'll not. I don't care if you crawl on your belly like the rattlesnake you are—I'll not grant it."

Callie stood abruptly and started for Darley, patiently waiting on the other side of the fence. Then she remembered the cape.

She returned to Hawk who was now half-sitting in the snow, a wide grin lighting his handsome face. Without a word, Callie yanked the cape from him and stomped through the deepening snow toward the fence, sorry the obstacle stood between her and a more graceful exit.

Within moments, however, she clambered over the fence and mounted Darley, her back still toward Hawk.

"Callie!" Hawk shouted. "Callie, wait!"

Ignoring him, Callie reined her mount toward Sun and Jeremiah's cabin.

"Callie!" he shouted after her again. "Don't forget—I won the race! I crossed the jump before you did."

The sound of Hawk's laughter echoed across the snowy meadow. Callie didn't look back.

Three

⤜⤛

Oberlin Collegiate Institute,
Oberlin, Ohio
Autum 1851

H awk rode into the small town of Oberlin, Ohio, and asked directions to the college. A few minutes later, he strode into the administration building.

"Can you tell me where I might find one of your students—Callasandra St. Clair?" he asked the serious-looking young man behind the desk.

The boy nodded, seeming to know immediately to whom Hawk referred. "She's staying over at Mrs. Gray's place. Can't miss it—two-story, white—just the other side of campus."

After thanking him, Hawk remounted and rode across the wide lawns to the house. As the student had said, the boarding-house was imposing; flanked by massive oaks and elms, its white-washed siding gleamed in the lowering sun. Hawk thought of Callie's and Juliana's Southern upbringing. Though he'd never seen a plantation, this large house somehow seemed fitting for Callie. She'd talked often of someday returning "home" to Natchez. Maybe attending college in this setting was the first step back into her old life.

Wrapping the reins around a rail, Hawk opened the front

gate, then bounded up the stairs and across the verandah to the heavy oak front door.

It didn't take long for Mrs. Gray, a small wiry woman, to greet him. She nodded amiably when he asked for Callie, then sent him to wait in the front parlor while she fetched Miss St. Clair.

Hawk sat down in a high-backed chair at the far end of the room. Mrs. Gray had left the parlor door open and he had an unobstructed view of the foyer and stairs that he assumed led to the young women students' rooms.

Looking up at the sound of light footsteps, Hawk caught his breath, watching Callie descend the stairs.

Suddenly, he realized he'd seen Callie in nothing but worn men's leather pants, old flannel shirts, and brown felt hats. Now, here she was, all but floating down the stairs in a frock the color of seafoam. Her cascading red curls, pulled up and off her slender neck, shone as bright as firelight.

When Callie reached the doorway, he stood. She saw him, and her face came alive. The look of her touched him someplace deep inside, and an unfamiliar longing swept over him. The feeling was so unexpected that for a moment he couldn't speak. He simply stared as Callie crossed the room to where he stood.

Her eyes seemed to shimmer with a depth he hadn't noticed before. Deep green with topaz flecks. The freckles he remembered from her hours spent in the New Mexico sun had all but disappeared from her white skin. With a pang, he realized he missed them. He'd always thought they spoke of vulnerability, even in the midst of her hot-tempered outbursts.

The missing freckles weren't the only change in Callie St. Clair. The woman standing before him was no longer the petulant child he'd known in New Mexico. He couldn't take his eyes from her.

"Hawk," she said, reaching for his hands in greeting. Her eyes crinkled in amusement. She seemed to read his thoughts.

He swallowed. "Callie," he whispered finally. "It's good to see you." His words sounded lame, overmatched by his feelings.

Still smiling, Callie pulled him to a small sofa where they both sat. She kept his hands in hers, a warm gesture of friendship and family ties, he assumed. "How long has it been? A year?"

Hawk nodded. It had been one year, two months, and three days since he'd seen Callie on his last visit to New Mexico. He'd figured it out on his way to Oberlin. "Around that," he said, smiling into her eyes. "Tell me, how do you like it here?"

"It's wonderful, Hawk. Academic life suits me." She laughed lightly. "And it's good to get back to civilization." The briefest shadow crossed her face, then just as quickly disappeared. She smiled again into his eyes.

"New Mexico was never to your liking, was it? You never really considered it home."

Before Callie could answer, Mrs. Gray bustled into the room, smiling at the two young people as she set the silver tray holding a teapot and two cups on a nearby table. Callie poured the strong liquid into dainty china cups, handed one to Hawk, then added a bit of sugar and cream to her own before removing it from the tray. She took a sip, watching him over the top of the cup.

Finally she said, "Home always seems to be someplace other than where I find myself. After Father died and we lost Stonehaven, it hurt too much to think that home was there. It had been stolen from us and there wasn't anything I could do about it. It stood to reason that Juliana and I needed to find another home for ourselves."

She took another sip of tea. "When we got to New Mexico and she married Parker, I realized that the cabin in the meadow was their home, not mine. Juliana—and even your mother—

made it clear that I was welcome with either of them if I chose to stay. But the meadow—New Mexico—never became my home."

"My mother's always loved you—you're the daughter she never had."

"I know. And I love her." Callie looked out the window for a few minutes without speaking. "But I had to leave. It's time for me to find the place I belong."

"Is it here?"

She turned her gaze to his face. He was again struck by the shimmering depths of her eyes. "There's a lot here that appeals to me. But I'm sure this isn't the place I'll stay." She poured him more tea, then filled her own cup. "I'll probably return to Natchez. Pay a visit to dear Uncle Caleb."

Hawk noticed a tone of bitterness in her voice. Her face paled as she spoke, making the few remaining freckles more pronounced. It made him want to gather her into his arms, to protect her. What her uncle had done to Callie when her father died had been unconscionable.

"You've always talked about returning," he said gently.

"I've never changed my mind. Stonehaven is mine. Someday I plan to fight my uncle for it."

And he knew she would. "For the same reasons?"

Callie nodded and said nothing more about the subject. They spoke for a few minutes about Hawk's plans to return to Harvard, graduate, and practice medicine.

"And then?" she asked, watching him intently.

"The same as before," he said. "Up the wide Missouri."

She nodded. "You've never changed your mind about that either." There was a touch of irony in her voice.

Hawk laughed lightly. "We're both pretty stubborn when it comes to mapping out our lives."

"It's a good thing we never fell in love with each other." Her tone was teasing, though she watched him intently as she spoke. "Think of the trouble we'd have trying to decide which calling to follow."

Hawk didn't smile. Though her words were meant to be lighthearted, she was right. His future had to be faced alone. He could never ask someone like Callie to follow him into the wilds of the upper Missouri River. The Mandans were his people, not hers.

He gazed at her, feeling a desperate sadness at what could never be. Again she seemed to read his thoughts. Something in her expression changed. She stood, seeming hurt. Or maybe confused.

They walked to the front door, then she faced him and took his hands in hers. She seemed to want to say something more, but didn't. After a pause she said simply, "It's so good to have you here. It's like having family—" She stumbled over the word, "—with me."

She smiled softly. "There's a social tonight. A picnic, dancing under the stars. Would you care to escort me?"

Her words and demeanor spoke of friendship and, as she said, family. Nothing more. It wouldn't hurt to stay one more day. It might be years before he saw Callie again. If ever. He winced at the thought.

"I'd love to accompany you," he finally said.

The evening passed delightfully. Laughing and talking, Hawk and Callie munched on fried chicken and drank their fill of lemonade. After dark, a group of students took out their fiddles and banjos. They played both ballads for singing and toe-tapping shuffles for dancing.

Once the faster music began, Callie didn't have a free minute. Young men lined up to ask Hawk's permission to dance with Callie. He nodded amiably, then watched as she whirled to the music.

Radiant in a gown of the palest lavender-blue, Callie moved as gracefully as wild lupines dancing in a meadow breeze. He imagined her life at Stonehaven, the fine clothes, the soirees and teas, the formal balls. She was right to want to return to Natchez. She was born to be the mistress of such a place.

He also realized that he was falling in love with Callie. He'd probably loved her from the beginning. Yet he knew his calling to minister to his mother's people. He smiled wryly to himself. Could there be two more different worlds?

As a giant harvest moon rose in the east and a breeze kicked up, rustling the leaves of nearby elms and sycamores, Callie approached him breathlessly. Her cheeks were pink from exertion, her eyes bright with excitement.

"Everyone's asked me to dance but you," she said, tilting her chin in the way he'd seen so often in New Mexico.

He grinned. "Then it must be my turn." He took her in his arms and they began to move to the music.

Around the grassy dance floor they circled, coming together with other couples, parting again, dipping and turning, grasping hands, lifting them skyward, laughing into each other's eyes, then whirling and bowing again.

Finally, Hawk led Callie away from the milling dancers to a nearby oak where they stood under its canopy of leaves, catching their breath. The moon painted a dappled pattern of silver light across Callie's face. Hawk reached for her hand.

"Callie, I must go."

She frowned. "Now? The evening isn't over. I thought—"

Hawk shushed her by touching her lips lightly. How could he

tell her that he simply couldn't look into her shimmering eyes another minute, that he couldn't draw her into his arms for another dance, or watch her tilt her face and laugh into his eyes one more time? He was too weak. And there was too much at risk. For them both.

"Callie, we must say goodbye." His voice was husky as he touched her cheek.

She covered his fingers with her own, watching him seriously, sadly.

"But Hawk, when will I see you again?"

"I don't know. It may be a long time. I've got my years at Harvard ahead. You've got at least two years here." He shrugged, not knowing how much more to say. About Natchez. About the Mandan villages.

"Promise me that we'll see each other again." The moonlight glistened in her eyes. She didn't shift her gaze from his. Something in her face stirred all the longings of his soul, but he couldn't answer her.

She continued. "I'll never forgive you, Hawk Jones, if you don't promise me that you'll find me again." Her tone was teasing, reminiscent of the other times she'd threatened the same— the spring morning in his mother's kitchen when she'd discovered who he was, the winter afternoon when he'd fallen from his horse and listened with delight as she declared her affection.

"That's something I can't promise you, Callie." It broke his heart to say it. "Neither of us knows what the future holds."

Her face fell, that beautiful face he wanted to look upon for the rest of his life. She pulled her hand from his and turned away. "Then just go," she whispered, her voice low and ragged. "Just go."

He touched her shoulder, but she stiffened and moved away.

"Callie, please. It's just that—" But he couldn't finish. How could he say all that was inside?

She turned again to watch him. But when he didn't speak, she simply whispered again. "Then leave, Hawk, if that's what you want. Leave me alone. Now."

"Callie, let's not part like this."

But she said nothing. Her face had paled and the sprinkling of freckles across her nose stood out in the moonlight. A breeze caught a wisp of her hair, and she tucked it behind one ear. Her deep green eyes shimmered with unshed tears and undeclared love.

After a moment, with the dying sounds of the fiddles and banjos in the distance, Hawk turned and strode from the place where Callie stood. But imprinted indelibly in his mind and soul was that final look of her.

Callie watched him walk away. Now she wished she had buried her pride and entreated him to stay.

"There is something else, Hawk," she whispered, half to herself, half to the wind. "I witnessed something terrible. I needed to tell you how it changed me—how it changed...everything. Why couldn't you have stayed just a few minutes longer?"

A sudden breeze caressed Callie's face. She gazed at Hawk until he had disappeared into the darkness. The wind seemed to whisper through the crisp fall leaves, "Nashtara...Nashtara."

Stonehaven

CHAPTER

One

✎

Oberlin, Ohio
Spring 1853

They're coming!" twenty-two-year-old Callie St. Clair whispered to the families hiding in the hay-strewn barn. "Everyone, get down. Cover yourselves with hay. Now!"

The movement and talking among the runaway slaves quieted. In one corner, a baby whimpered. And nearer to Callie, another child sobbed, "I'm scared, Mamma." The mother crawled through the hay and gathered the little one into her arms. A nervous silence settled across the group.

Outside, the voices of the slave hunters drew nearer. They would soon be in earshot of the barn.

Suddenly, a baby mewed pitifully as if sensing the terror.

"Quiet!" Callie's tone was harsh. The fugitives' lives depended on their silence. "You must keep the baby quiet." The baby's cries were muffled, then stopped abruptly. Callie pictured the child held tightly against his mother's breast and for a frantic moment wondered if he could breathe. More than one infant had suffocated in its parent's arms while on the Underground Railroad— its life sacrificed to keep the whole group from being discovered. Callie shivered at the thought.

"Callie, hurry! Get in beside me," Sheridan O'Brian whispered. Her Irish brogue was more pronounced than usual because of her fear. The sounds of shifting hay in the loft followed her words. "Hurry, Callie. They'll soon be here."

Callie settled under the hay, picturing the hunters as they carried their torches, searching out fugitives and returning them to their masters in the South for a reward, imprisoning those who helped them. Callie knew that, if caught, she'd probably be tarred and feathered. For certain she'd stand trial and go to prison. Even in Ohio it was a federal crime to assist runaways—it had been the law since 1850.

But Callie did it anyway. She had been a part of the Underground Railroad for two years, almost as long as she'd been studying to be a teacher at Oberlin Collegiate Institute. She had taken over as the group's leader a half-year before. Many of her friends—all students at Oberlin—were part of the Railroad. They had helped dozens of runaway slaves reach Canada. None in Callie's group had been caught, at least not yet.

Usually, two or three student "conductors" took charge of the "station" or stop on the Railroad. They switched stops often, using farms, homes, or abandoned shacks to keep the slave hunters off guard. Tonight it was Callie's turn as captain of the station, with help from her friend Sheridan and another student, a newcomer, Jake Smyth. Jake was now crouched in a nearby thicket, waiting to give the all-clear signal to the wagons that would carry this group north to their next station and one day closer to freedom.

Callie listened carefully. The sounds had died down, but that didn't mean the men were gone. In the barn, no one moved. She couldn't even hear the sounds of breathing.

It was too quiet.

Callie raised her head and pulled bits of straw from her matted curls. Squinting through the cracks in the barn's wood siding, her heart caught in her chest. She could see the glow of bobbing torches. The slave hunters had dismounted and were creeping toward the barn. "Oh, no," she breathed. "They're coming." Sheridan clutched Callie's hand.

Again there was silence. Callie felt her heart's mad pounding. She stared into the darkness and waited.

Outside, the frogs stopped croaking. The crickets hushed. Callie listened for footsteps in the eerie quiet but could hear only the rush of blood through her veins.

"What will we do?" Sheridan breathed.

Callie didn't answer, but quickly shook her head, a signal to keep silent. The truth was, she didn't know the answer.

A few moments passed, then someone shouted. The sound carried from the thicket where Jake had been hiding.

Sheridan caught her breath audibly. She had figured the same thing. With Jake caught, they were next.

More shouts. Someone let out a whoop followed by coarse laughter and the sounds of people running. Then another hoot. Cheering and guttural laughter followed.

Jake was caught. There was no doubt now. The hunters would guess the Underground station was nearby.

Callie peered into the night, watching, waiting for the inevitable.

First she saw the torches then heard heavy boots on hard-packed dirt nearing the barn. Lone footsteps. One of the hunters was headed toward the barn's double doors.

The rusty hinges creaked as the door slowly opened. The room flared with light from the man's flaming torch.

Callie squeezed her eyes closed, not daring to breathe, hoping against all hope that a child wouldn't sneeze or cry out. The runaways remained as still as death.

The man with the torch chuckled, then slowly closed the

door. A few minutes later someone began knocking at the side of the barn.

Callie looked at Sheridan quizzically.

"Aye! A hammer it is." Sheridan's voice was flat. "They are nailing shut the door."

"But, why—" Callie began, then knew before the question had left her lips. The smell of smoke drifted through the cracks. "Oh, no," she whispered frantically. "They wouldn't." She scanned the barn for an escape. There was none. "They wouldn't!" she repeated.

Smoke rapidly filled the barn. A child began to cough, then whimper. It was followed by others crying out in fear.

"Come out," Callie commanded the runaways, struggling to keep her voice calm. "Get down on the ground—you can breathe better there. Please, remain calm. We'll get out of here. I promise. We'll get out."

The three families came out from their hiding places, fathers and mothers carrying their babies. The older children clung to one another as they followed Callie's instructions and quickly lay on the dirt floor.

A soft glow from the outside fire illumined the room. Callie glanced frantically at Sheridan. Her friend's dark blue eyes were wide with fear, her face white against the black of her hair. They could hear crackling flames shooting up the barn's outside walls.

"We don't have much time, Callie."

"I know." The flames grew brighter. Heat filled the barn. The smoke grew thicker.

"There's only the window." Sheridan's voice remained steady. "I don't see flames there. It's our only chance."

Callie nodded. "That's what they're counting on."

"I know. But it's the only way."

"We've got to get the families out first." Callie's voice caught.

"But we'll be sending them right into the hands of the slave hunters."

"It's better than dying."

"Is it, Sherrie?"

Sheridan nodded, her eyes sad with understanding. "It's our only choice."

Amid the coughing and crying, Callie spoke calmly to the families, explaining what needed to be done. One of the runaways, a big man named Israel, moved quickly to the roughly shuttered window. He pulled off the shutters. One by one he began lifting people over the ledge.

The slave hunters' yells could be heard as the children ran from the burning barn straight into the arms of their captors. The women and men would be the last to leave.

Bright orange flames now licked higher. The heat was growing unbearable. Holding her cape against her face, Callie struggled to breathe as she helped Israel with the children.

One little girl clung to Callie's breeches, wailing in fear. Callie scooped the tiny girl into her arms, holding her close for an instant.

"Dadda! Dadda!" the little girl cried, reaching beyond Callie to Israel, who was helping the last of the children over the ledge.

Tears coursed down Callie's cheeks as she looked into the big man's eyes. She knew the tragedy ahead. The family wouldn't be together for a long time, maybe never. They would be herded like cattle—with no thought of keeping them in family groups—back to their Southern owners. She knew from her own plantation childhood that runaways would be sold and purposely scattered. Collectively, they were too strong; they knew too much. Separated, they were weaker.

The men, and probably some of the women, would serve as public examples. Whippings for first offenders, maiming for the others.

Callie handed the child to Israel. The big man held his daughter close for an instant, then his eyes met those of his wife, a pretty woman at his side. She climbed over the window, then he placed their little girl in her arms. "Run to the woods if you can," he said softly, though there was no hope in his voice. "We'll meet there." Without a word she turned and ran.

Israel's broad face crumpled as the shouts and whoops of triumph carried back to the burning barn. Without a word he helped the remaining runaways crawl through the window.

The hollering, punctuated by jeers, grew louder with each one who ran from the burning building. Within minutes all had climbed from the window except Israel, Sheridan, and Callie.

The building crackled with the flames that now enveloped it.

"Do you want to go first?" Sheridan smiled softly at Callie.

Callie nodded then touched Sherrie's arm as if to say goodbye and started toward the window. Just then a wooden beam fell in front of her, pulling down the roof. Sparks flew. Dark smoke billowed as new flames soared, instantly catching the loose hay.

Gasping for air, Callie looked around frantically. No escape route now.

Israel grabbed for Callie, pulling her out of the way of another falling beam. With his other hand he grabbed Sheridan. All three dropped to the dirt floor and moved to the other side of the barn, to the door that had been nailed shut from outside.

Israel put his shoulder to the door, ramming his big body against it again and again. The door didn't move.

Sheridan leaned against the door and Callie joined her. They pushed hard. Flames licked closer. They tried again.

"Together now," Israel breathed. "Move together."

It was their last chance. The heat was too intense, the flames too close.

Closing her eyes and calling upon every shred of strength in her body, Callie threw herself into the door.

Seconds later she felt the rush of cool night air as the doors flew open and the three of them stumbled from the barn.

Without looking back, they ran. No one stood waiting for them. No one followed. They ran in a straight line to the thicket of woods where their friend Jake had waited earlier.

After a few minutes, Israel, who was in the lead, held up his hand as a signal to stop. They silently took cover in a copse of willows.

Callie fought to catch her breath along with the others.

"There—" Israel panted, looking back toward flames, now barely visible through the trees. "Look there. They think we died inside."

The hunters stood silently watching the inferno that had once been a barn. The rest of the roof had caved in. Even the doors from which they had fled had burst into a wall of flames.

"Let's hope they don't notice the doors are open," Callie whispered.

"They're on the other side, the window side." Sheridan's voice sounded hopeful. "Maybe they won't think to look anywhere else. With those flames—Israel's right. They probably don't believe anyone could have escaped."

"They're figuring we're dead now." Israel squinted into the darkness. "But they won't for long. When the flames die down, they'll look for bodies."

"Then they'll start looking for us," Sheridan added.

"That's right, child. That's right." The big man was solemn. "We need to move on."

"Before they get the dogs." Callie knew they needed to move quickly. But where would they go? She wondered if the wagon that was supposed to meet the runaways might be still hidden nearby. She mentioned it to the others. If they could get Israel to the wagon and on his way to the next station, she and Sheridan could slip back to their rooms at the college undetected. And they could see about getting help for Jake Smyth.

"I worry about Jake," Sheridan whispered after a few minutes.

"What do you mean?" Callie looked at her, sensing what her friend was about to say.

"Jake is new. They will try to get him to tell who else was helping him."

"I don't think he would do that."

"And why not? He has nothing to lose. They may promise to go easier on him if he tells."

Israel nodded in agreement. "And they have other ways." He paused, still watching the distant flames. "Ways that bring pain. She's right"—he glanced at Sheridan—"he'll tell."

"We'd better move on." Callie looked at the other two, wondering if they had a better idea than she did which direction to run.

Israel spoke first. "No. The two of you must take care of yourselves. Let me be on my way. I can move faster alone." He looked at them kindly. "Go on now. Get moving. Do what you need to do to save yourselves."

"You'll be heading north?" Sheridan asked, as he stood. "Maybe you can find the wagon that was supposed to meet us. You'll be in Canada within days."

The shoulders on the black man's body sloped downward. He shook his head slowly. "No, child. I'm not going north."

"You're not thinking of going back, are you?" Even as she asked, Callie knew the answer.

He nodded. "After my family. They'll be sent back to Mississippi. Vicksburg. Where we started from. That's where I'll find them—my Bethenia and our baby, Cody."

"That's not far from Natchez—" Callie began. The big man looked at her quizzically, but she didn't go on.

"Godspeed," Sheridan whispered. And before either young woman could say anything more, Israel turned and, without looking back, took off through the woods with the agility of a deer.

Callie looked at Sheridan, the knowing expression in her friend's eyes a mirror of her own feelings. "We've got to get away from here."

"You're meaning Oberlin?" Sheridan sounded worried.

Callie nodded. "As far away as possible. If we're found out—not even the college can save us."

"I know."

Callie knew they were both picturing the unthinkable—being tarred and feathered, perhaps worse. Standing trial. Going to prison. She swallowed hard. "We've got to go back to our rooms for clothes, money. And we've got to move fast."

"Where will we go?"

Callie reached for Sheridan's hand and pulled her up to stand beside her. "We'll decide that later. For right now, we've just got to get our things—and hope that Jake doesn't tell—at least till we are miles away from this place."

With one last glance toward the now-dying embers, the young women moved swiftly through the night.

Jake Smyth struggled against the ropes that bound him. Two hours earlier he had been dragged with the runaways to a house not far from the burning barn. Then a rag had been stuffed in his mouth and a hood pulled over his head. He had been shoved against something that felt like a barrel or tree trunk to await what he knew was the inevitable. Through the ensuing hours his captors discussed their plans for him, seeming to take pleasure in laying out the details.

Several men had ridden off to bring back wagons for transporting the runaways. And now, off in the distance, the captured families waited. Some of the children were crying. Now and then a young one called out, asking its mamma to explain what was happening. Still others whimpered in fear or fatigue.

Jake smelled the tar as it bubbled over a hastily built fire. Shuddering, he willed himself not to think of the hot liquid blistering his naked flesh.

Suddenly someone pulled the hood from Jake's head, and a toothless, grinning face greeted his blinking eyes. "Hello, son," the gravelly voice said softly, menacingly. "We're just about ready for you." The man shifted his eyes to the pot of boiling tar, then back to Jake. He grinned again slowly. "You're gonna wish you'd died in the fire, son, before we're done with you."

Jake could feel beads of sweat form on his upper lip. The gag was removed, but the young man said nothing.

"Now, it can be easy. Or it can be painful. It's up to you. You're lucky we've thought to give you a choice." The man paused, looked again at the boiling tar, then spat loudly at the pot and chuckled as his spittle sizzled. He moved his gaze back to Jake. "After all—we don't need to do nothing on your behalf on account of your being the criminal and all. It really makes no never-mind to us, son, one way or the other."

"What do you mean?" Jake wished his voice hadn't quavered as he spoke. He cleared his throat, then started again, trying to sound braver. "I don't know what you're talking about. I don't even know why I'm here. I was just waiting for someone in the woods. I didn't know what was going on in the barn."

A burst of laughter interrupted him. "You had no idea about them n—— in the barn, son?" He snorted. "I s'pose you're just waiting to join in a Sunday school picnic."

"I was waiting for my girl. We'd planned it. We were both sneaking away from the college. But we couldn't come together—" Jake's words tumbled out, sounding unbelievable even as he spoke them.

"From the college, eh?" The man grinned. "One of them young upstart rabble-rousers that give our village a bad name. I should've figured." He spat again. "And you were going to meet your girl. Mind telling me her name?"

Jake said nothing.

"It's names we want, son. Just names." His voice softened. "We'll go much easier on you if'n you'll tell us who was working with you."

"I said I was waiting for my girl. Why do you want her name? She—we—had nothing to do with the Undergr—" His voice faltered.

"With the what, son?"

Jake knew he'd blundered. He fell silent.

"What do you know about the Underground?" The man paused, letting his gaze linger on the pot of tar. "Do you know what it feels like to be tarred and feathered, son? It ain't pretty. And it sure ain't easy." He began to describe in detail the worst he'd ever seen happen.

Jake drew in a ragged breath. The man watched him intently.

"Now, then. Don't you think it's time to tell me all I want to know?"

Jake felt like crying, but he held his ground and shook his head no. "I can't," he said simply.

"All right then. Have it your way."

Nearby, several of his captors had been watching and listening. At the man's nod, a few sniggered in anticipation as they moved closer to Jake.

Jake looked up at their eager expressions. "Stop," he shouted.

"I'll tell you what you want to know."

"Everything?"

He nodded, ashamed of his weakness. "Yes," he whispered. "Everything."

"Start talking."

"Their names are Callasandra—Callie—St. Clair and Sheridan O'Brian. We were the team for tonight's work."

"You're all students at Oberlin?"

"Yes."

"Are there others in on this? Others who take turns at this station?"

"Yes."

"Give us their names."

Jake Smyth listed them one by one, tears springing to his eyes at his betrayal.

"Who's their leader?"

He didn't answer.

The man looked to the others standing nearby. "Maybe y'all ought to stir up the tar real good now. Get it ready."

Jake cleared his throat. When he spoke, his voice was barely audible. "Nashtara," he said. "She's known as Nashtara."

"I didn't hear you."

He spoke louder. "Nashtara."

"You said, 'known as.'"

Jake nodded.

"Then go on. What's her real name?"

The boy gulped, hesitating.

"What's her real name, son?" The man's face was just inches from Jake's.

"Callie St. Clair," Jake whispered. "She is the one known as Nashtara."

"The same that was here tonight." It was more a statement than a question. "And how will we find this Miss St. Clair?"

"I told you, she's at the college."

"There's lots of young ladies at Oberlin. How do we find her without askin'? We don't want to alert anyone about why we want her. We wouldn't be wantin' her to get away before we get her, now would we?"

Jake nodded, understanding. "She's pretty," he said. "She's small but looks strong. She's got bright red hair that falls down her back in curls. Some freckles across her nose. You can't miss her—she's the only one at Oberlin who looks like that."

"And the one who was with her? What was her name again?"

"Sheridan. Sheridan O'Brian."

"How will we know her?"

Jake paused, thinking of Sherrie. He'd always been sweet on her, though he'd never been brave enough to tell her so. He tried not to picture her pretty face as he betrayed her to save his own skin. "She's Irish," he said quickly. "She's got a thick brogue. Sounds like she just got here straight from Ireland."

The man grinned with one side of his mouth. "You did the right thing by telling us, son." Then he looked at the rest of his men. "Okay, boys. You know what you gotta do." Then he turned his back as the men fell upon Jake and prepared him for tarring.

As Jake alternately cried out for help and yelled accusations of trickery, the man called out: "Stuff in the gag! I don't want to hear any more."

Then he pulled aside his three best hunters. "Ride to Oberlin. As soon as it's daylight, search the campus for this red-headed Callie St. Clair." He spat and chuckled. "And find the one who was with her—the Irish gal. Sounds like you can't miss either one."

The men mounted and rode into the ash-gray dawn.

51

CHAPTER

Two

D id you—bring money?" Callie's words came out in short
bursts as she and Sheridan sprinted through the woods south
of Oberlin. They had left the college an hour before, slipping
from their rooms in the darkness with only what they could
carry on their backs. Neither had taken the time to change from
the men's clothing they had worn at the barn—leather britches,
old hats and shirts, and sturdy boots.

Sheridan patted her vest pocket as she ran. "It's all that Aunt
Fiona last sent to me. And you?"

Callie nodded. "I brought everything that was supposed to
last me till the end of the term." She dodged a low-hanging
branch. "I'm not sure how far it will take us."

"We've not talked about—where we're headin'." Sheridan
panted, jumping over a small boulder in their path.

"Let's stop—and rest a minute." Callie fell to the ground,
fighting to catch her breath.

Sheridan dropped beside her, gulping for air. "I don't think
I've run this hard since leavin' Ireland. Shamus and I would often
run across the bogs, but I think you've got my twin brother beat
in speed, Callie St. Clair."

Callie leaned back against a large rock, listening for sounds of pursuit. Satisfied they were safe, at least for the moment, she spoke again. "I think we need to head south."

"We *are* heading south."

"No. I mean into the deep South—Mississippi."

Sheridan tilted her head. "Wouldn't that be—how do you say?—leapin' from the pan straightaway into the glowin' coals?"

Callie smiled at her friend's rendering. "It would be dangerous. But then anywhere we head would be. If Jake identified us to the hunters, there's probably a warrant out for our arrest complete with our names, descriptions, everything. I think it would circulate mostly in Ohio. Especially northern Ohio. If I were the authorities I'd expect us to head to Canada, not Mississippi."

"If we're caught in the South, worse things than prison could happen to us, Callie."

"I know. Chances are, though, word of us won't get that far." Callie sighed and didn't speak for a moment. "You once told me about a cousin who lives in Natchez."

"Aye. A second cousin. His name is Liam. Liam Sheridan." She settled back against a large rock across from Callie. She laughed softly at Callie's quizzical look. "Sheridan was my mother's family name. Though my papa's name was O'Brian, she wanted me to always be a Sheridan. My real name is Mary Elizabeth Sheridan O'Brian." She smiled shyly. "From the time I was a wee tyke, I fancied being called Sheridan. I've been Sheridan ever since."

"That will make for a convincing introduction—if he doesn't remember you." Callie turned to place her elbow on the rock where she sat, then rested her chin in her hand.

"I think he will. Aunt Fiona says I'm the spittin' image of our great-grandmother. I never met her. But Liam, being older, knew her well." She paused. "I take it you're thinkin' we should head to Natchez?"

Callie nodded. "It makes sense. Would Liam take us in?"

"I don't know. He's a cotton trader. He's made a fortune since he came here from Ireland years ago. Aunt Fiona boasts of his fine town house in Natchez. Sheridan Hall, it's called. But I don't know how kindly he'd take to poor, unfortunate relatives appearin' on his doorstep."

"When was the last time you saw him?"

"It was in Ireland—before the potato famine." Sheridan's face grew sad. "I was only seven years old, and I believe Liam must've been nearly twenty. He came to our farm with his mother—my own mamma's cousin. I don't remember much about him except that he was exceedingly handsome. He ignored me completely, he did."

"Let's hope he won't ignore you now." Callie tossed a few pebbles at the base of a slender willow a short distance away.

For a few minutes neither young woman spoke. Then Sheridan, her face still serious, turned to Callie. "Why are you thinking about Natchez? Surely not just because of Liam. Is it Stonehaven?"

"I've always wanted to go back. Now seems to be the time."

"You told me once that your uncle, the senator, stole the plantation from you. Are you still intendin' to prove it—to try to get it back?"

Callie nodded. "Yes, but for a different reason than before. When Juliana and I first ran away from Stonehaven back in '46, I was convinced that Caleb had something to do with my father's bad investments and losing everything. Caleb is connected to every bank and political leader in Mississippi. It would have been an easy thing for him to do—adjust some investment figures here, call in some early payments there. Payments he knew my father was unable to handle in bad crop years."

"Why would he want to?"

"That's the part I could never figure out. I don't think Juliana could either. She finally decided it must have been Father's fault after all."

"Aye, but you weren't convinced."

"No. During the years I spent with my sister and her husband in New Mexico, I couldn't let go of the idea of returning to Stonehaven, taking back for Juliana and me what is rightfully ours. And proving to the nation what a crook the high and mighty Senator Caleb Benedict is!"

"What changed your mind?"

"I never really changed my mind about that. I still feel driven to prove my uncle's guilt and take back Stonehaven."

Sheridan waited for her to go on.

"It's the reason I want Stonehaven that's changed. Once, I wanted to return to the days of grandeur as mistress of the finest plantation in Natchez. Even as a child I enjoyed the richness of the place—the balls, the gowns, the beauty of the lands. I wanted to take possession of it and the hundreds of slaves that once belonged to the St. Clairs. But now—"

"It's the Underground Railroad," Sheridan interrupted. "That's why you want to go back."

Callie nodded vigorously. "Stonehaven could become a major station in the South. Think how many families we could help get to Canada. We already know the northern connection. We could find out local station names. We'd begin working from your cousin's—while I get information about Caleb and Stonehaven." Callie's voice was triumphant. "What do you think, Sherrie? Do you think we could make it work?"

But she didn't need to ask. Sheridan's face brightened visibly.

"Think about it, Sherrie, before you agree. You could return to your aunt's in New York. It would probably be safer."

Sheridan smiled sadly. "Aunt Fiona sent me to Oberlin

because she thought me incorrigible and didn't know what else to do with me. She doesn't want me back. If she knew I was a fugitive from the law, she'd probably turn me in herself." Her deep blue eyes, clear and unafraid, looked straight into Callie's. "No, Callie St. Clair. I believe in the Underground Railroad as much as you do. I want to go to Natchez. We'll go and make our plan work." She stood and helped Callie to her feet. "Nobody can stop us, you and me."

Callie gave her friend a quick hug. "Then we'd better get started." She looked around. "Now that it's light, let's find a farm where we can buy some horses. I don't know about you, but I'm tired of running."

Days later, Callie stood alone on the deck of a small steamer, heading south on the Ohio River. She and Sheridan had boarded in Cincinnati and were halfway to Cairo where they would transfer to a larger riverboat and head down the Mississippi River for Natchez. Sheridan had retired early to their room, giving Callie a chance to be alone with her thoughts.

She looked across the deep green water to a wooded riverbank, marveling at the swiftness with which the steamer moved along. How different from the slow riverboat trip she and Juliana had taken when they fled Stonehaven six years earlier! At that time they had been moving upstream at what seemed to be a snail's pace. Now, heading downriver, Callie felt the stiff breeze against her face and the lift of her hair in the wind. She closed her eyes, relishing the smell of the river and the feeling of steadily moving forward. She smiled to herself, feeling more secure with each nautical mile the riverboat placed between her and Oberlin.

Oberlin. Her eyes opened wide at the thought of Oberlin Collegiate Institute. With the danger-filled days following the incident at the barn, she hadn't let herself dwell on her loss at having to leave so suddenly.

She had been within weeks of receiving her teacher's certificate. She and Juliana had spent most of the money from the sale of their mother's jewels for Callie's travel from New Mexico to Ohio and for her school expenses.

How can I tell Juliana what I've done? How can I tell her that Mother's money is nearly gone, wasted on an education that will do me no good? Not only is my education worthless without the certificate, now I'm a fugitive as well.

Callie thought about writing to Juliana and Parker to explain, to ask their forgiveness. But she knew she wasn't ready to do that yet. Maybe she wouldn't be for a long time. She drew in a deep breath. Perhaps after she won back Stonehaven. Yes, she suddenly decided. That's exactly what she would do: temper the bad news with the good. Maybe Juliana would forgive her more readily if she knew that Stonehaven once again belonged to the St. Clairs.

Her thoughts settled on Juliana and Parker. Callie had lived with them during their first few years of marriage. She helped them build their cozy little cabin in the meadow, just down the lane from Morning Sun and Jeremiah Jones. She pictured the vivid New Mexico skies, the sun beating hot on her shoulders as she worked in Juliana's garden, the sense of freedom as she rode Darley across the meadows and mesas.

Callie smiled, remembering the love she had felt there: Juliana and Parker's deep passion for each other (they still behaved like newlyweds) and the joy and delight that surrounded the births of their children, a son they named Richard after Callie's and Juliana's father, and a daughter (born just before Callie left for Ohio) named Morgan, the German word for "morning." The little girl had been named after the family's dearest friend, Morning Sun, a Mandan Indian. Callie smiled in remembrance. It had been she who thought of Morgan's name.

Love. Callie thought of all that word meant as she considered New Mexico. Juliana's family. Sun and Jeremiah. And of course, Hawk.

Callie's heart quickened at the memory of him. She remembered the way he'd ridden bareback across the meadow, the bright New Mexico sun catching his sun-streaked hair and casting a sheen on the bronzed muscle coils of his arms and chest. His raw strength had always impressed her: How incongruous for someone who spent hours each day with his nose buried in medical books.

It no longer surprised Callie that when she thought of New Mexico, her thoughts always returned—and stayed—with the image of Hawk riding in the wind. Something about the scene caused her heart to beat faster.

Besides, she thought with deep sadness, it was easier to think of Hawk riding across the New Mexico mesas than it was to picture him in the moonlight at Oberlin, looking into her eyes and telling her goodbye.

More than a year and a half had passed since that night. Callie hadn't seen nor heard from him since. At first Callie refused to consider that she might never see him again, even though he'd made the possibility—no, the probability—very clear.

But now? Callie sighed, looking out across the river. She knew that Hawk was soon due to leave Boston for the West and his work as a doctor among his mother's people. She tried to tell herself that it didn't matter what Hawk did or didn't do with his life, that it was none of her concern. After all, if she considered that Hawk was right, they would never meet again.

Callie didn't wonder at the tears filling her eyes. She'd felt their sting before when she'd thought about a lifetime without Hawk.

Two weeks later, Callie and Sheridan stood at the riverboat's bow as they rapidly steamed toward Natchez on the muddy Mississippi. It was late afternoon and the sun hit the river at a slant, casting bright glints of light on its ripples.

While in Memphis, the young women had sold their horses and spent most of their remaining funds on clothing appropriate for entrance into Natchez society. They set aside enough money for the riverboat fare with only a few hundred dollars to spare. It was a gamble to deplete their funds that way. But early in their journey they had schemed to enter Natchez with aplomb, determined to avoid looking like poor, plain country bumpkins. "Besides," said Sheridan more than once, "when Aunt Fiona finds I'm with her favorite Cousin Liam—and not returning to live with her in New York—she'll be so happy she'll probably continue with my allowance." And she laughed. "We'll not consider, of course, that she's paying me to stay away!"

Now Callie wore a frock of emerald green—"an exact match for your eyes," Sherrie had declared in the shop—and had pulled her mane of copper hair upward, letting the curls cascade down her back.

Sheridan's ivory skin and black hair, sleek and shiny, were set off by a deep purple dress. Her dark blue eyes danced as the riverboat steamed deeper into the South.

"It's beautiful," she whispered, as Callie pointed out the mansions on the cliffs above the river. It was late spring, and the azaleas and dogwood and magnolias spread like frothy banks of pale pink and white snow around the stately homes. The branches of the weeping willows hung low, green and lacy frames above the profusion of blossoms. Fields of tender and pale corn and cotton seedlings spread for miles on the rolling hills beyond the mansions.

"I've missed it." Callie couldn't take her misting eyes from the sight. "I had forgotten." She was lost in thought for a moment, then continued. "When Juliana and I left, it was late fall—the trees had mostly dropped their leaves and nothing was in bloom. Even so, I remember my sister telling me to look around and memorize its beauty. We stood at my bedroom window and looked out across Stonehaven—the oaks, the ivy, the magnolias shining silver in the moonlight." She turned to Sheridan. "I was so sad. Our father had just died. We were forced to leave the only home we'd ever known. But even though it seemed impossible, I knew I'd be back someday. I swore I'd come back to Stonehaven."

Sheridan smiled softly, understanding. "And here you are, Callie. You're almost home."

Callie stared out across the river. Emotions swirled inside her, just as muddy as the river. "You know, don't you, Sherrie, that we have to act differently than we really are."

Sheridan tilted her head. "It's our role in the Underground you're worried about?"

Callie nodded. "We can't reveal our sympathies."

Sheridan waited for her to continue.

"You don't know the South. It's very different from Ohio—or New York where your aunt lives. First of all, certain behavior is accepted—no, *expected*—among women."

"Go on."

"Southern women are strong, but they accept the way of life here."

"You're meaning slavery and such?"

"Yes."

"Callie, I already knew that, I did. You're not telling me anything I hadn't figured out for myself."

"It's not just that we can't speak out against it. We have to go along with it, condone it, if necessary."

Sheridan studied Callie as she spoke. "Go on," she repeated.

"We have to play the part of Southern belles."

"Do you think that will be so hard?"

"It might be." She took a breath. "In Natchez you will see slaves sold. You may see whippings or worse. Negroes being branded—their ears or noses notched or teeth knocked out for identification." She took her friend's hand as a look of horror crossed Sheridan's face. "But—you can't react, Sherrie. No matter what you see and how sick it makes you feel, you can't let on. Above all, you can't speak out against it. Not to anyone."

Sheridan nodded. "I understand, I do."

"If either of us lets on—it could jeopardize our work with the Underground. In the end, we'll save more lives, get more people out, if we simply play the role of mindless, silly belles."

"And we can't trust anyone. We'll have to move slowly in finding out about the Underground in Natchez. If we ask the wrong people—well, I don't have to tell you what could happen."

Sheridan nodded, her face pale.

"We'll tell your cousin Liam Sheridan that we're here for a visit. We're simply friends from school on holiday. I once lived here. I have good memories and want to look up old friends. I want to see my dear Uncle Caleb. I'll hire a carriage and visit him, playing the loving niece that I am." Callie smiled wickedly. "We'll pull it off, Sherrie. I know we will."

Sheridan grinned, her color returning, and slipped into an exaggerated drawl, looking up at an imaginary Cousin Liam. "Why, honey. I just love it here so much I've decided to stay." She fluttered her thick black lashes and fanned herself with a gloved hand. "I do believe it's the most wonderful place on earth. I want to make Natchez my home, I do. Cousin Liam, sure, won't you-all help your little ol' Irish cousin find a place to live?"

Callie burst out laughing. Sheridan's Irish brogue and southern drawl had even caused other travelers on the riverboat to turn and smile.

"I do declare, Sheridan O'Brian," she said. "I believe these little ol' belles will have quite a time in the South."

Still laughing, the two young women looked out at the river. In a few moments, though, they were again speaking low and seriously, planning every detail of their stay in Natchez.

Three

A short distance from St. Louis, the young doctor, Jedediah Jones, dressed in fringed buckskins and carrying a leather doctor's bag and a Hawkin rifle, nudged his horse's flanks. The Arabian mare reacted with a movement so fluid, so filled with raw power, that the young man marveled again at her magnificence.

Hawk—as Jedediah still preferred to think of himself—patted the animal's delicately arched neck and thought of the man who had given him the horse. She had been a gift upon completion of his studies at Harvard from Dr. Noble Jackson Hill, his mentor and dearest friend. Dr. Hill had taken Hawk into his home years before to prepare him for a career in medicine, to teach and drill him so that he could enter Harvard, the elderly doctor's alma mater. Dr. Hill had then sponsored his admittance to the elite institution. Hawk had no illusions that he would not have been accepted otherwise.

And now the Arabian. Dr. Hill wasn't a wealthy man; most country doctors weren't. Many times patients paid their bills with chickens, eggs, and sides of salt pork. Hawk knew the horse had cost the good doctor at least a half-year's income. But his mentor shared Hawk's love of horses, and the Arabian had been a gift telling of the high regard in which he held his young student. Dr. Hill had probably searched from St. Louis to the Atlantic coast for the perfect piece of horseflesh, then, too excited to await Hawk's return to St. Louis, had the bay delivered to Harvard.

Hawk had left Boston soon after the commencement ceremonies. After weeks on the road, he would arrive at Dr. Hill's home in St. Louis by nightfall. He had promised in his last letter to Dr. Hill that he would spend the summer helping with his patients.

Since the California gold rush had begun, St. Louis was bursting with folks heading west and with Easterners who came that far, then decided to stay. The few doctors in the town couldn't keep up with the demand. Hawk felt he owed Dr. Hill at least a few months work before he moved on to the Mandan villages in the upper Missouri.

To find his way to his mother's people, Hawk had already contacted Thomas Fitzpatrick, "Broken Hand," as he was called by the Indians. The old trapper hired himself out as a guide, as many of them did after the bottom dropped out of the fur market. Hawk looked forward to spending time with the rough old man who had trapped with Hawk's father during his younger years.

It would be difficult to find the remaining Mandans. They had been nearly wiped out by the diseases of the white man. Only a few hundred remained, and most family groups had purposely scattered into areas they hoped were inaccessible by whites. But Fitzpatrick knew the region better that most. If anyone could find the Mandan villages, it would be old Broken Hand.

Hawk reined the Arabian around a bend above a small canyon, then rode to a rise slightly to the north of the trail. A slow smile spread across his face as he reached the top. Below him flowed the Mississippi, swift, turbulent, untamed. As it always did when he saw it, the river evoked longings of wild freedom within him, longings for the home of his ancestors far beyond the Mississippi, beyond the reaches of the place where the Missouri entered it. Yes, even beyond that to the snow-covered mountains that created the headwaters of the Missouri, the place where Morning Sun, his mother, had been born.

He dismounted and stood silently near the Arabian, his face immobile, his body still, as he watched the swiftly moving currents. They were the same that flowed by the Mandan villages. Perhaps his cousins drank from these same waters. An agitation matching that of the river welled up inside him, though he didn't understand why. After a few minutes, Hawk mounted and rode down the trail leading to the ferry crossing and the final leg to St. Louis.

By nightfall, Hawk was riding toward Dr. Hill's house on the western edge of town. He took the mare to the barn, unsaddled her, left her with the groom, then bounded to the front of the house and up the porch, taking the stairs two at a time.

Before he could call out, the door opened, and the grinning face of the white-haired doctor greeted him.

"It's about time you got here, young man. I'd about given you up." The old man's voice was gruff, but his eyes were bright with tears.

"Sir." Hawk took Dr. Hill's hand in both of his own.

Then the doctor brought him to his barrel chest in a rough embrace, slapping him heartily on the back. "Jedediah, you're a sight for these sore old eyes. It's good to see you, son."

"Thank you, sir. It's good to be back."

Dr. Hill ushered Hawk into his parlor. "Sit. Tell me about Harvard. Your commencement. Everything."

Hawk paused. The mention of the commencement reminded

him of Dr. Hill's generous gift. He was embarrassed at his oversight. "Sir, I nearly forgot—you must come see the Arabian."

The older man laughed. "Do you think I bought her sight unseen? I inspected her from ear tip to tail tip, inside and out, in Richmond." He paused, a wide grin still covering his wrinkled face. "Naturally, I'd like to set these eyes on her again—see how she fared the trip. But that can wait. I'd rather hear about you first. And you look to be starving, son. I'll get Eula to fix you some victuals."

Hawk began relating details of his final days at Harvard, the closing of classes, the final goodbyes to the friends he'd made there. Before he had finished, Dr. Hill's housekeeper had set the table and served up a steaming venison stew and a hearty bread. The two men continued their conversation over supper.

"I've got something for you, son," Dr. Hill said, when they were through eating. He moved to a desk at the far end of the room, rummaged around, then came back with an envelope. He handed it to Hawk.

Hawk saw that it was from New Mexico. The script was delicate. Even before he saw the signature, he recognized it as belonging to Juliana James, Callie St. Clair's sister, and his mother and father's dearest friend in New Mexico.

He frowned. Something must have happened to his parents.

"Bad news?" The older man watched him read.

Hawk scanned the first page. It was filled with greetings from them all. "No. No bad news." He shook his head slightly as he continued reading through the letter, becoming more alarmed as he read.

Finally, he spoke. "This is from Juliana on behalf of them all. It seems it's been some time since they've heard from Callie. They're worried."

Dr. Hill nodded sympathetically, waiting for him to go on.

Hawk sighed. "They're asking me to ride up to Oberlin College and check on her."

"That's not exactly on your way."

"It's five hundred miles the opposite direction. If I had known, I would have swung by on my way from Boston."

"You're angry that you've got to go?"

Hawk shook his head slowly. "No. Just worried. Juliana's right to wonder why they haven't heard from her."

"I only asked because the last I remembered, you thought of the young lady as a 'self-centered, hot-headed, spoiled brat.'"

"I once thought that."

"And now?"

Hawk looked straight at his friend. "She's still high-spirited." He chuckled. "And feisty, opinionated…unpredictable. There's no doubt about that."

Dr. Hill threw his head back and laughed. "She sounds delightful."

Hawk felt himself color. He nodded. "That she is."

Dr. Hill raised an eyebrow, waiting for Hawk to continue.

But the young man didn't want to speak of his feelings for Callie, feelings he himself didn't understand. So instead he returned to the situation at hand. "Callie's always been conscious of others' feelings. There's got to be something wrong if she hasn't contacted her sister for this length of time."

Dr. Hill nodded in agreement. "There's something you must know about Oberlin College, son. It's true that it has a good reputation. When it was founded back in the 'thirties, it was the first college of its kind to admit women—completely academic, rather than simply a finishing school."

"I agree. I was impressed with it when I stopped by to see Callie a couple years ago."

Dr. Hill's face turned serious. "Oberlin College has another reputation, Jed." He paused as if watching for Hawk's reaction.

Hawk settled back into his chair. He had no idea what Dr. Hill was referring to.

"Its students are active abolitionists. I've heard they're openly part of the Underground Railroad."

It was Hawk's turn to laugh. "That's one thing we don't need to worry that Callie would get involved in. She's a Southerner down to the tips of her dainty little feet. A Southern belle through and through. You should have seen her in action at the college. Believe me, she was born to be a plantation mistress."

"That was a few years ago. What do you know about her views now?"

"I know Callie very well. She was raised in Mississippi. Natchez. Grew up on a plantation called Stonehaven with hundreds of slaves at her beck and call. I know she's talked of going back. For years she's claimed that the plantation was stolen from the St. Clairs." He sighed. "As I told you, this young woman is as single-minded as a stampeding buffalo. I don't think she's changed. She'd more likely be out trying to convince the abolitionists and free-soilers they're both wrong."

Dr. Hill pulled his spectacles from his nose and cleaned them with his handkerchief. "How long has it been since her family's heard from her?"

"They don't really say. But I get the feeling that they had letters from her every few weeks until several months ago. Of course, with the distance between them, by the time the mail was delivered they might get several letters at once. But at least they were hearing from her." Hawk paused, realizing how strange it was that communication had stopped so abruptly. "They haven't received word from her for quite some time."

"It might be serious." Dr. Hill watched him intently. "I think you need to leave as soon as you can."

Hawk nodded slowly. "It's just that—"

The old doctor interrupted. "Don't worry about leaving me, son. I'd looked forward to having you work with me—but this is more important. The young woman could be in real danger. Her family was right in asking you to look in on her."

"It's not just having to leave here, not being able to give back a little of what you've given me—" he began.

"It's your trip up the Missouri, isn't it, son?"

Hawk nodded. "I've got it set up with Fitzpatrick. We were to leave in September. I might be back from Oberlin by then, but I need the summer to prepare—gather the medicines and equipment I'll need." He realized even as he spoke that he was afraid to see Callie again, afraid that just looking in her eyes would cause him to put aside his dream, his mission, forever.

"Son, sometimes we don't know why we're shoved off course. The path you've laid out for your life is a godly and noble one. It's your dream. I know better than anyone what it means to you to serve your mother's people.

"Truth is, God knows better than we do the direction we should go. We fix our compass on something distant and, though it may be a godly direction, it might not be the right time. It might not even be the right calling.

"I've never seen anyone who was so sure of his course at such a young age. When you came to me, you were still a child. But you knew that you wanted to be a doctor. You wanted to help those in pain. You wanted to find a cure for the diseased—especially the Mandan.

"I always knew that God had placed those desires in you, son. I saw you overcome great obstacles to achieve your dreams. I observed your great talent and growing skill. You learned, first from me, then later at Harvard, all those fine touches that made a physician good.

"I've seen your compassion. I know firsthand your drive. I've seen you kneel in prayer, seeking God's will." Dr. Hill paused, his dark eyes piercing Hawk's. "But son, I don't think you ever considered that God's will might be different from your own. That his timing might be different from yours." He smiled gently as he spoke the last words.

"You think I'm impatient."

Dr. Hill nodded slowly, his face kind, but said nothing.

"How can I wait for 'God's timing' when my mother's people are dying? There are fewer every year. Once there were tens of thousands. Now there are only hundreds left. Maybe not even that." Hawk paused, then added, his tone solemn, "Of course I'm impatient. How can I not be?"

Dr. Hill remained silent. The clock on the mantel ticked loudly, slowly. Finally, he spoke, a touch of irony in his voice. "We doctors sometimes place ourselves in a lofty position. We have healing powers—maybe not admitting even to ourselves that those powers are acquired, not innate—that place us on a plane above the ordinary man. We may even go so far as to invite God to walk with us as we set our life's course—as long as he keeps in step with us on the path of our choosing." He gazed straight into Hawk's eyes. "Not we with him on his path."

"You know me too well, sir."

Dr. Hill laughed softly. "I know myself too well."

Neither man spoke for a few minutes, then Dr. Hill leaned across the table. "Tell me this, son. Is there anyone else whom you would trust to find Callie? Someone who would care enough to make sure of her well-being? Or—if she has met with tragic folly—someone who would give his life for her rescue?"

Hawk smiled slowly. Dr. Hill knew him even better than he thought. "No," he said, simply. "No one."

"Sometimes when I'm given no choice, I see God's hand in

the direction I'm pointed toward." He laughed again. "It's probably because I'm too stubborn to find his will any other way. And you're as stubborn as I am, Jed." He stood and slapped the young man on the back affectionately. "We're alike, you and me. I think God did that on purpose, too."

The two men went outside to the barn, picked up grooming brushes and combed down the mare. They spent the rest of the evening in easy camaraderie, speaking of the growing popularity of the new Arabian breed in America, and of course, about Callie St. Clair and her possible whereabouts.

Three days later, Hawk, dressed once more in the fringed buckskins he preferred for traveling, swung into the Arabian's saddle, touched his hand to his hat in a goodbye to Dr. Hill, and headed north. Folded in an inside jacket pocket was the letter from Juliana.

Three weeks later he rode into Oberlin and straight through town to the campus.

A student, a young woman dressed in drab skirt and blouse, looked up as he rode onto the tree-lined grounds. She gazed at him, a polite but puzzled expression on her face. Hawk smiled to himself. He knew he looked more Indian than white when dressed in his buckskins. But it was his light-brown hair and blue eyes that confused most people.

"I'm looking for a Callasandra St. Clair," he said. "You might know her by the name Callie."

The young woman's open expression suddenly went blank, purposely blank. Maybe she was afraid of him. He glanced at his clothing again. After all, the way he was dressed might put off any genteel young lady.

He began again. "I'm sorry. I should have introduced myself.

My name is Dr. Jedediah Jones." He patted the everpresent black leather bag tied behind the saddle. "Callie is a friend of my family's in New Mexico. We haven't heard from her in quite some time. I'm wondering if you could direct me to her rooms."

The young woman looked uncomfortable. She moved her gaze from his, a pink flush rising to her cheeks. "She no longer attends Oberlin," she finally said, her discomfort obvious.

"Do you mean the school is on a holiday break?"

"No. Miss St. Clair left last term."

"After she received her certificate."

The young woman leveled steady gray eyes his direction. "No. It was too soon for that. She just left."

By now two other students, a young man and another young woman, had joined her. Hawk swung off his saddle and stood closer to the group. They stared at him with identical guarded expressions.

"Do any of you know where she might have gone?"

They shook their heads in silence.

"Then tell me this: Is there anyone around here who might know? Maybe a friend of hers? A teacher?"

Again, no answer. Only silent blank stares.

Then the young man spoke up. "You should talk to the president."

"All right. Point the way."

The young man mumbled that he would, and Hawk, leading the Arabian, followed him to an ivy-covered building nestled amidst oaks and willows. The student nodded toward its wide porch. "In there," he said. "The president's name is Welland. Daniel Welland."

Hawk climbed the stairs and rapped at the door. It was opened by an assistant who showed him into Welland's office after he explained the purpose of his visit.

A dignified older man stood and greeted Hawk. "Sit down, sit down," Welland said, as he seated himself behind his desk. "And what can I do for you?"

Hawk repeated his questions about Callie, told of his family's interest, and watched the president's face for any signs of discomfort such as he had noted in the students.

The man looked perfectly at ease. He smiled and shook his head. "Young people these days..." He shrugged. "It seems they just can't make up their minds about what they want in life."

Hawk waited silently for the man to continue.

"This friend of your family's, Miss St. Clair. In my recollection, she was one of the flightiest students to enter Oberlin." He sighed as if embarrassed. "We did what we could for her, but very honestly, she just wasn't academic material. She struggled for several terms, then finally gave up and left."

"Left?"

Welland nodded. "She left in the middle of last term. It was very sudden. Right before exams, as I recall. It seems the final academic push just became too much for her."

Hawk thought of his recent words to Dr. Hill about Callie being busy attending soirees and teas. Welland's explanation of Callie's troubles fit the high-spirited young woman Hawk remembered. She had probably sworn her friends to secrecy to save embarrassment for her family. Perhaps she'd run away, too ashamed to return to New Mexico.

"Do you know where she went?"

Welland shook his head sadly. "I assumed she had returned home. Home to—" he hesitated, "—New Mexico, was it?" His tone dropped, as if asking what else could be expected from the godforsaken place. Hawk disliked the man for it and wondered if Callie had too.

"Would she have confided in anyone? A friend perhaps? Is

there anyone who might know where she went when she left?"

Welland cleared his throat. His light skin colored slightly. "Not really. No, I can think of no one."

"She had no friends?"

The college president tapped his spectacles on the desk's highly polished surface. "There was one friend—" he began.

"Was?"

"I say 'was' because her friend left at the same time as Miss St. Clair." He shook his head sadly. "Of the same mind, those two. I assume that if you find one, you'll find the other, pursuing... well, who knows?" He gestured with one hand, then shrugged. After a moment he stood, concluding their meeting. "Good luck," he said, extending a hand. "I do hope they are finding gratification in their new pursuits."

Hawk left Welland's office deep in thought. As he walked down the hall to the door, the president's assistant—the same who had earlier greeted him—looked up from his desk in a separate office. The young man nodded, then went back to his work.

Abruptly, Hawk stopped, then stepped across the hall. "Would it be possible to see Callie—Callasandra St. Clair's records?" He hadn't asked Welland the exact date of Callie's departure from Oberlin. Her records would tell him. It wouldn't be much to go on, but it would at least be something.

The young man didn't hesitate. "Of course," he said, and stood to go through his files.

Hawk smiled to himself. The records office at Harvard would never allow such an intrusion. This young man, probably a student himself, must be new at his job.

"Here they are—'Callasandra St. Clair,'" he said, reading her name at the top of the folder. He spread it open on the desk in front of Hawk.

Hawk thumbed through the papers, expecting to see the

record of the "flighty" young student Welland had described. He looked closer. "Are you certain these are her records?" Hawk rechecked the name at the top of the record file as the young man nodded vigorously.

Consistently, from the first term Callie had attended Oberlin, her marks were high. Extremely high. There were notes of commendation from her teachers. He read through them. Again and again they praised her academic achievement.

Why had Welland lied to him? Had he confused Callie with another student? As Hawk scanned the marks on Callie's final exams—exams she had passed with noted honors—a voice at the doorway interrupted him.

"Our student records are confidential." President Welland, redfaced and grim, strode across the room and yanked the folder from Hawk's hands. "You had no right to request them." Then he turned to the cowering student assistant. "And you, young man, had no right to show them to this—this—" he stammered, "—this bounty hunter."

Hawk turned and grabbed the man by the top of his shirt. "Bounty hunter? What are you talking about?" His voice dropped. He'd had enough of the man's duplicity. "I want answers. And I want them now." He shoved Welland against the wall, glaring into his frightened watery eyes. "Where is Callie St. Clair?"

"I don't know."

Hawk tightened his hold on the man's collar. Welland gulped, and whispered again. "I really don't know."

Hawk believed him, but he didn't loosen his grip. "Why did you call me a bounty hunter?"

Welland stared at him, his eyes turning cold, hard, filled with hate. "Because that's what you are," he muttered. "You can't fool me with your tale of family friendship. You're not the first one

75

who's nosed around here looking for Miss St. Clair, hunting the fine young woman like dogs after a coon. All for a price. You disgust me, you and your kind." Welland spit in Hawk's face.

Shaken, Hawk backed away, dropping his hold on the man. He wiped his face with the back of his hand and studied Welland. The man was protecting Callie. He had lied to protect her. But from what? He had to admire Welland for his tenacity.

"I'm not a bounty hunter. Whatever Miss St. Clair has gotten herself into, I'd like to help. Please believe me. Help me find her."

Welland stared at him, venomous hate still written on his face. "I've heard that before, too." His voice dropped when he continued. "As I said, you'll not get anything else from me. From any of us."

Hawk turned to go, then looked back at Oberlin's president. "For what it's worth, sir—thank you for what you're doing for Callie."

The man looked stunned at his words but said nothing.

Hawk mounted the Arabian and rode to Mrs. Gray's two-story house at the edge of the campus.

Mrs. Gray, wiping her hands on her apron, opened the door at his knock. She didn't seem to recognize him.

"I'm looking for Callie St. Clair," he said.

"I've never heard of her."

Hawk fought the exasperation welling inside him. "She lived here with you. Barely a little over a year ago. I saw her here myself."

"You're mistaken, sir. I've never heard of anyone by that name."

"Please, ma'am. It's important I find her. I know she was here. We sat inside together, visiting. You brought us tea. Surely you remember me."

Her face was blank, but there was fear in her eyes. "I most

certainly don't, sir. Now if you'll excuse me. I have work to do." She started to close the door.

Hawk blocked it with his foot. "Please. I'm Callie's friend—" he began.

"That's what they all say." For the first time, a shadow of recognition, then sadness, crossed her face. "Now, if you will excuse me—" and she closed the door firmly.

Hawk started to knock again, then let his hand drop. It was no use. Mrs. Gray was obviously afraid of something. Or someone. She had probably said all she intended to.

Later, after Hawk had mounted the Arabian and was heading south to his camping spot, the perplexed look on Welland's face came back to him. And the expression of fear and sadness on Mrs. Gray's face. They were both guarding some door that Callie had exited. But why? What were they covering up?

The unsettling fear that had been lurking within him since reading Juliana's letter weeks ago now struck deep into his soul. What if something terrible had happened to her? What would he do?

It was hard enough to think of a lifetime without her. It was unbearable to think of a world without her in it—even if she were nowhere near him.

He suddenly remembered the prayer she had whispered that winter day long ago when she'd thought him mortally injured after falling from his horse. "Oh, God," she'd implored. "Please let him be all right." Her voice had trembled with fear.

Now, Hawk found himself echoing her words. "Dear God," he breathed. "Please let Callie be all right." But this was no prank. She wasn't here to squeeze his hand—as he'd done to her that day—and laugh into his eyes.

He bowed his head again. "Please, God. Let her be all right," he prayed, as he rode.

The night following Hawk's visit to Oberlin College, he made camp outside town near a thicket of willows. After a supper of pemmican he had brought from St. Louis, he lay down next to the dying embers of his campfire and stared at the starlit heavens. He wondered if Callie might be gazing at the same sky. But from where?

Unable to sleep, Hawk thought about the enigmatic young woman. From the first moment he'd set eyes on her, Callie had alternately exasperated and delighted him with her hotheaded temper one minute and tender insights the next.

He smiled at the memory of their first meeting. He would never forget the look of her as she had rounded the curve—eyes closed, flame-colored hair flying, riding faster than the prairie wind. She'd had no thought that anyone else might be on the trail.

In that split second before she looked up and saw him, he understood the pure abandon written in her face, the freedom and raw joy she was feeling as she rode. He'd felt the same emotions while riding under the high mesa skies, especially after living so many months in his cramped quarters at Harvard.

Callie's fleeting look changed abruptly when the horses met, reared, and whinnied. Surprise turned to fury when she saw him and his horse in front of her. She hadn't even considered that the accident could have been caused by her reckless behavior. When her horse stumbled and headed down the cliff, she had yelled at Hawk all the way to the riverbank.

But then his behavior hadn't been exactly chivalrous. Once he determined that Callie wasn't injured, his concern had been more for the horses' well-being than for that of the angry young woman. Barely more than an overgrown child, she had stomped and fumed at him for *his* recklessness. He knew now that he shouldn't have ridden off the way he did. In silent irritation he'd left her, dusty and disheveled, to get herself out of the canyon. At the time, it seemed she deserved it for the way she had treated him.

Through the years, though he returned to New Mexico only a few times, she seemed never to forgive him, first for leaving her stranded, then later for her chagrin at railing on to Sun and Jeremiah about the brute she'd met on the trail—only to have him step through the door and be introduced as their son.

And she never let him forget it. Each time Hawk visited New Mexico and rode into the meadow, his heart leapt at the thought of seeing her again. But their meetings were always the same. Callie, with flashing eyes and a toss of the head, made it obvious she still thought him an uncouth brute.

Until the horse race. He chuckled at the memory. Callie had shown him nothing but contempt until that day. But after the fall, when she had knelt over him ashenfaced, holding his hand, touching his cheek, the moment had been so sweet that he hadn't wanted it to end. His laughter had broken the spell. Within moments the hot-tempered, unforgiving, unpredictable Callie St. Clair had been resurrected.

Hawk rolled over and tossed a branch on the embers of his

dying campfire, watching the sparks fly into the black sky. Settling back into his bedroll, he again attempted to sleep. It was no use. His thoughts returned to Callie.

It had been less than two years since he'd last seen her at Oberlin College. But not a day had passed, even at Harvard, when he didn't think of her, remembering the look of her as she stood in the silver moonlight.

Hawk sighed, staring into the heavens with its canopy of stars. What kind of danger had Callie gotten herself into? From Welland's words he figured that Callie must be a fugitive from the law. Otherwise, why would there be a price on her head?

But what could she have done to get herself in such a fix? She wasn't a criminal. Hawk did know that about her. Dr. Hill had mentioned the Underground Railroad stations in Oberlin. But Hawk quickly dismissed Callie's involvement in such activities. Plantation blood ran deep in her veins. He knew firsthand that her Southern upbringing affected most of her views. Hawk decided he could stake his life on Callie having nothing to do with helping runaway slaves.

But then, what had she run from? She obviously had left in a great hurry—so shortly before the term's end. He'd seen the date of her last exam. It was only days before she would have received her teaching certificate. Why would she leave without it? And why was the president of Oberlin College protecting her?

The answers simply were not there. Hawk stared into the night sky thinking of Dr. Hill's words about God's direction. Since Hawk's childhood and his earliest dreams of becoming a doctor, he'd thought nothing would deter him from ministering to the Mandan. He loved God and wanted to serve him. But had he been wrong about his calling?

Here he was in Ohio instead of in a keelboat on the upper Missouri. He was chasing after a hotheaded young woman who obviously didn't want to be found.

But no power on earth would keep him from trying to find Callie. He again pondered the mystery of her disappearance, trying to place himself in Callie's thoughts as she left Oberlin. Where would he go? Farmhouses were scattered throughout the countryside. Callie had been there long enough to make friends with the villagers. Perhaps one of them had taken her in. She could be within minutes of where he now lay. If that was true, he might find her sooner that he thought.

Then, just as he was about to fall asleep, Hawk remembered Stonehaven. He stared unseeing at the blaze of stars overhead. Of course. If he put himself in her position, that's exactly where he would go. He knew with a sinking realization that's where Callie would go, too.

She would ride horseback to the Ohio River and catch a steamer to Cairo, then head down the Mississippi to Natchez. It would take her weeks. But if anyone knew how to travel—on covered wagons or riverboats—it was this young woman. And she was fearless. A thousand-mile journey to her childhood home would be nothing to Callie.

He closed his eyes again and sighed. He would get an early start, ride the Arabian to the Ohio River, board a riverboat, and head to Natchez where he was certain he would find Callie St. Clair.

Hawk finally fell into a restless sleep. But his dreams were filled with Callie's image, cascading hair the color of molten fire, eyes flashing like priceless emeralds in the sun. Then he and Callie danced, whirling and dipping to the music of fiddles and banjos, laughing into each other's eyes.

The music faded and Callie made Hawk stop dancing. She pointed to the stone houses of the Mandan that suddenly surrounded them. Near the small, dark houses, the sick and dying reached their arms out for help. Feverish babies whimpered pitifully. Aged grandmothers wailed in mourning.

Then the fiddles played again. And Callie danced by, silver in the moonlight. Hawk ignored her, determined instead to reach the babies, the children, the village elders. But his legs had turned to stone. He looked desperately to Callie for help, watching her dance with the lightness of wildflowers in the wind. She could help, if only she would. But he couldn't ask her. She had disappeared. No one knew where she had gone.

He turned again to the villagers. They began to fade, with only the images of their hands remaining stretched out to him, calling to him. Soon nothing was left of the dream but darkness and the haunting cries of the sick and mourning.

CHAPTER

Five

❧

Four high-stepping grays pulled the hired carriage down the main street of Natchez. Inside, Sheridan looked over at Callie, her eyes shining.

"I'm feeling like a grand lady, Callie. I never thought I would be headin' to the grandest house in all the South." She suddenly looked stricken. "Mind you—the grandest only according to my own Aunt Fiona. She was saying that not knowing anything at all about Stonehaven."

Callie grinned and patted her friend's hand. "You'll have to be the judge, Sherrie, after you see them both!"

The carriage rumbled past a slave auction in the town square. A wooden platform with stairs at either end dominated the scene. An auctioneer was in place at its center with a group of slaves roped together, some young, some aged, to his right. The black men and women stood, faces without expression, shoulders slumped. A few traders stood guard nearby, talking among themselves, sometimes nodding toward this slave or that. Below the platform a noisy crowd had gathered.

Sheridan gasped. "Animals," she whispered, her voice low. "Animals."

"Slaves are thought of as cattle—" Callie began, misunderstanding.

"No! I mean the others. The auctioneers. *They* are the animals. How can they treat people that way? Look at them, Callie. Their bodies are barely covered. That one—there! Look what they're doing." The vehicle had stopped to let traffic cross. Sheridan peered through the open window.

A skinny girl, maybe fourteen years old, was led to the platform. The crowd watched the auctioneer examine her. He pried open her mouth, loudly pointing out the soundness of her teeth. Lifting one small arm then the other, then each of her bony legs, he attempted to draw attention away from her sickly appearance and spoke about the strength of her limbs as if she were a prize piece of horseflesh. Then she was turned from side to side, back to front, with hands tethered, her head hung low.

Callie felt the heat of angry tears spring to her eyes. Growing up in Natchez, how could she have been blind to the horror of such treatment?

"Who'll start the bidding?" the auctioneer called out to the crowd.

"You're gonna have to pay someone to take her off your hands," someone in the crowd yelled, "being she's so all-to-pieces bony!" A few laughed at his words and called out their opinions to the auctioneer. No one started the bidding.

Callie fought to keep her expression immobile. Across from her, a pale Sheridan turned her face away, covering her mouth with a lacy handkerchief. "I never knew," she whispered, when her color had returned.

The carriage rumbled past the auction and turned east. Neither young woman spoke for several minutes.

"Callie," Sheridan finally managed, her voice trembling. "Do we have any money left?"

"A few hundred dollars." Callie knew why Sheridan asked. "But we'll need every penny if Liam won't take us in."

"I'm willing to take the chance if you are." Tears glistened in Sheridan's eyes.

Callie nodded, then called to the driver to turn around. "I hope we're not too late."

Within minutes the carriage had again pulled close to the slave auction. The bidding for the same young woman was up to a mere two hundred dollars.

The auctioneer had already raised his gavel to pronounce the girl sold when Callie called out, "Two hundred twenty dollars. I'll give you two twenty."

The crowd turned and watched as Callie opened the carriage door and stepped down from the vehicle.

"Two hundred twenty. I have a bid for two hundred twenty. Do I hear more?" The auctioneer looked out expectantly at the crowd.

There wasn't a sound.

"Then this girl is sold for two hundred and twenty dollars to the woman in green." He nodded in Callie's direction and tapped the gavel smartly on the table before him.

Callie walked to the platform, paid the money, then nodded toward the girl to follow her. With head still down, the child walked behind her new mistress to the carriage.

They settled inside, Callie and Sheridan across from the girl. The driver flicked his whip above the grays and the carriage again moved down the main road through town.

"What's your name?" Callie's voice was gentle.

The girl kept her eyes downcast. "Rebecca, ma'am."

"Rebecca, you will be safe with us."

"Yes, ma'am." Still she did not look up. Her soft voice sounded indifferent.

"She'll be needin' proper clothes, Callie."

Callie nodded. They couldn't take a servant child into Sheridan Hall dressed in rags. Again, she called out to the driver, this time to stop at the nearest clothiers.

"I've got enough," Sheridan whispered, not wanting Rebecca to know they were down to their last few dollars. She patted her pocketbook.

When the carriage halted, Callie and the girl waited while Sheridan disappeared into the store for a few minutes, then reappeared with a bundle under her arm. "Rebecca, these are for you," she pronounced, and placed the package on the girl's lap.

Her thin fingers trembling, Rebecca untied the package, then looked up with a shy smile. Sheridan had picked out a pale yellow day dress with a white pique collar and matching apron. The astounded girl lifted the soft dress to her face then suddenly giggled, spotting beneath it a lacy petticoat, dainty pantaloons, and stockings.

"And these." Sheridan produced another small package. "A well-dressed woman always needs good shoes. Matching shoes. I guessed at the size"—she looked down at Rebecca's feet—"but I think these will do."

This time Rebecca tore open the package and pulled out finely stitched lace-ups. She hugged them to her pitifully thin chest and gave Callie and Sheridan another shy smile.

"Now," Callie said, as the carriage bumped along through town. "Where can she change?"

"I've thought of that, too." This time Sheridan gave the instructions to the driver. Within minutes the carriage had pulled into a deserted alleyway. Callie and Sheridan exited, leaving Rebecca to dress in privacy. The driver moved away from the carriage and stood by the team.

A short time later, the girl opened the door and stepped from the carriage, daintily holding her skirts, admiring her shoes with each step she took.

Sheridan glanced at Callie and they both smiled at the transformation. The girl was beautiful and now looked older than they had originally guessed. Maybe as old as sixteen. The pale yellow suited her.

At first Rebecca's gaze met theirs, her smile wide and open. Then she seemed to remember her place and promptly looked at the ground, the smile gone.

Callie stepped toward her, gently cupped her hand beneath the girl's chin and turned her thin face toward hers. "Please look at me, Rebecca."

The girl tried again, then quickly looked away. She had been taught to avoid eye contact.

"Rebecca?"

"Yes, ma'am?" Her eyes remained downcast.

Sheridan stepped forward. "Rebecca, we bought you. But not to be our slave."

This time Rebecca looked up and her gaze lingered on Sheridan's face. She tilted her head slightly.

Sheridan went on. "Sure, we can't tell you everything right now. But please believe we mean you no harm. We'll be seein' to it that no one ever hurts you again."

The girl nodded and kept her gaze level.

Callie broke in. "Around others you will do for us just as any other house servant would. But in private, we will drop the pretense. We will wait on ourselves."

Rebecca's eyes were bright, intelligent.

"Have you had any book learnin'?" Sheridan asked.

"No, ma'am." Again Rebecca looked down.

"Aye, then, we'll be fixin' that straightaway."

Rebecca looked up in surprise, examining Sheridan's face. Her expression brightened. The reaction was stronger than when she'd seen her new clothes. Again, Callie caught a glimpse of the girl's intelligence.

"Yes. We both studied to become teachers. You'll be our first student."

This time Rebecca's face broke into a wide smile. "I don't know if that'll be good or bad, Miss Sheridan," she said. "Bein' the first I mean." The three laughed together.

Several minutes later, the carriage halted in front of Sheridan Hall. The two-story structure with its ornate double-columned entrance, wrought-iron scrollwork, and impressive height, stood out among the other town houses that lined the street. The white of its walls gleamed like fresh-hewn alabaster in the bright spring sun. Dogwood trees provided a canopy of lacy pink on either side of the stone walkway lined with a neatly trimmed boxwood hedge. An English garden of wild roses, hollyhocks, irises, foxglove, tiger lilies, and black-eyed Susans grew in well-planned disarray between the front of the house and a low wrought-iron fence that ran the length of Sheridan Hall. The look of it all was enchanting, friendly.

Callie smiled at Sheridan as the driver opened the carriage door. "Your Aunt Fiona may be right—this may well be the most beautiful home in the South."

Sheridan seemed too nervous to answer. She took a deep breath as the three young women stepped from the carriage in front of the gate. Callie placed a few coins in the driver's hand, then turned to walk with the others to the wide porch.

Moments later, Sheridan rapped the sterling silver knocker at the center of the ornately carved mahogany door.

A tall, dignified house servant with graying hair opened the door. "May I help you?"

After asking for Master Sheridan, Callie and Sheridan were ushered into the front parlor. Rebecca was shown to the kitchen, a separate room attached to the main house by a covered walkway. She would wait for them there.

For several minutes the young women stood waiting for the master of Sheridan Hall. The room, with its dark wood floors and trim, was tastefully furnished with pale blue-and gold-brocaded furniture. A grouping of two high-back wing chairs and a sofa were arranged opposite a large fireplace with an ornate silver andirons and firescreen frame. Liam Sheridan must have a penchant for sterling, Callie decided. Even the door handles were silver, adding an elegant touch to the soft sheen of the polished mahogany.

Sheridan stepped to a floor-to-ceiling window that opened onto the front porch, and beyond that the English garden. She fingered the lace at the window.

"It's Irish," she said softly, with misty eyes. "Irish lace."

Just as Sheridan spoke, the double parlor doors opened. Standing between them was one of the most handsome men Callie had ever seen. He had Sheridan's black hair and deep blue—nearly violet—eyes. His skin was ruddy. An outdoorsman, she figured. He wasn't tall but seemed to contain power in his build, even in the way he moved as he strode across the room toward the young women.

"How is it that you recognize the lace?" He directed his question to Sheridan. When he spoke, his voice held a touch of the same brogue as his cousin's.

"Why, Liam Sheridan. Don't you know your own cousin?" Sheridan tilted her head, watching him expectantly.

Liam looked puzzled for a moment then broke into a wide grin. "Why, of course I do. You're little Sherrie O'Brian—the one who stole my surname." He opened his arms and gathered Sheridan into an embrace.

"How is it you're here?" he asked, after a few moments of misty-eyed and noisy laughter. "But first, you must tell me— who is your beautiful traveling companion?" He cast an appraising gaze in Callie's direction.

Sheridan introduced Callie. Taking her hand, Liam bowed formally, then motioned for Callie and Sheridan to sit on the gold-brocaded sofa. He sat opposite them on one of the high-backed chairs that flanked the sofa. Something told Callie that although Liam's demeanor was lighthearted, beneath the facade was a shrewd businessman.

"Tell me," he was saying, "what brings you to Natchez? The last I heard from Fiona you were about to finish the term at Oberlin."

Sheridan cast a wary glance at Callie as if looking for support. Callie nodded with a slight smile then noticed that Liam hadn't missed either movement.

"Well," Sheridan began, after taking a deep breath and smiling sweetly. "After the rigors of our studies—Oh, Cousin Liam, you just don't have any idea how hard we worked at Oberlin— we, that is Callie and I, wanted to take a holiday." Her words rushed together and Callie had the awful feeling that Liam—as shrewd as she already guessed him to be—would surely know a well-rehearsed yarn when he heard one. Sheridan went on without pause. "Many of our friends decided at the term's end that they would travel. Why—Cousin Liam—some were even sailing to Europe—England and France. I just knew Aunt Fiona would say no to that. I'm sure you know how she feels about me, all of that nonsense about being incorrigible and all.

"But I digress. The point I was making, Cousin, is that with everyone else off on their travels, my friend here—Callie—and I started discussin' where we could go on holiday. Oh. I didn't tell you yet that Callie is originally from Natchez. Grew up on a plantation not far from Sheridan Hall. Well, as soon as we discovered our mutual interests here—here in Natchez, I mean—we decided to head down the Mississippi. Of course we had to head down the Ohio River first." Sheridan laughed lightly, then without missing a beat, continued. "And that's how we ended up, hoping to spend our holiday with you, Cousin Liam." She gave him her brightest smile. "We were hoping—and we're sorry that we didn't send word ahead—we're hoping you could take in your little ol' Irish cousin and her friend for a few weeks. We promise we'll be no trouble. No trouble at all."

In the silent moments that followed Sheridan's speech, Callie forced herself to keep her gaze on Liam, willing him to accept her friend's words. Sherrie's tale—mostly because of the way it spilled from her like milk from a dropped china cup—sounded false.

Liam's eyes twinkled when he finally spoke. "Aye, but it's taken you some five weeks to get here."

Callie's gaze met Sheridan's in alarm. "How would you be knowin' that?"

He went on. "Five weeks gave plenty of notice for Fiona—who expected you in New York at the term's end—to contact Oberlin and find that you'd left. Seems you escaped in the middle of the night. Though no one could—or would—say why. Sure now, Fiona, being the smart Irishwoman she is, figured that if you'd gotten yourself into some scrape you might end up here. I received a telegram a week ago askin' me to watch for you."

Sheridan hung her head for a moment. When she looked up her eyes were flashing. "Then why the pretense, dear cousin? You actin' like you didn't know me, when all along you knew who I was and why I was here. Then letting me rattle on the way you did, making a bloomin' idiot of meself."

Liam broke into laughter. "Aye, I did. And I found that one thing you're not, little Sheridan O'Brian, is a good storyteller. You'll need lessons while you're here. Lessons from one of the best." He laughed again before continuing. "But you're wrong, child. I *don't* know exactly why you're here, now do I?"

Sheridan glanced at Callie as if seeking a way out of the web she'd spun.

"We'd better tell him the truth, Sherrie." Callie met Liam's gaze calmly. "You see, sir—"

"Please. Call me Liam," he interrupted, then nodded for her to continue.

Callie smiled innocently. "All right, Liam." She was determined to do a better job of her tale than Sheridan had with hers. He would hear only what she wanted him to hear. "I'll call you Liam—only if you will call me Callie."

He nodded, not taking his shrewd blue eyes from her. "You see, it's my fault that Sherrie left school so abruptly. What Sherrie told you about my being from Natchez is true. I grew up on a plantation outside town. You may know it—Stonehaven."

"Stonehaven?" Liam sat straighter in his chair, then leaned forward, his expression no longer benign. His eyes pierced hers. "Go on."

"When I was sixteen, my sister Juliana and I were forced to leave Stonehaven. We were told that our father—Richard St. Clair—had made some bad investments. Borrowed against the land. When the banks called in the notes it was during a bad crop year and Father didn't have the means to pay. He lost everything. His heart failed. He died—very suddenly. Juliana and I were left with nothing but debts."

Liam didn't speak. Callie couldn't read his expression.

"Juliana and I left Stonehaven after our uncle and guardian—"

"Caleb Benedict," Liam murmured, almost as if to himself.

Callie was surprised. "You know him?"

"Everyone knows Senator Benedict." He didn't elaborate.

"As I was saying, after Uncle Caleb arranged a marriage for

me and a governess position for Juliana, we decided we'd had enough of his 'help.' We left Stonehaven one night and never returned."

Liam Sheridan still watched her intently. "You've returned to visit your old home?"

Callie nodded.

"You're aware that Benedict is now the owner of Stonehaven?"

"My sister and I had heard that."

"And you're here to visit—even after the pain he caused you?" His laugh was bitter, his voice mocking as he continued. "Oh, I see. The long-lost niece returns home."

"Yes." His tone angered Callie, but she kept her voice calm, unemotional, and narrowed her eyes at him. "Why do you assume my uncle caused us—me—pain?" He knew more than he was telling. "I said that I fled after he'd tried to find me a husband. That wasn't painful. It was simply an error in his judgment."

Liam Sheridan suddenly laughed. The sound was hollow, false. "Ah, yes," he said. "Maybe it's just my suspicious nature, but for a moment I assumed you'd come here to reclaim your plantation. But I see now how absurd that would be. I mean, the two of you?" He gestured toward Sheridan and Callie.

Sheridan took the bait. "What do you mean, 'the two of you,' Liam Sheridan?" Before Callie could stop her she went on. "As if the two of us couldn't do anything we put our minds to? I'm ashamed to be callin' you my cousin if you're going to toss about such accusations. If Callie wants to take back the land that is rightfully hers, that's exactly what she'll be doing. Nothing will stop her, dear cousin. Nothing."

This time Liam's laughter was genuine. He put up his hands. "Aye. You're right, Sherrie O'Brian. And shame I admit." He thickened his brogue.

But he didn't fool Callie. He had extracted the information he'd set out for the moment he laid eyes on them. She wasn't surprised when, after a moment of light banter with Sheridan, his gaze settled on Callie and he continued to probe.

"You're here to look into the fate that befell Stonehaven and your father." There was no question in his tone.

"Yes." Callie made a quick decision to tell him that much. She had planned to ask him later to recommend a lawyer to look into the matter. He had simply moved her plans forward a bit. "Yes," she repeated, sighing. "That's the real reason we're here. As I said earlier—I talked Sheridan into leaving Oberlin and traveling here with me."

"You couldn't wait until the end of the term?"

"Well, no sir. The school setting wasn't much to my liking. And I—I just couldn't wait any longer to come home." She gave Liam a sweet smile, moving gently, ever so gently, into the role that she and Sheridan had planned for her. She would have to be careful. This shrewd man seemed to sense motives and plans. Sherrie's cousin or not, Callie didn't know how much they could trust him, if at all. Well, two could play his game.

Callie looked up at him prettily. With a delicate hand she touched the red curls at the base of her neck then settled the folds of her emerald dress around her. Her voice took on a low breathy tone in its earnestness. "Liam, I think you've already guessed that I'm convinced Caleb Benedict had something to do with my father's losing Stonehaven."

One side of his mouth curled upward. He nodded. His expression said that she wasn't fooling him with her soft Southern manners.

She determined not to let that stop her. "I need your help." She appealed to the gentleman in him. "I will need a lawyer. Someone who's not 'owned' by my uncle. I've made inquiries to those I've met from here. It seems that Caleb Benedict is, shall we say, well connected? Eventually, of course, he will know I'm here. He'll also know what I'm after. But for now, I want to keep my investigation quiet."

Liam nodded. "I understand your concerns." For the first time he looked sympathetic. Callie briefly wondered if she'd been wrong about him. They spoke about Natchez lawyers for a few minutes; he mentioned one by name and said that he would contact him on her behalf the following morning. He picked up a bell from a nearby table, rang for a servant, then smiled at the young women. "Forgive me for my lack of manners. You must be terribly tired from your trip. Please…" He gestured toward the door as the tall servant who had met them earlier came in. "Follow Benjamin to your rooms."

Callie and Sheridan stood to do as they were bid. "Liam, we have a—" she stumbled at the word, "—a servant. Rebecca. We'd like her with us."

"Of course, dear. She's out in the kitchen?"

Sheridan nodded.

"Benjamin will get her. There's a maid's room between the two of yours. She'll stay there."

They had started to leave the room when Liam spoke again. "Your baggage, ladies?" He looked at them, one eyebrow raised, as if suspecting they had arrived with practically nothing.

Callie brushed a strand of hair from her face. "We left it at the dock. Could you send someone for it?"

"Of course." Then he addressed Benjamin. "You'll see to it that it's fetched?"

The black man nodded then led the way to the foyer. As they climbed the wide circular staircase, Callie felt Liam's gaze. She turned to see him standing in the foyer, a half-smile on his handsome face. But she also saw something else, something cold. Calculating. She shivered for the second time since meeting him.

"Supper will be served at eight," he called up to them. "We'll speak more of your plans then. There is something else I need to tell you about Senator Caleb Benedict. Something you should know."

Callie turned sharply to ask him to tell her now. She would gladly return at once to the parlor. But Liam Sheridan had disappeared through one of the elaborately carved mahogany doors leading from the foyer.

D ark clouds settled on Natchez by late afternoon, causing the servants to light the hand-painted French lamps and set logs in the fireplaces. By the time Callie and Sheridan joined Liam in the dining room for supper, a light rain had begun to fall.

Callie caught her breath when she saw the sumptuous meal: oysters on the half shell, roast suckling pig, collard greens, beaten biscuits with apple butter, and sweet potato pie. The servants had set the table with bone china plates and dishes—purchased on his last trip to London, Liam told them proudly. Sparkling crystal goblets held the Madeira.

Afterward, Liam, with Callie on one arm and Sheridan on the other, walked them to the library. Logs crackled in the fireplace as the three settled into comfortable leather chairs nearby.

Benjamin appeared within minutes, offering either brandy or hot, sweetened tea.

Callie once more admired Liam's elegant taste as the servant poured her tea from a sterling teapot. Sheridan's brandy was served from an equally beautiful crystal decanter.

Liam lit a sweet-smelling pipe and leaned back in his chair, his brandy on a table to one side. "Ah, 'tis good to have life in this house again," he said with a sigh.

"Now, you can't lead me to believe, Cousin Liam, that you've turned into a lonely old bachelor. Not someone with your good looks and obvious fortune," Sheridan teased.

Liam chuckled. "Sure, you know how to flatter an old man now, me sweet lass." The exaggerated brogue rolled from his tongue.

Callie couldn't help smiling.

Sheridan continued, her accent as pronounced as his. "What are you now, Liam? Thirty-five? Why, you've barely begun life's journey. And my goodness, man, surely you would be married if you'd desired. What woman wouldn't think you a fine catch?"

He threw back his head and laughed. "Ah, me sweet Sherrie. You're medicine for the soul, you are." He laughed again.

They continued the lighthearted banter. Callie settled back to watch, enjoying the sweet camaraderie between the two, the warmth of the elegant room with its crackling fire, the sounds of rain pelting the windows.

She wanted to believe Liam was just as he seemed at this moment. For Sheridan's sake more than for her own, she wanted him to be a good, honest, hardworking man.

"Ah, this one's a thinker, this flame-haired lass."

The repartee had stopped and Liam was looking in Callie's direction. Embarrassed, Callie met his gaze with a smile. "I was just enjoying watching the two of you together," she said honestly. Her voice took on a more serious tone. "Liam, you mentioned earlier that you have something else to tell me about my uncle. I'm curious. What is it?"

Liam's expression changed. There were grooves in his face that Callie hadn't noticed earlier. He somehow looked older, harder.

"I know your uncle well." The brogue had disappeared. His

tone was as brittle as his expression. "Very well."

Callie tilted her chin. "You said earlier that everyone knows Caleb Benedict. I take it that you know him better than most."

He nodded. "Yes. You might say that."

Callie waited for him to continue. Sheridan slipped her a sideways glance with raised eyebrows and a barely perceptible shrug.

"When you first arrived and told me how you were forced to leave Stonehaven, I wanted to stay out of it. I told myself it was your business—however you wanted to go about seeking revenge, retribution, restoration—" His voice broke off as he tamped new tobacco into his pipe, relit it, and drew in the smoke. "—whatever it is that you're after."

He leaned forward, his blue-eyed gaze locked on hers. "But after listening to your story—the unfair manner in which you were treated, I felt I couldn't remain silent. You see, Callie, he's done this to others. Stonehaven was the first. In the last few years, he's helped plantation owners, shopkeepers, even bankers themselves, borrow. They begin making low-interest payments. He gradually increases the interest until they can no longer pay their bills. Of course they've used their plantations or businesses as collateral. When they can't pay, it all belongs to Caleb Benedict." He puffed on his pipe, watching Callie intently. "It's done through banks here in Natchez—even upriver as far as Vicksburg."

"He owns all these banks?" Callie was incredulous.

"He owns the bankers."

"They're in debt to him?"

"In one way or another."

"What do you mean?"

"He finds out things—things they'd rather not have anyone know. Sometimes he threatens to tell their wives or says he'll drop a notice of their 'affairs' in a local newspaper. If he can't find anything, he makes it up. Word has it that he simply suggests—shall we say—an indelicate story. He tells his victim a few of the details he's 'discovered' about them. Most already know his reputation. He can ruin a man's character in a few day's time. They're ready to do as he says."

Callie shook her head slowly. "I can't believe my father didn't know this about him. Why wouldn't he have taken precautions? Not borrowed from him?"

"You have to remember, Stonehaven was the first. And, after all, Caleb Benedict was a relative."

"My mother's brother." Callie was quiet a moment, watching the flames lick the fire. "I wonder if Caleb would have been so cruel as to have threatened my father with some trumped-up story. Would he have been that cruel?"

No one spoke. Only the sounds of the rain and the fire filled the room.

"Maybe that's what killed him—not only losing Stonehaven, but the thought of losing his reputation as well."

"You may never know, Callie." Liam's voice was soft.

"Will you help me? Not only get Stonehaven back—but take down this self-centered, cruel monster?"

Liam nodded. "That's what I had to tell you. I'll be more than glad to. I've had my share of run-ins with your uncle myself. I know how he operates. I don't think we need a lawyer to get our evidence. We can do it ourselves." Smoke from his pipe circled upward as he drew in a breath. "There's one more thing."

Callie scrutinized the man before her. His eyes had narrowed and his handsomely ruddy face had taken on a calculating look. The cut of his jaw looked almost menacing in the flickering firelight.

"As much as I would enjoy your company at Sheridan Hall, I

think it would be beneficial for you to plan a visit—perhaps an extended visit—to Stonehaven."

Callie's eyes widened. She waited for him to continue.

"I can send a servant to Caleb with a note from you, asking to visit." His lip curled briefly. "You will write of the anticipated pleasure of seeing him again. After all, he is your mother's brother. He's family. If your words are filled with innocence and affection—how can he resist?"

Liam smiled. For a moment the harsh lines disappeared. "When you meet him, you will play the role of the dutiful niece, grateful for whatever hospitality he might offer." He watched Callie, waiting for her reaction.

She nodded. "Do you think he would offer me a home at Stonehaven? Why would he trust me?"

"Why would he not trust you? You were barely more than a child when Juliana whisked you away in the dead of night. You didn't want to go. In fact, you cried for him and Stonehaven all the way to—where was the godforsaken place she took you?"

Callie grinned. "New Mexico."

"Aye, it was a terrible thing to be yanked from your childhood home at the whim of your sister. And now you've finally returned to see your beloved uncle, delighted that he was able to 'save' Stonehaven from the creditors who threatened."

Sheridan broke in. "Does Caleb have any way of knowing that you are suspicious of him? Did you or Juliana ever write to him? Accuse him of any misconduct?"

"No. We've had no contact with him whatsoever."

"Ah. There it is then." Liam looked triumphant. "And I might add, me lass,"—he lapsed into the Irish brogue that so charmed Callie—"you're a much finer actress than me little Sherrie here."

Sheridan glanced at Callie and they both burst into laughter.

He had seen through them from the beginning.

"I'll do it!" Callie announced. Liam's idea was sound. In her mind she skipped ahead beyond the initial visit to a time when she would win Caleb's confidence. She might gain access to any records he kept at Stonehaven, records of illegal transactions that could condemn him. "It makes perfect sense." And she could see from the glow in Liam's eyes, he was thinking the same thing. "Aye, 'tis a good plan you've thought of, Liam Sheridan," she said, attempting to match his exaggerated brogue.

Liam's eyes twinkled as he moved nearer the fireplace to stoke the fire, then rang for Benjamin to bring the writing materials.

"Seat yourself at the desk, child," he said, looking at Callie. "We'll put our heads together and write your uncle Caleb Benedict a missive"—Liam smiled wickedly—"with words that will make him seek you out like a weasel does a chicken coop."

Much later that night, Liam Sheridan sat alone in his library. The young women had long since retired upstairs for the night. Before him the dying embers of the fire glowed orange-red against the dark room.

He stared into the fire, thinking about the man he hated more than any other on earth, even more than any who had caused his family pain in Ireland.

No. This was different than those troubling days of the Irish famine. Caleb Benedict owned him as no man had ever owned him. Owned him to the point of making him sick with his own weakness. And that was the thing that caused the hatred to grow.

Liam had built his cotton trade from nothing, built it into one of the most successful money-making ventures in the South in a mere dozen years. It had started out as a small trade operated from the back room of a mercantile. From the beginning, Liam had a knack for picking opportunities that allowed him to expand without touching his capital. He bought out other businesses, hired on more workers, brought in partners (who eventually sold out to him) up and down the Mississippi. He dreamed of building a cotton warehouse larger than any other in New Orleans. He wanted even more expansive growth: Sheridan and Associates would own its own fleet of ships. His company—built by his own keen skill and sweat and calloused hands—would be known on both sides of the Atlantic. As far away as Ireland.

That's when his company caught the attention of Senator Caleb Benedict. At first Liam was flattered that a man of such political prominence invited him to fancy dinners and soirees at Stonehaven. They spent time riding and hunting together. They developed an easy friendship. The man was old enough to be Liam's father, and maybe that's why Liam's usual acute reading of other men failed him so miserably when it came to Caleb. After losing his own father at such a young age, he mistakenly—unconsciously—thought of the elder statesman as a replacement.

Liam was caught off guard when the social events turned so gradually, so smoothly, to business. Caleb spoke of a silent partnership. He would back an expansion that would allow Liam to realize his dream: the warehouse in New Orleans, the fleet of ships that would sail the Atlantic.

Caleb called him son as he explained that he knew how much it would mean to Liam. It would be a risk, but he wanted to help Liam build the largest shipping empire in the world.

The rest was easy. Of course he trusted the man who had befriended him. Of course he signed the papers giving Caleb the partnership he sought. Only, this time, there would be no buying him out as Liam had done with partners in the past. This time it would be too late. Because, on Caleb's advice, they borrowed extensively to expand.

It would have worked, except that the orders for cotton

inexplicably began to dwindle. Some of Liam's oldest, most reliable customers began buying cotton elsewhere. Then ships began to refuse his goods cartage. Within months, business had dropped by 50 percent. Liam used his savings to make payments on the loans. A year passed and, with it, all he had in reserve.

Caleb offered to find other loans for the company through bankers he knew. Disheartened, Liam agreed. What else could he do?

Then Caleb began to forecast the demise of Sheridan and Associates. He offered to buy Liam out—at a rock-bottom price.

Liam refused. But by then he was clearly aware that Caleb Benedict had set out coldly, most calculatingly, to destroy him from the first day of their acquaintance. How could he have been such a fool?

Now all pretense was gone. Caleb openly mocked the Irish, pointedly laughing at Liam in the presence of others.

Liam avoided further contact with his partner and continued selling off divisions of his company to make payments on the loans. All the while he kept meticulous records of Caleb's business affairs. He contacted those who had been duped by the man. So far, nothing illegal had been discovered, only questionable, shady dealings. Just as he had in Liam's case, Caleb made certain all transactions for properties and businesses were legally signed and sealed.

But Liam hadn't given up hope that Caleb's greed might cause him to disregard the legalities. Somewhere, somehow, Liam would find that overlooked detail. The tables would turn.

And now? He watched a flame lick up from the dying embers. Now? His thoughts moved to Cousin Sheridan and that delightful creature Callie St. Clair.

Luck was smiling his direction. He stood and grabbed the poker to stoke the fire then settled again into the leather chair.

Reaching for his pipe, he tamped in the tobacco and lit it, watching the smoke curl upward as he puffed.

Callie St. Clair would fit nicely into his plan. Living at Stonehaven, she would have the motive—*and* the opportunity—to find the information that would destroy her uncle.

Callie was a comely lass. He would not object to pursuing the romantic stirrings he'd noticed within himself since meeting her. If Stonehaven became hers, he'd have only to marry her to make Caleb's plantation his own. Law dictated that upon marriage a woman's property became her husband's.

It was pleasant to consider: a beautiful young bride whose dowry would provide the final coup for his dealings with Caleb Benedict.

Liam let out a long, satisfied sigh. The coals burst into a quick flame, then died again. He took another puff on the pipe. Aye. Fate was smiling upon this Irishman once again in the form of this flame-haired lass, Callie St. Clair.

Yes, he would make Callie his own, he decided. This was one time he wouldn't let heaven rest until his heart's desire became reality.

$\mathcal{S}even$

On the cobblestone street outside Sheridan Hall, Callie daintily lifted her skirts and stepped into Caleb Benedict's family-crested brougham. Rebecca settled into the opposite seat, fluffing the flounces of her yellow dress.

It had been just three days since Callie had written to her uncle. His reply had been immediate and warm: He wanted her to come as quickly as possible. He would send his carriage for her. And he was quite clear that Stonehaven was to be her home for as long as she liked.

It was midday by the time the vehicle rounded the corner and turned into the tree-lined road winding up a small rise to Stonehaven. As they crested the hill, a small gasp escaped Callie's lips. Tears stung her eyes. There before her stood the imposing mansion of her childhood, more beautiful now than she had remembered.

Its whitewashed brick walls gleamed against the purple sky of spring. The sprawling edifice stood proudly on an emerald hill, surrounded first by lawns and oaks and azaleas then farther out by fresh-plowed fields of cotton and corn.

As the carriage drew closer, Callie could see that behind the columned portico that ran the full length of the house the windows were open to catch the breeze. Drapes swayed and danced to its rhythm just as they had done in her childhood. They had always looked friendly, as if the house was glad to see her family return after they had been away.

She thought of the years—nearly seven—that had slipped by since she last saw Stonehaven. Even now the house seemed to welcome her. And from the tone of his invitation, her uncle would also. But he didn't know the real reason she had come. She thought of Liam, the help he was offering. He didn't know her real reason for wanting Stonehaven. It didn't matter that he was Sheridan's cousin, Callie wasn't ready to trust him with knowledge of her work with the Underground Railroad.

The carriage rounded another curve. Within minutes she and Rebecca would step down at the front portico. Her heart beat faster.

Then she saw him. Caleb Benedict. The man who had caused her nightmares and grief. The man who had once driven her from her beloved home.

He strode down the front steps, looking expectantly toward the brougham. He looked much the same as she remembered, though perhaps a bit more stout and with considerably more white in his hair. Callie gave him a big smile and waved as the driver halted the team.

"Uncle!" Callie cried, running to his open arms. She hugged him fiercely, then stepped back and smiled into his narrow, lined face. "Oh, Uncle. I thought I'd never see you again." Almost unconsciously, she slipped into the drawl of her childhood.

Caleb's small eyes searched hers. He was shrewd and didn't trust her. She could see it in his eyes. She would have to work hard to convince him. She gave him a tremulous smile.

He finally spoke as he took her hand in both of his. "Callie St. Clair. You're the livin' image of your sweet mamma." Callie thought his eyes teared, but she couldn't be sure. "I'm quite over-come with emotion." He smiled, but it seemed a foreign expression and a hollow sentiment.

"I understand just how you feel, Uncle," Callie said with a sniffle.

Caleb put his hand under Callie's elbow, turning her toward the steps leading to the portico and front entry. "I'll have Titus get your luggage. I have housemaids who will be at your disposal—or would you rather keep your girl?—" He let the question hang.

"I would like my—" Callie faltered as she usually did when forced to refer to Rebecca as her servant, "—my—ah—Rebecca placed in a room near me, please." She would have to be more convincing than that. She went on, attempting to play her role with greater confidence. "She can unpack my things and freshen them. Would you have one of your maids take an iron to my room?"

Caleb nodded. "As you wish." He dropped her arm to hold open the door.

Callie stepped through the entrance and into the house her father had designed and built. In awe she looked around. Nothing had changed. It had the same light, open feel. The sun flooded the foyer through the floor-to-ceiling windows. Beyond the doorways leading to the front sitting room, the library, the dining room, the same play of sunlight dazzled and brightened.

A small cry of delight escaped her lips. "Uncle Caleb, it's just as I remember it!" She gave him a quick smile, hoping her dimple showed. "How did you ever manage to save it from creditors? Oh, but I shouldn't even ask. It's none of my business, I'm sure. But"—she squeezed his arm affectionately—"I'm just so delighted you managed to do it."

She looked up into his face, forcing her expression to be guileless and filled with admiration.

He responded at last. Laughing, he took Callie's hand in his. "I'm so glad you think so, Callie. Come, let's retire, shall we, to the sitting room. I'll have Delilah get you something to refresh your parched throat." He ushered her to the front room.

Callie settled into a high-backed chair of satin and carved mahogany and fixed her skirts prettily around her ankles. Caleb sat across from her.

"Tell me about what's happened to you and your sister. Where did you go when you left here so suddenly? What did you do?" He sounded sincere.

"It wasn't easy, Uncle." Callie looked at her hands as if embarrassed, then shyly back into his face. "We should have listened to you. I didn't want to leave my home. I didn't want to leave you. But Juliana thought it would be best." She pulled out a lace handkerchief. "You told me that you had found someone who would take me as his wife." Her lower lip trembled. "I was so frightened. Papa had just died. We were penniless. I should have trusted you." She gazed at him with tear-filled eyes, then continued, her voice barely audible. "I was just so frightened."

Caleb's voice was gentle. "Where did you go?"

Callie explained about Juliana's wild scheme of traveling to New Mexico. She embellished the dangers and her fears as she told the tale of their wagon journey west.

Caleb shook his head in disbelief. "I had no idea. You poor child," he murmured more than once.

Callie told how she'd been beaten and left for dead along the way. She threw in words about how she had begged Juliana to take her back to Caleb. She told how Juliana had met and married the rugged wagon captain, leaving Callie alone and lonely, then finally shipping her off to college in Ohio.

Caleb asked Callie questions about New Mexico and her sister. She could see he wanted to know how interested Juliana was in Stonehaven, though he never came right out with it. He was gracious, even charming, as he probed for information. Callie matched his grace and charm word for word, smile for smile.

Finally he seemed satisfied that Juliana had no real interest in Stonehaven or in returning to Natchez for any reason. Not even to see her, Callie added with a sniff.

Though his eyes remained cool and assessing, Caleb's voice was kind as he began to speak of Callie's role at Stonehaven should she decide to make it her home.

"I have an overseer of the household, Miss Wilhelmina Holt. She's been with me for years—takes care of my bookwork and runs the house. I don't know what I'd do without her. But the truth is, she's getting older and could use some help." He smiled broadly. "I see you as a godsend, Callasandra. If you could take over the oversight of the house—run it as Stonehaven's mistress"—he raised an eyebrow—"it would relieve some of her duties."

Callie tilted her head. "Tell me more."

"Miss Holt, of course, would continue on in her oversight of the financial affairs of Stonehaven. You would manage the goings-on within the house itself—overseeing the servants' activities, ordering the household supplies, running the day-to-day chores, planning the social events I put on from time to time." He looked at her expectantly.

Caleb removed his spectacles, cleaned them, then wiped his bulbous nose, a gesture of his Callie remembered from childhood. "It might seem an overwhelming position for you right now," he went on, "but with your education and understanding from your early years here—I have no doubt that you would soon find it second nature." His eyes were bright as his gaze met hers. "Of course, you would work into the position gradually. Miss Holt would oversee your training."

The room fell silent as she thought over his offer. It seemed to come rather abruptly. Why would this politically astute and historically calculating man trust her so quickly? Was this a trap? Or a test? He was watching her as she considered his offer. He seemed to sense her skepticism.

She smiled sweetly at him. "This is quite a generous offer, Uncle."

"It's actually a business proposition, dear."

"How do you mean?"

The smile left his face. "I'm offering you a home here at Stonehaven for the rest of your life—if you desire. In return, you will be the plantation's mistress—at my side to welcome guests, to help run my household efficiently and economically..." His voice trailed off as if there would be more to consider.

"And?"

"I see it as a business proposition. We both benefit."

There had to be greater benefit for Caleb than simply her running his household. There were probably dozens with Wilhelmina Holt's experience from Natchez who could be hired to fill the position.

Of course, Callie was a blood relative. He might think that she would add a touch of family grace to the household.

No. There had to be more. She was sure of it. There was something he wasn't telling her.

"Think it over, my dear, if you like. We can speak of it again later." He rose and indicated it was time for her to do the same. "But for now, let me introduce you to Miss Holt. She'll show you to your rooms, and you can settle in. Dinner is served at two o'clock, supper at seven-thirty." He cupped his hand beneath Callie's elbow and guided her through the doorway, across the foyer toward Wilhelmina's small office.

Before tapping on the office door, he looked down at Callie.

His expression had suddenly changed, even more unreadable than before. "There will, of course, be some papers for you to sign before you start. I'll have them prepared as soon as you give me your decision."

"Papers?"

He laughed lightly, his expression softening. "Don't look so worried, dear. I promise I'll explain them to you. We'll get all this out of the way after supper tonight. Plan to meet me in the library."

Callie nodded, puzzled.

He rapped lightly on the heavy oak door. It was immediately opened by a tall, sour-looking woman. Her brown-gray hair was twisted, then wound severely at the back of her head. The cut of her gray dress emphasized her gaunt frame, and the gray of it suited her colorless skin.

"Yes," she said simply.

"Miss Holt, I would like to introduce my niece." He turned to Callie and completed the introductions.

The woman nodded at Callie without expression, though her sharp eyes didn't miss an inch of Callie's dress. The set of her thin lips told her that Wilhelmina Holt had better things to do than to meet the frivolous niece of her employer.

Callie smiled, attempting to be pleasant. Wilhelmina's cool expression didn't change.

"As you know, Wilhelmina, Callasandra has returned home to Stonehaven—perhaps permanently. Please make her welcome. If Callie decides to stay, the two of you will be working closely together." He looked from one to the other. "But of course, we don't need to rush into the business of it all right now." He smiled brightly. "For now, I'm sure Callasandra is tired from her journey. Would you show her to her room?"

Wilhelmina nodded.

"She is to be given her old room."

The older woman looked at him sharply but said nothing.

"It was to have been readied."

"It has been, sir. The young woman was expected."

Callie didn't like the way Wilhelmina spoke as if Callie herself were not in the room. "Miss Holt, if you'll please take me there now I'd be grateful."

Wilhelmina raised her head in a gesture of superiority. For the first time she smiled, a cool, calculating smile. Then she nodded for Callie to follow her up the stairs.

Callie was unprepared for the rush of emotions that overtook her as she opened the door to her old room. Surprisingly, little had changed. Caleb had kept her old furniture—the polished mahogany high-poster bed and matching wardrobe, the oval dressing table and ornately carved looking glass. Light filled the room from the large bay window above its padded seat. A swag of lacy cotton drapes framed each side.

As soon as Wilhelmina left her alone, Callie strode to the bay window and looked out across Stonehaven's vast lands. For as far as she could see, slaves were working the fields. A hot sun blazed down on it all, causing a shimmering across the deep greens of summer growth.

Callie remembered the last time she stood by the window, Juliana seated on the windowseat below her, and gazed at the moonlit scene. It was the night they were forced to leave Stonehaven. Juliana had said they might never see their childhood home again. Even then Callie had declared she would someday return, that she would someday reclaim Stonehaven as their own.

Now, here she was at the brink of an uncertain future.

Reclaiming Stonehaven? Creating a safe haven for runaway slaves? Destroying Caleb Benedict for what he had done to her family and others? What did she hope to gain by being here? What did she hope to gain by playing this duplicitous role?

Callie looked out at the cotton fields, the tender-green corn plants, the gardens below her. Yes, of course she wanted Stonehaven to be hers. There was the love of the land her father had instilled in her. That would never change. But even if she had to give up the plantation to realize her plan for the Underground, then so be it.

She looked again at the slaves, bent nearly double as they worked the cotton fields in the blistering sun. If she did reclaim Stonehaven, it would be a vastly different plantation, run by freed slaves who were paid wages, free to go if they pleased. She didn't know if it ever had been done. If Stonehaven went to paid labor there would be a great loss of profit. And the social repercussions would be devastating. But it could be done. It *had* to be done.

Callie again looked out across the fields. She noticed a pregnant woman stooping to her backbreaking labor, weeding and hoeing. A child followed behind her, picking insects from the plants. Callie shuddered, thinking about how many times she'd looked upon the same scene without noticing.

As a child, she had taken pride in the St. Clairs' treatment of slaves. Many were cared for as if they were part of the family. There were gifts at Christmas, warm clothing for winter, good medical care from Dr. Greenleaf Meade who visited the slave quarters weekly. Her father hadn't separated families. If a courting slave fancied a girl from another plantation, her father made sure to buy the girl so that they could be together.

But no matter how well they were treated, they weren't free. Should any slave run away, there were beatings carried out under the overseer's direction. Sometimes severe beatings. And knowing

Uncle Caleb, she supposed that under his direction swift and brutal punishment was often meted out in much the same way.

Callie watched the young mother as she began hoeing another row. She didn't know how or when, but if Stonehaven did become hers, she would free them all, then hire them back with an offer of fair wages. But that would be in the future. Probably the distant future.

Sighing, Callie sank to the window seat and leaned against the window, turning her thoughts to the tasks at hand. First, there was the Underground Railroad to consider. And she needed to win her uncle's confidence to gain access to the evidence of his illegal activities.

A light knock on the door between her room and Rebecca's interrupted her thoughts.

"Come in," she called.

Poking her head through the door, Rebecca flashed Callie a dimpled smile.

"I'm glad to see you, Becca. I need to talk with you about something important." Callie patted the window seat next to her. "Come, sit down."

Rebecca smoothed her skirts as she settled into the seat.

"First of all, I want to caution you about life here at Stonehaven."

"Yes, ma'am." Her dark eyes were curious.

"I want you to stay away from the overseer, Rebecca," Callie began after a few moments. "If anyone gets the idea that you are being treated as if you are free, the results could—" She stopped, searching for the words to continue.

"—bring us harm?" Rebecca finished for her.

Callie nodded. "And you know what the punishment would be if you're discovered learning to read?"

Rebecca frowned. "Yes, ma'am. I know."

"I know you're proud of what you're learning, Becca. But I'm trying to protect you. Please don't tell anyone about the reading."

Rebecca kept her dark eyes on Callie's. For a moment she didn't speak and reached down to smooth her yellow skirt. Then she seemed to be searching for the words she needed. "Why do you care, Miss Callie?" she finally asked softly.

"Becca, I bought you to give you your freedom. Miss Sheridan and I planned it from the beginning."

"Freedom?"

"As far as I'm concerned, you're free now."

The girl looked too stunned to speak.

"I'm planning to have the papers drawn up as soon as we can find a lawyer we can trust."

Rebecca tilted her head, not understanding.

Callie took a deep breath. "Because my actions can't be known. What Sherrie and I do for you must be kept a secret."

"Why?"

"Before Sherrie and I came here from Ohio, we were helping out as station masters in the Underground Railroad."

Rebecca's mouth fell open, her eyes widened. "You were?"

Callie nodded.

"Miss Callie, I should've known—after everythin' you've done—"

Callie walked over and sat on the bed, motioning for Rebecca to sit in the tapestry chair opposite her. "Now I've got some hard questions for you, Rebecca."

Rebecca nodded. "Yes, ma'am."

"Sherrie and I would like for you to work with us in the Underground Railroad here." She paused, watching Rebecca's expression, the lively interest in her face. "But more important is your freedom. As soon as we can, we'll have the papers drawn

116

up. Then you will be free to go—or stay and work with us."

Rebecca's dimples showed again. "I'll stay and help you!" she declared without any hesitation. "But I'll be free, Miss Callie! I'll be free." She stood and danced across the room, her thin arms out, her small hands palms up. She whirled, laughing and crying at the same time.

Then she grabbed Callie's hands and pulled her up twirling her into a dance.

Just then the door opened. A grim-looking Wilhelmina stood watching as the young women quickly stepped apart.

"Yes?" Callie stared at the older woman.

"I came to remind you that luncheon will be served in fifteen minutes," she said, without expression. There was no acknowledgment that she had witnessed anything out of the ordinary. But Callie had the feeling that the woman would store it all for future use. She would need to be more careful.

The midday meal passed pleasantly enough, and afterward Callie asked her uncle if she might borrow a horse to ride around the grounds. He said that not only would he be delighted for her to do so, he would join her. Callie nodded in agreement, though she was mildly disappointed. She had looked forward to her first ride alone.

She met Caleb at the stables just as the late afternoon breezes off the river had begun cooling the air.

Caleb was an excellent horseman, and Callie actually enjoyed his company. He seemed to dare her to make the same jumps at breakneck speed that he did. She complied, of course, showing off her skills as an accomplished rider. Riding Darley in New Mexico had given her a taste for pushing a horse's velocity and jumping ability to the point of near danger.

Callie closed her eyes, remembering the feel of the ride under the purple New Mexico skies, Darley's power beneath her, galloping across the high mesas. She had raced Parker on his Appaloosa and Jeremiah on the roan. But none had been as challenging as the day she raced Hawk.

Eyes still closed, Callie relived the moments of their race across the snowy meadow, horses' hooves pounding across the icy, hard ground, steam flowing from the beasts' nostrils, their mutual joy of matching gait to thunderous gait as they rode.

Oh, Hawk! she nearly cried aloud. *How I miss you!*

When she opened her eyes, she was almost surprised to see Stonehaven's fields instead of New Mexico's high mountain meadows. And a familiar ache had returned, the ache that filled her heart with sadness whenever she remembered Hawk.

At the end of the ride, a new appreciation seemed evident in Caleb's demeanor as they dismounted and walked from the stables toward the house. When they reached the side door entrance to the library, he suddenly took her hand in his.

"Callie, I do hope you consider staying. Just now, out riding, you reminded me so of your mother. You look like her, and you've got her spirit. I'm glad you've come home, dear girl. It's like having a bit of Anne Marie here with me again." He seemed sincere.

Callie squeezed his hand. "I plan to stay, Uncle Caleb."

"Good, child. Good." he said. "We'll discuss the details tonight—as I said before." He stepped from the porch into the library. Callie noticed his halting gait and the slump of his shoulders. The ride must have been hard on him, she decided. She fought a feeling of pity; this was no time to soften her feelings toward the man.

After supper, Callie joined Caleb in the library. It was too warm for a fire, but Caleb nodded toward the chairs arranged near the marble fireplace. Callie sat in a high-backed chair, and her uncle settled into a small matching sofa, stretching his short legs to rest his feet on a nearby hassock.

"Well, now," he sighed. "You said earlier that you're interested in staying on at Stonehaven." He raised an eyebrow toward her.

Callie smiled sweetly, waiting for him to continue.

"I watched your face as you rode with me today. It's obvious you love this land."

Still she didn't answer. The best way to get information, she'd learned long ago, was simply to be silent, uncomfortably silent.

Caleb cleared his throat. "You do love Stonehaven?"

This time she nodded.

"And you want to stay."

She nodded again. There was a long pause.

"Well, yes. I told you about some papers—an agreement that is—that you will need to sign. It's only a formality, you see."

Callie kept her gaze evenly on him.

Caleb reddened, obviously unused to a controlling silence such as hers. Then he stood and moved to his desk—the same desk that had belonged to her father.

He rummaged through a drawer, pulled a document from it and handed it to Callie.

Callie took it without comment and began to read. He was careful. No wonder he'd not been brought up on any charges. If this paper was any indication of his normal business procedures, he made sure that all legalities were locked up tighter than a chicken in a weasel-proof coop.

Callie read on without speaking. Finally she looked up at

Caleb, who watched her intently. "You want me to sign away any claim I might have to Stonehaven."

This time he nodded silently.

"Why?"

"Is that why you came here? To look into your rights as the offspring of the former owner?"

So he had guessed one of her motives. Callie willed herself not to color. Well, two could play this game. "Is that what you think, Uncle Caleb?"

He let his gaze rest on the document. "This is to ensure that you haven't. That's all, Callasandra. In exchange for your signature, I will draw up a separate document leaving Stonehaven to you upon my death—providing there is no contest to my ownership during my lifetime."

"That's a generous offer, Uncle. Why would you want to do that? You barely know me."

His voice softened. "Maybe it's because I'm growing older and want kin around. Perhaps its because I see a bit of your mother—my little sister—in you." He again seated himself in the velvet chair. "Whatever it is, my dear, perhaps it is wisest to 'not look a gift horse in the mouth' as they say."

He suddenly grinned at her, his eyes lively. "It's also time we brightened up this place again with a beautiful mistress of the house. Though I'm out of politics and no longer need to entertain for political reasons, we can still make soirees at Stonehaven the talk of the county."

They talked on into the night, Callie asking questions about her duties and her rights should she sign the document. Then she asked if she could have a few days to think it over. Caleb looked surprised, but nodded in agreement.

It was close to ten by the time Callie, tired of stifling her yawns, kissed his cheek at the library door and headed up the stairs to her room.

A few minutes later, Callie pulled back the covers and slipped into bed. Her mind whirled with confusing thoughts. If she signed Caleb's document, would that mean she couldn't seek information that would condemn him and win back lost property for other victims? She didn't think so. The paper said nothing of those circumstances.

What if, after signing, she found proof that Stonehaven had been taken from her father illegally? Would this document still be legal and binding? It might be.

But what choice did she have? If she didn't sign, she would be forced to leave Stonehaven. Caleb was shrewdly testing her loyalty, and she would have failed his test.

As she began to drift off to sleep, she suddenly thought of what she would do. She'd draw up a document of her own. A paper outlining her rights—such as the oversight, buying, and selling of the house servants. That would at least give her some control over their treatment. And the ownership of those she bought would remain in her name. That way she could someday see to their freedom.

She would also see to it that she eventually would control the activities of Miss Wilhelmina Holt. She wanted access to the accounts; her oversight would ensure that as well.

Callie settled deeper into the feather mattress, the document's wording already forming in her head. Then a muffled voice caused her to start and sit up in bed.

What was it?

She listened again. The sound came from Rebecca's room. She slipped from underneath her covers, padded to the door between their adjoining quarters, and quietly opened it.

There in the moonlight, Rebecca knelt, facing a small window. She was speaking aloud as if to a friend, her eyes open, her face lifted heavenward. There was an expression of pure joy on her face, a glow that seemed to come from someplace deep inside.

Callie couldn't hear her words, but she knew Rebecca was praying. Once in a while she heard snatches of something like "precious Jesus" and "sweet Lord." As Callie silently closed the door, she heard Rebecca thanking God for the gift of his deliverance that day.

Once again in bed, Callie pulled the covers under her chin. But this time her mind wouldn't let her drift so easily to sleep. The image of Rebecca praying in the moonlight reminded Callie of her family in New Mexico: Juliana and Parker and Jeremiah and Morning Sun Jones. They all spoke to God as if he were their friend—the same way she'd just heard Rebecca pray.

Especially Sun Jones. She remembered how the Mandan woman's every breath and every step was reason to praise her God. One time she had even prayed for Callie's healing after her accident by the creek. Callie had been unconscious at the time, but Juliana told her in vivid detail how Sun's prayers on Callie's behalf had been answered.

Callie had decided long ago that she and God had come to an understanding of sorts. She wouldn't bother him if he wouldn't bother her. Truth was, she really didn't need him. She was perfectly capable of handling the crises she'd been through in her life.

Juliana credited God for getting them through all the scrapes and twists and turns it took to get to New Mexico. Callie knew better. It was their own hard work and common sense that got them through. God might have been there watching it all from a distance, maybe even applauding them as they moved their wagon across the prairie, found themselves in the middle of an Indian uprising, and even built their house in the mountain meadow. But it was their own blood and sweat and good sense that had brought it about.

She turned toward her window and gazed up at the silver moon, thin and lacy clouds drifting across it.

God…the creator of the moon and stars and world and universe? Yes, of course.

But God…a loving friend who cared about every breath she took, every step she walked?

No. That was a childish notion.

She didn't begrudge Rebecca, Sun, Juliana, Hawk, or any of the others their fantasies; however, she had a better understanding of herself and her world.

But when Callie finally closed her eyes and began to drift into a dreamless sleep, she wondered about that place inside that felt lonely and cold.

 Eight

❧

A few days later, in the presence of Caleb's attorney and Wilhelmina Holt as a witness, Callie St. Clair signed away her rights to Stonehaven. In return, Caleb, seated at his library desk, signed a new will, granting her ownership of the plantation and all its holdings upon his death. Callie presented her own document that initially caused Caleb to sputter in anger. Then after reading it, he looked up at her, his eyes filled with admiration for her astute countermove.

After the signing, Callie assumed some of the household duties, with more promised for the future. Caleb called the house servants together and announced Callie's new position. Smiles of recognition came from some who remembered Callie from her childhood.

She began working closely with Delilah, a wiry and muscular, seemingly ageless woman, who ruled over the other house servants with an iron hand; the dignified, graying Titus, head butler, who had worked for Callie's father; the spirited maids Delcie, Diana, and Tryphena; and the army of kitchen servants headed up by the rotund, jovial cook named Pleasant, whose ten-year-old son Abe, dressed in a starched linen jacket, operated the tall peacock feather fan at mealtime.

Within weeks, Callie had comfortably slipped into her role as Stonehaven's mistress. Working from a small walnut secretary in the dining room, she planned menus with Pleasant, ordered supplies with advice from Titus, and managed the house servants through Delilah.

One night as they settled into the velvet library chairs, Caleb poured himself a brandy and Callie brought up the illnesses she'd noticed among the servants.

"I'd like to hire Dr. Greenleaf Meade to stop by weekly," she told her uncle.

"He worked for your father, didn't he?"

Callie nodded. "Yes, and I noticed he's still in practice in town."

Caleb shrugged. "Makes no difference to me. I've gone through a lot of doctors out here. None of them seem too eager to treat the Negroes. Not that I blame them—seems to ruin their other practice." He sipped his brandy. "But you go ahead, Callie. See if Meade'll make regular stops."

Callie spoke of other household needs, then Caleb smiled. "You're doing a fine job, Callie. I'm hard to please—but I must say—you've pleased me greatly since your arrival." He settled back into his chair.

"It's time to introduce you to Natchez society as my kin," he said simply, "and the new mistress of Stonehaven. It will be the grandest weekend event of the season—perhaps the year. We'll start preparing immediately. I want you to oversee the party from start to finish—sleeping accommodations and meals, music and musicians for dancing—everything." He narrowed his eyes; they seemed to brighten in anticipation. "What do you think?"

"It's a wonderful idea, Uncle. But I know something like this will take weeks to plan. Do you have a date in mind?"

"How about mid-September?"

She nodded. "I'll start working on it immediately." The idea did appeal to her, but not for the reasons her uncle would assume. With the intricate details of the party ahead, she had more excuses than ever to spend time in Natchez. She and Rebecca might find greater access to information about the Underground Railroad.

"You may need assistance," her uncle was saying. "Let me know and I'll arrange it."

"Actually, I was thinking the same thing. I would like to invite my friend Sheridan to help me out."

"Sheridan?"

"Yes, I told you about her—my friend from Oberlin. We stayed with her cousin Liam when we first arrived in Natchez. He's—"

Caleb interrupted. "You don't need to tell me about Liam Sheridan. I know who he is." He took a sip of brandy, a pensive expression crossing his face. "Yes, of course," he said, after a pause. "By all means, invite your friend out for a visit. She's welcome to stay and help for as long as you like."

They spoke for a while about the party, then Callie announced that she would take the carriage into Natchez the following day. She wanted to visit Sheridan, enlist her help, and begin the party preparations.

Caleb suddenly seemed distracted, though he nodded in agreement. When Callie left him, he was lost in thought, staring into the empty marble fireplace. She closed the library door behind her and climbed the spiral staircase to her room, wondering if her trip to Natchez had anything to do with his demeanor.

After she left, Caleb stood and moved slowly to his desk, seated himself, and held his head in his hands.

Callie St. Clair, with her flame-colored curls and snapping green eyes, caused him to dwell on Anne Marie. His sister, as an adult, looked nothing like Callie. No, the unruly red hair and freckles had been the bane of Anne Marie's childhood. By the time she had married Richard, the red had faded to auburn and the freckles had all but disappeared.

Ah, but Callie. She was the image of her mother—the sister he raised—in Anne Marie's early years: high-spirited, intelligent, sweet, and innocent. A person could see clear through to Callie St. Clair's soul in those green eyes. And it was the look of her that he was afraid would be his undoing.

He rubbed his eyes, then wiped his spectacles before placing them on his nose. The truth was, he only wanted Callie at Stonehaven so that he could watch her. Her efficiency at running the household was a bonus, and he intended to keep her as busy as possible during her stay.

During her stay? He stared again at the marble fireplace, the cold ashes in its yawning, empty mouth. He thought about his future plans for Callie. He'd intended to rid himself—and Stonehaven—of her all along. Find that place of vulnerability, discredit her, or worse. He hadn't decided exactly how or when.

But he'd known all along that the time would indeed come—just as it had for her father, the arrogant Richard St. Clair, who'd taken away pretty Anne Marie. Wealthy, educated, erudite, Richard was everything that Caleb Benedict was not. There was something of his haughty demeanor in Callie. The same had also been true of Juliana.

Caleb pushed back his chair, strode to the mantel, and drained his brandy. His prey needed careful watching while he lured her into his velvet trap. Then he would strike when she least expected it.

The following morning after breakfast, Callie kissed her uncle lightly on the cheek and left for town in the brougham.

It was a glorious morning, the sky nearly violet, the earth alive with high-summer color, the smell of sun-warmed soil drifting from the fields where the slaves were already stooped along the rows of nearly ripe cotton.

By noon the driver, Josiah, halted in front of Sheridan Hall. Callie hadn't seen Sherrie for several weeks. In her hurry, she didn't wait for Josiah but let herself out the door, then ran up the walkway to the ornate entrance. Within minutes her friend met her in the foyer with an enthusiastic hug. Then Sherrie led her to the parlor and rang for tea. They chatted for a few minutes before Callie brought up the barbecue and her invitation for Sheridan to stay at Stonehaven and help.

Sheridan grinned as she tucked an errant strand of black hair behind her ear.

"Of course I'll help. When do you want me there?" She looked around the exquisitely decorated parlor and gestured toward the rest of the Hall. "Believe me, Callie. I'm goin' stark, ravin' mad in this place. Cousin Liam is gone more than he's home." Sheridan's brogue made Callie smile. How she'd missed hearing it! "I'm telling you, Callie St. Clair, it's a good thing you came today. I don't think I could've stood it another minute. I've been feeling I'm the only livin' thing in a graveyard."

"A graveyard?"

Sheridan nodded. "Aye. A graveyard." Suddenly she didn't look so lighthearted. Her voice lowered. "Cousin Liam isn't here right now, so I can speak plainly." She stood, closed the parlor door, than again seated herself opposite Callie. "Liam's in some sort of trouble."

"What do you mean?"

"Callie, I don't think he's bein' honest. Even with me bein' his cousin." She shook her head incredulously.

"Honest about what?"

Sherrie's dark blue eyes looked troubled as she continued. "I think he's got problems. Deep problems."

Callie thought of Sherrie's charming and handsome cousin, the quick repartee they'd shared the week she'd spent at Sheridan Hall. "How do you know?"

"Sure enough. I can tell by the way he's actin', I can. He's glum."

Callie smiled. "Maybe that's just the way he is. After all, Sherrie, you don't know him well."

"Aye. But there's more. Much more." She again stood and walked to the door, opened it and peered out to see if anyone was near. Satisfied, she turned back to Callie.

"A visitor came at midnight a few nights ago. He was ushered in as if Cousin Liam was waiting for him. They came in here—to this very place we're sittin' now." She paled a bit, looking guilty as she went on. "Believin' this to be strange, I crept down the stairs. I know I shouldn't have, Callie, but my curiosity got the best of me. Well, as I was sayin', I came to this door, which was closed, of course, just as it is now." She glanced at it again. "That's how I know you can hear through it."

"I would've done the same thing," Callie agreed, hoping to relieve some of Sherrie's embarrassment. "And don't forget—we did much worse in Oberlin."

Sherrie laughed lightly, grateful. "Aye, that we did!"

"What did you hear?"

"I heard arguin'. Loud voices. Liam's and someone else's."

"What were they saying? Could you hear their words?"

"Sure enough, I could. The same as if I had been standin' next to them."

"And?"

"They were arguing about some money that Liam owes. A lot of money, Callie. I could tell by what he said that he's about to lose everything."

"Money he owes to the man who was speaking?"

"Aye."

"Do you have any idea who the other man was?"

"No. None at all."

"Did you ask Liam anything about it the next day?

Sherrie's cheeks flamed. "I did not! I'd be a fool to let on that I ever eavesdropped. I at least learned that much in Oberlin."

Callie nodded. "I know. You're right. But what are you going to do?"

Sherrie looked sad. "There's nothin' to do. I'm just feelin' sorry about my cousin. I wish I could help."

The muffled rattle of carriage wheels on cobblestones caught their attention. Sherrie stood and moved to the front window. "Here comes Cousin Liam now," she said.

Within minutes Liam Sheridan had joined the young women. He greeted Callie with the same charm and exquisite manners as before, attentive when she spoke, eyes bright with interest as he watched her. He readily agreed to Sherrie's extended visit to Stonehaven, with the stipulation, he added, that he be allowed to call on them both from time to time. Callie detected no despondency in his manner.

After Sherrie finished packing her trunk, Liam gave instructions to one of the house servants to load it on the back of the carriage.

He kissed Sherrie on the cheek, bidding her goodbye, then turned to Callie, with a warm expression in his deep blue eyes. He kissed her hand, keeping her fingers a bit too long at his lips. Flustered, Callie withdrew her hand and stepped backward, feeling her cheeks redden.

He smiled a bit wickedly, acknowledging her discomfort. "I'm looking forward to calling on you at Stonehaven," he said.

As the vehicle clattered along the cobbled street leading away from Sheridan Hall, Sherrie settled into the plush leather seat with a satisfied look. "Aye! I knew it would happen sooner or later," she said, chuckling.

"What do you mean?" Callie asked, though she was sure she knew.

"Cousin Liam's sweet on you, Callie St. Clair. Aye, that he is!"

Callie said nothing, just turned to stare out the window as they neared the center of town. Sherrie was right. Callie had felt Liam's interest right from the start. He was handsome, charming, amusing. She had a feeling that life with Liam Sheridan would be exciting, no matter the state of his finances.

A few minutes later, Callie dismissed the driver for the afternoon, and she and Sherrie visited the clothiers. The young women spent two hours examining fabrics and designs. Finally, Callie ordered three new dresses, one in pale green organza with matching crinolines for the barbecue. Sherrie ordered a delicate floral print for herself with money taken from the latest allowance sent by Aunt Fiona in New York. "She's forgiven me for leaving Oberlin," Sherrie explained, "now that I'm visiting Liam."

Afterward they stopped in the stationers and bought parchment paper and envelopes for the barbecue invitations.

Leaving the shop, Sheridan pointed to a slave auction just starting in the town square. Ten or twelve slaves, roped together, stood off to one side, guarded by a group of white men. After a few minutes they were herded to a tent near a tall wooden platform.

The auctioneer stepped to his place at a center table. The gavel lay to his right.

"We've got to find out about the Underground," Callie whispered to a pale Sheridan. "Rebecca's doing her best to ask around without drawing suspicion. But it's as if nothing exists." She took a deep breath as the auctioneer called for the first slave to be brought to the block. "We may have to simply start our own."

Sherrie nodded, angry tears gathering in her eyes. "I don't think I can watch this again, Callie. Let's go." She turned abruptly.

Callie started to follow her friend, then glanced once more at the platform. The slave, a tall, well-muscled black man, was brought to the block. When he was turned to face the audience, Callie gasped.

"Sherrie," she whispered hoarsely. "Look!"

Sheridan turned and narrowed her eyes. "Who—?" She turned to Callie, her eyes unbelieving. "Is it Israel?"

Callie nodded. "It's him! I know it's him. He's been caught." Her voice dropped sadly. "We knew he would be."

"He was going back to save his family in—where was it?—Vicksburg?"

"Yes, Vicksburg. Not all that far from here. Remember, Sherrie, he told us that night that he was sure they'd be returned to his old master—and that he was going after them."

Callie turned to again watch the proceedings. The bidding began, and the price was already high.

The young women exchanged glances briefly, smiled slyly at each other, then moved closer to the crowd.

"I hear fifteen hundred—" the auctioneer began.

A young man in the front row interrupted with "Sixteen hundred."

A moment later a distinguished gentleman at the rear called, "Seventeen."

There was a pause. Then Callie called out, "I bid two thousand."

The crowd grew silent as people craned their necks to look at the newcomer. Callie and Sheridan stepped toward the crowd. Callie kept her face immobile. She didn't dare look at Israel.

"Two thousand. I hear two thousand dollars. Is there another bid?"

For a moment no one spoke. Then someone said loudly, "Twenty-five. I bid twenty-five hundred."

"Three thousand. I bid three thousand dollars," Callie declared in a loud, clear voice.

There was murmuring from the crowd. Three thousand was considered high for a field slave, even for an obviously muscular and healthy specimen such as the black man standing before them.

"Thirty-one hundred," someone declared.

This time laughter followed. The crowd waited expectantly, still turned toward Callie and Sheridan.

"Three thousand, one hundred dollars, going once, going twice—"

"They're trying to raise the price because you're a woman, Callie," Sheridan growled under her breath.

"Three thousand, five hundred!" Callie shouted.

Silence. Callie could feel Israel watching her. She kept her chin high and her gaze on the auctioneer.

"Thirty-five hundred once. Thirty-five hundred twice." He paused, his greedy eyes searching the crowd. When he got no response, he pronounced the slave sold to the "pretty little lady in the back."

Callie moved to the record keeper at the side of the platform, arranged for payment from the Stonehaven accounts, then signed her name to the bill of sale.

She nodded for Israel to follow her back to where Sheridan stood waiting. Without a word or glance exchanged the three walked toward the livery stables where they would find the waiting brougham and its driver.

In the shade of a magnolia tree near the slave auction, Hawk Jones stood leaning a shoulder against the trunk, his legs crossed at the ankles. He'd slung his hat low over his eyes and chewed on a long stem of grass.

He'd been in Natchez for a week. His first day in town he'd headed for the office of Dr. Greenleaf Meade, a fellow student Dr. Hill had known at Harvard. But the doctor had left a notice on his door that he was visiting outlying plantations and wouldn't return to Natchez until the end of the week. So Hawk asked around town about Callie St. Clair. His inquiries drew only blank stares until, on the second day, he made it a point to mention Stonehaven. Suddenly there were smiles of recognition.

"Callie St. Clair? Of course. She's the new mistress of the mansion," said one shopkeeper.

Others added even more detail. "Ah, Caleb Benedict's dear niece who's returned home after years gone."

"Ran away from her sister out west," one woman related. "The poor girl was abducted from her home years ago. It's a wonder she made it back alive. She lived among the savages, you know."

With that, Hawk shook his head and turned away, figuring that the scheming Callie he remembered was alive and well. But still he'd been disappointed. He had hoped to find the answers to her puzzling behavior, solid reasons that would explain the mystery of her disappearance. *Lived among the savages?* He and his gentle mother were the only Indians Callie had come in close contact with in New Mexico. A slow anger boiled inside. No matter what the trouble she was fleeing, how could she toss out such untruths?

Now, leaning against the tree, Hawk debated whether to stay in Natchez for a few more days, ride to Stonehaven to see Callie, or simply catch the next boat north to St. Louis. He now knew her whereabouts. Whether or not she was a fugitive from the law, she was obviously safe at home in the place where she'd always said she would return.

What good would it do to make contact? It would only cause him more pain. He had at least learned that much about himself when it came to a certain Miss Callasandra St. Clair. He was lost in thought about Callie when a commotion from the slave auction caught his attention.

He winced as a large black man was led to the auction block, turned from side to side, back to front, arms held up to show off his biceps. Then the bidding began. Hawk felt sick.

He'd started to turn away when he heard a female voice call out a number. He would've known that voice anywhere. He turned his head.

It was Callie!

There she was, her thicket of red curls as unruly as ever, the tilt of her chin, the graceful elegance of her neck as stunningly beautiful, as mesmerizing as he remembered. Just as she had captivated him the first time they met, she held his heart now. He wanted to run to her, make himself known, gaze into her eyes once more.

All the unpleasant thoughts disappeared that had settled into his mind since he'd begun his quest to find her. If only she would turn.

But her gaze remained fixed on the auctioneer; she called out another number.

Slowly, the sick realization struck him, bringing bile from his stomach into the back of his throat: Callie was bidding for the slave who stood bound and scarred before the crowd.

Hawk looked at the ground, ashamed for her, ashamed of her, ashamed that he knew her. He was unable to watch a moment longer.

The bright world of a few minutes earlier suddenly seemed only cruel, harsh, cold.

As the auctioneer pronounced the slave sold to the "pretty little lady in the back," Hawk turned away.

CHAPTER

Nine

For several minutes Hawk couldn't leave the auction site. Too sick to move, he could only think of the ugliness he'd just witnessed. How could he have thought himself in love with such a woman? Had he never known her soul?

Slowly, he walked to the livery where he'd left the Arabian mare. He planned to saddle her and head straight to the docks to board the next riverboat heading north.

It was more than the stifling heat that threatened to suffocate him in this place. The scene at the auction reminded him of all that was abhorrent about slavery. He'd discussed it with his classmates and professors while at Harvard and understood both sides' reasoning—the economics of the South, the morality issues brought up by the North. But none of it had prepared him for seeing another human being sold as if he were nothing more than an animal.

Hawk drew in a shaky breath, trying to steady himself. The air around him felt hot, thick, unbearable. He ran the remaining distance to the livery, rounded the corner, and stepped into the dim light of the hay-strewn, rough-boarded building.

Out of breath, he halted at the doorway, letting his eyes

adjust, his breathing become normal.

Then he heard Callie's voice again.

There, on the other side of the cavernous stables, she stood with a dark-haired young woman and the slave she'd bought earlier. There seemed to be no one else in the livery.

Hawk crept silently into the darkness of an empty horse stall, watching the trio. They were obviously waiting for their team to be hitched. An empty carriage stood waiting on the street beyond the open door Hawk had just entered.

Callie was animated as she spoke, though Hawk could catch only snatches of her words. He heard the word "Vicksburg" once, and "family" twice.

The slave listened attentively, contributing to the conversation from time to time. The dark-haired woman seemed to be questioning him. He saw the black man bow his head as if in some emotional pain. Then silence followed.

Callie St. Clair obviously had much to learn about treatment of slaves, at least from what Hawk had already observed. This was the first conversation he'd witnessed between master or mistress and slave. He'd seen orders given and received. Eye contact by the slave was strictly avoided. Social conversation did not exist.

Yet here was Callie conversing with—and listening carefully to—her newly purchased slave as if he were an equal. As Hawk watched her, he softened somewhat. Perhaps she was a plantation mistress who treated her slaves well. At least that was something, he thought.

After several minutes the dark-haired young woman left to see about the carriage. The slave leaned toward Callie as if telling her something in confidence. Hawk didn't have time to consider what they might be saying, because the young woman again stepped into the stables, calling to them that the team was hitched and ready. Then Callie, the black-haired girl, and the slave passed without noticing him on their way to the carriage.

Hawk kept himself hidden until he heard Callie's slave swing himself up to sit with the driver and the young women settled themselves inside. Then, as the driver popped his whip over the team, Hawk stepped to the livery door, thinking they were on their way.

Callie looked through the carriage window at the same moment the team jerkily pulled the carriage away from the stables.

Her eyes met his. Time stopped. An eternity seemed to pass in that brief moment.

Callie's lips parted in disbelief. And could he be imagining it?—her eyes reflected a deep joy at seeing him. There was something else, he realized, as the carriage rumbled from his sight. Her look was beseeching. And it held a mysterious sadness.

Hawk stood rooted to the spot, unable to move, unable to shake Callie's image from his mind. His emotions clashed: the abhorrence at what he'd witnessed at the slave auction; the mysterious enchantment her presence stirred within him.

How could he leave Natchez without seeing her again, without speaking to her?

Hawk saddled the Arabian and headed to the docks. By the time he'd halted the mare beside the riverboat, he'd decided to spend a few more days in Natchez, to try again to make contact with Dr. Meade and to find out what he could about Callie's position at Stonehaven.

And of course, he would see Callie. He wasn't sure how or when. But he would gaze once more into those clear green eyes before heading back to St. Louis, the upper Missouri River, and the Mandan villages.

Just before sundown, Hawk knocked at the office door of the elderly Dr. Meade. He noticed that the "closed" sign from a few day's earlier had disappeared.

A tired-sounding and muffled "come in" floated through the painted wood and glass-paned door.

A small bell tinkled as Hawk opened the door and entered. Dr. Meade, a distinguished-looking, slightly graying gentleman, was heading to his desk in a separate, smaller area off to the side of the waiting room. He turned, surveying Hawk quizzically.

"I'm sorry, I'm through seeing patients until after my midday dinner. You'll need to come back later this afternoon." Though his words were clipped, his drawl was soft, pleasant.

"I'm not here to see you for medical reasons."

The older man frowned. He looked distrustful. "I don't have much time. State your business, then."

"My name is Jedediah Jones. I'm a friend of Dr. Noble Jackson Hill's in St. Louis."

"That so?" The older gentleman's manner didn't change. Hawk could see a wariness in him.

"Dr. Hill has been my mentor for the last several years—saw to it that I got into Harvard."

For the first time, Dr. Meade smiled, then nodded his head slowly. "Ah, yes. Of course. You must be the one he calls Hawk."

"I am he."

Dr. Meade stood, moved across the room, and vigorously shook Hawk's hand, then patted him on the back and nodded to a nearby chair. "Sit. Tell me about yourself. Why didn't you just say you were Hawk in the beginning?"

Hawk sat, grinning at the man who didn't stop talking long enough to let him answer.

"I don't think I've ever heard Noble call you Jedediah—only Hawk. And he's mighty proud of you, too, son. Mighty proud. His last letter was full of bragging about your finishing up at Harvard. I hear your scores were among the highest in your class." He shook his head slowly. "Brings back memories, I tell you, Hawk—is it all right if I call you Hawk? I'd be happy to call you Jed, Dr. Jones, whatever you like. Well, as I was saying, seeing you—knowing what you accomplished—conjures up the past right in front of these old eyes. Doesn't seem like that long since Noble and I were there."

"Hawk, sir. Just call me Hawk," the younger man said, when he could finally get a word in.

"Good, good. And just call me Doc. Everyone else does around these parts. Now, tell me, what're you doing here? Nothing's happened to Noble, has it?"

"No. Dr. Hill is in good health. I left him just weeks ago. He's busy, though. I regretted having to leave. I'd hoped to help him out during the summer months."

"We all work too hard," Dr. Meade said solemnly. "It comes with the profession. Why couldn't you stay? It must have something to do with you being here in Natchez."

Hawk explained about Callie St. Clair, her sister's concern, and his quest to find her whereabouts. When he mentioned Oberlin College, he noticed a flicker of recognition in the doctor's eyes. Then it was gone, and Hawk continued.

"Callie has returned to her childhood home, to a plantation called Stonehaven."

"I know of it," Dr. Meade said, without expression.

"I saw her briefly yesterday—at an auction. She bought a slave."

"Nothing unusual about that. From what I've gathered, Caleb Benedict has turned over much of the day-to-day running of the household to his niece. Buying slaves fits into the category of her duties."

"I suppose it's not unusual. I was surprised to see her in that role."

Dr. Meade didn't comment.

"She left Oberlin College so suddenly—actually right before the term ended. She told no one where she was headed—not even her sister. I only guessed that I would find her here. Then the next thing I know, I find her comfortably settled into her role as plantation mistress, working closely with the uncle Callie believed cheated her father, stole the family home, and caused her and Juliana to run away."

Hawk realized, as he attempted to explain Callie's behavior to Dr. Meade, that there were still many unanswered questions, questions he was as determined as ever to answer. He'd been looking at the surface facts, what Callie obviously had wanted others to see—and be fooled by—if they examined the evidence closely. Could it be that she had calculatingly left the trail of a thoughtless young woman too filled with self to bother with even a letter to her sister? The thought stunned him, though he realized it had been dormant in his mind since he'd left Oberlin College. Callie was playing a role. Why hadn't he thought of it before? Or was he thinking of it now because he willed it to be that way?

He transferred his attention back to Dr. Meade, who watched him intently. "I want to see her—find out if she's faring well. I need to urge her to at least write her relatives in New Mexico, let them know she's all right."

Dr. Meade smiled. "There aren't other reasons?"

"No, sir," he said quickly, feeling himself color slightly.

"Doc," Dr. Meade corrected with a knowing grin. "Actually, I'm acquainted with Miss St. Clair."

Hawk waited for Doc to go on, wondering why his heart seemed to skip a beat.

"Years ago I worked for her father, Richard. Made weekly trips out to treat the slaves. Miss St. Clair remembered me, and when she recently started working for her uncle, she stopped by to ask me to resume my visits."

"So you'll be going out to Stonehaven?"

Doc smiled, nodding.

"Soon?"

He smiled again. "Tomorrow."

"Mind if I go along?"

"I could use your help, son." Dr. Meade began to describe the conditions at Stonehaven and the other plantations in the county. "Stonehaven's always been considered better than most. Richard St. Clair set a precedent that Benedict has followed. Taking care of your slaves pays off in their efficiency in the long run." He sighed. "As they say, a healthy slave is a productive slave."

Hawk watched the older man as he spoke, trying to figure his sentiments. So far, they were no different from the standard patter he'd heard from Harvard Southerners.

"I'd be happy to help you out while I'm here."

Doc brightened at his words. "You don't know what you're in for, son. I get a few patients in here—but for the most part, I travel around the county treating the plantation slaves." He let out a deep sigh. "Not many doctors will treat them, you know. Once you start, you lose your other patients. They don't want the same hands touching them that've touched a slave."

"How will they feel about being touched by a half-breed Mandan?"

Doc Meade threw back his head and laughed. "Who? The Negroes or the local citizenry?" He laughed again. "Well, now, we'll just have to let them figure it out on their own, I suppose."

Doc brought out some cold fried chicken and corn bread, offered some to Hawk, then spoke to the younger doctor about his dreams for the future.

"Someday I'd like to set up a facility devoted to medical research. No one's paid much attention to the ailments of the poor," Doc said. He related in great detail the strides by modern medicine to treat the wealthy and, conversely, the lack of care for meeting the needs of the poor.

Nodding, Hawk said he understood, telling him of his call to the Mandans.

"We're cut from the same cloth, you and me," Doc said, after a few minutes. He wiped his face with a large cloth napkin. "Noble was right to send you here."

Finally in the waning light of the afternoon, Doc closed the door and pulled down the shade. "You're welcome to stay with me, son. I live in town not far from here. I live a simple life—just myself and the Missus, but it'll beat all to tarnation your staying in a boarding house."

Hawk thanked him and left to pick up his belongings at the hotel where he'd spent the previous two nights. He was welcomed warmly by Doc's wife, Bea, who said it felt as if she was meeting Noble Hill's son. He quickly settled his spare but comfortable room, glad for his decision to stay on in Natchez.

His bedroom opened onto a small balcony facing downtown Natchez. After supper, he opened the French doors and leaned against the doorjamb for a long while, watching the town slip into the gathering darkness. The square was empty now, and all signs of the slave auction had disappeared.

With oil lamps and candles illuminating the paned windows of nearby houses, the scene seemed deceptively innocent, like a picture in a child's storybook, he thought. Fireflies flitted beneath his window, and he could see their glittering presence here and there along the cobblestone street in front of Doc's house. A breeze had kicked up from the river, and now the air, though still heavy with moisture, felt cool against Hawk's skin. Crickets and frogs chanted their late summer arias. Once in a while a carriage rumbled along the street and the clacking of horses' hooves added to the soft cacophony.

Somehow, though he was far from the destination he'd planned when he left Harvard, Hawk felt at peace. Dr. Hill had counseled him well about seeking God's will. He'd been right about sometimes finding it where you don't expect it. Hawk still didn't understand why it wasn't for him to go directly to the Mandan villages as he had planned. For that matter, perhaps he would never know why God had led him here instead.

He lifted his face heavenward, setting his gaze far beyond the sights and sounds of town, far beyond the crescent moon just now sliding from behind the clouds. Wordlessly, but with a depth of emotion he rarely showed to anyone else, Hawk began to speak to his God in praise, supplication, and adoration. He brought the details of his life, his feelings, his concerns, his hopes, and his dreams before his Friend.

For several minutes Hawk stood leaning against the doorway, thinking of Callie. He thought about the expression he'd seen on her face as her carriage rolled away from him, and suddenly he feared for her.

Long after he had lain down on the high iron bed and closed his eyes, he couldn't shake from his thoughts the beauty he'd seen in Callie's face... or the beseeching look she'd given him.

A ye! Me own grandmother's nightcap! Who was that?" As the carriage rattled along the road leading from the stable, Sheridan craned her neck to look back, her eyes wide with awe.

Feeling lightheaded, Callie took a deep breath. "His name is Hawk."

"Hawk? What kind of a name is that?" Sheridan was still looking out the brougham's window, watching the buckskin-clad figure disappear in the distance.

"It's Mandan. He's a Mandan Indian."

Sheridan finally turned from the window. "But his eyes...his hair—" she began. "He doesn't look like a savage."

"The Mandans are known for their light eyes. They're the only tribe in North America to have them. Besides, only his mother is Indian." Stunned by Hawk's surprising appearance, Callie's voice was barely audible. She swallowed hard. "And he's anything but a savage. He's a doctor. Harvard-educated."

Sheridan's eyes widened with interest. "How do you know this?" Then she noticed the stricken look on Callie's face and smiled. "Ah, 'tis coming to me, it is. He's from New Mexico. You knew him there."

Callie nodded, regaining her composure, though she could still feel her cheeks flaming. "He's a friend of my family's. His parents live near Juliana and Parker."

"And I'm wishing my family had friends who look like that!"

Callie laughed, a surprising joy filling her as she spoke of Hawk.

Sheridan giggled. "Aye. Never have I seen such a man! But what's he doing here?" She craned her neck for a last look, finding that the carriage had turned onto the road leading from town and the livery was far behind them.

"I was just wondering the same thing."

"You said that his parents live near Juliana?"

Callie nodded.

"It seems to me he could have been sent to find you."

Sheridan was right. He'd been sent by Juliana and Sun to find her as if she were an errant school child. She narrowed her eyes as she thought about it. Of course. Why else would he be here? "Last I heard from Juliana, Hawk was to finish his studies at Harvard in early spring. Then he was planning to head up the Missouri river to the Mandan villages."

"Why would he be wantin' to do such a thing as that?"

"His mother's people have died by the thousands from diseases brought by the white man. He studied medicine so that he could go there and help them."

Sheridan's face reflected her remorse. "I shouldn't have said what I did about him going there." She was silent a moment. "Did you ever write your sister Juliana about where we are?"

"No."

Sheridan frowned. "You should've done it before now, Callie St. Clair. I wrote me Aunt Fiona. You should've done the same with Juliana. I'm sure that's why your friend has come—and here we are keepin' him from his noble mission. His people are dyin' now while he's searchin' for poor Juliana's missin' sister."

"He's not my friend."

"What?"

"Hawk's not my friend," Callie repeated with a sigh. Everything Sheridan had just said was true, but she might as well straighten her out on this detail first before trying to explain the rest. "When we last saw each other—in Oberlin two years ago— he made it perfectly clear he wanted nothing to do with me."

Sheridan rolled her eyes. "Why not, in heaven's name?"

"I don't know. I never did understand. It seemed that all of the harsh words and feelings from our days in New Mexico had been put aside. We danced in the moonlight—then he left abruptly. No explanation. Nothing. He just walked away from me after saying we'd probably never meet again." She sighed, remembering the sadness of that moment.

Sheridan touched Callie's hand. "You still…care for him?"

For several minutes Callie didn't answer, but gazed through the carriage window, out across the fields of ripening cotton and corn. Finally she nodded slowly. "Yes," she whispered, "I do."

Then she explained why she hadn't written to Juliana. "I've been so sorry about using up our inheritance on an education I didn't complete. I thought if I could do something here"—she gestured toward the cotton field out the window—"to finally settle the mystery of our father's losing the plantation…" her voice dropped.

"Then when you wrote her, you'd be able to say something of redeeming value." Sheridan reached for her hand. "Am I right?"

Callie nodded, grateful as always for her friend's under-standing.

"You need to write her straightaway, Callie. It's not fair for her to be a-worryin' after you—no matter how bad the news is that you send her."

"Now I wish I had. Then they wouldn't have sent Hawk. And I wouldn't have to account for my actions."

"I wouldn't mind explaining anything to that man." Sheridan laughed lightly. "Not for a minute."

"Well, I do mind." Callie set her lips in a straight line and stared out the window as the carriage rattled on to Stonehaven through the lengthening late-afternoon shadows.

An hour later the young women stepped from the brougham at the front portico. Callie sent Israel to the stables with Josiah. She intended to make the newly purchased servant her new driver. His freedom would follow.

After Titus opened the ornate doors for them, Caleb and Wilhelmina Holt greeted them in the foyer. As Callie made introductions, she regarded her uncle with alarm: His behavior toward her seemed noticeably cool.

But he was ever the gentleman with Sheridan. He bowed and kissed her hand, charm falling from his lips like honey. Sherrie, however, paled noticeably and seemed flustered.

Callie didn't have time to sort it out. Caleb turned abruptly, his small unblinking eyes fixed on hers. "I need to speak to you immediately, Callasandra. Privately." She felt her palms moisten, wondering what he'd discovered.

Callie kept her expression pleasant. Ignoring Wilhelmina, she asked Delilah, who had just then bustled into the foyer, to show Sheridan to her room—the one on the far side of Rebecca's, she said. She then followed Caleb across the polished wood floor to the library.

He sat heavily behind his desk and frowned at her, running his fingers through his thin white hair. He pulled a paper from the top of his desk. "What is the meaning of this?" His voice was low, controlled.

It was the bill of sale for Israel.

She looked up at him, smiling in relief. "What do you mean, Uncle? It's obviously the bill of sale for a servant I bought today." It hadn't occurred to her that news of her purchase would arrive at Stonehaven before she did.

He sputtered. "I've never spent thirty-five hundred dollars on a slave in my life!" His face was nearly purple. "Why did you think this was necessary?" His eyes held hers accusingly. "Why was this slave so—extraordinary?"

"He looked healthy," she answered lamely. "I had hoped to speak to you about a new carriage—and a driver of my own. I saw this slave on the auction block and decided he would do."

"Would *do?*" Caleb banged his fist on the table. "You made a laughingstock of me. The auctioneer himself brought me the news. He was still laughing when he got here. Said he wanted to see my face when I read the bill of sale. It seems the entire audience knew on whose behalf you were bidding." He squinted his eyes at her. "Why did you bid such a fortune? You had to have had a better reason than simply wanting a new driver."

Callie took a deep breath, meeting his fierce gaze. "Why, Uncle Caleb," she said. "I saw nothing unusual about it at all. The bid beneath me was already close to this amount." She kept her voice in a sweet drawl. "I didn't think thirty-five hundred was exorbitant for someone of your means."

He looked at her, his anger seeming to fade. Appealing to his vanity had helped. "He wouldn't bring over two thousand if we sold him at the same auction." He sighed. "But it's obviously too late to do anything about it now."

Callie waited for him to go on.

His lip curled on one side as his eyes again scanned the bill of sale. Before he spoke the words, Callie had the terrible feeling that she knew what he was going to say. "I can't see spending this much on a stable hand—a driver. You said you bought this man because he looked strong and healthy. I'd say he's more suited for field labor—not sitting behind a horse on a fancy brougham. Don't you agree, Callasandra?"

"You didn't hire me on to buy field slaves, Uncle. You've put me in charge of the household. I purchased this slave with that in mind. I do believe you're undermining my authority in violation of our agreement—and I must insist that the slave be left at my disposal."

She met Caleb's gaze, hoping that her fear didn't show. "I have a lot to learn in running a household—buying and selling slaves are probably at the top of the list. But I'm new at this. I simply made an error in judgment." Standing, she drew in a deep breath and managed a tremulous smile. "I apologize, Uncle Caleb, for any distress I caused you. I will try to do better."

Callie stepped toward the door, then paused and looked back. "I will be expecting Israel—that's the name of the slave in question—to begin driving for me tomorrow. And he will be driving Rebecca around the county by week's end to deliver the invitations to our barbecue."

She smiled sweetly and turned gracefully with her chin up, leaving a dumbfounded Caleb still seated behind his desk.

Caleb stared at the door long after Callie had closed it behind her. He admired his niece's gumption, the way she had turned the tables on him. Again, he thought how like his Anne Marie she was—a bit like himself as well. But it didn't matter. What needed to be done would be done. He had to protect himself.

A few minutes later, the door opened slowly, and Wilhelmina Holt, with a knowing look on her narrow face, entered and primly seated herself opposite the desk.

"You heard?" he asked, though he knew she had.

"Of course."

"I think you're right about her sentiments."

"I know I'm right. I saw what I saw," Wilhelmina sniffed as if there were a putrid odor in the room. "I saw your niece embracing the girl Rebecca."

Caleb handed her the bill of sale for the slave named Israel. "I want you to find out everything you can about him. Why he was sold. Where he's been. The trouble he has been into. Everything. There was a reason behind my niece's actions today. I want to find out exactly what it was."

Wilhelmina nodded.

"And I want this information in my hands soon."

"I'll get started right away."

Caleb nodded. "The sooner, the better."

As soon as Callie reached her bedroom, Sheridan joined her. The young women sat down together on the window seat, the deepening shades of dusk falling behind them. They could hear Diana and Delcie lighting the hall candles outside Callie's room.

Before Callie could tell of her distressing conversation with Caleb, Sherrie reached over to touch her friend's arm. Her eyes were wide, her face still holding the pallor Callie had noticed when she was introduced to Caleb.

"Callie, it was him. Your Uncle Caleb."

"What do you mean?"

Sheridan took a deep breath. "Remember how I told you about Liam's midnight visitor?"

Callie nodded slowly, beginning to understand a lot of things.

"It was Caleb," said Sherrie.

"Liam owes him money."

Sheridan confirmed it with a nod.

Callie let out a long sigh. "That explains why Liam is so anxious to help us bring my uncle to ruin."

152

Sheridan's dark blue eyes were troubled. "I heard their conversation clearly. Liam's about to lose everything—his cotton shipping business, Sheridan Hall, everything!"

"Why didn't Liam tell us?"

"Pride, maybe. Or maybe he didn't know whether he could trust us or not."

"We've got to contact him, Sherrie. And we need to move faster—go through Caleb's papers. Try to find something."

"Tonight?" Sheridan's creamy skin had turned an even paler shade of white.

"No. The day after tomorrow. I overheard him telling Titus he has an appointment in Natchez that day."

"What about Wilhelmina?"

Callie grinned. "Between the two of us, I think we can take care of her." She paused, then added more seriously, "But we must get word to Liam. He's got to hold off any transactions he may be making with Caleb. I'm worried that he may be the appointment my uncle has."

"How can we get word to Liam?"

"I've got a plan." Callie knit her brows together in thought. "Tomorrow morning we'll start writing out the invitations for the barbecue. By afternoon some will be ready to send." She tilted her chin, feeling more confident. "And—I think I'll try out my new driver on the delivery run. We'll send Rebecca with him. Of course, Sheridan Hall will be included as one of the stops."

A short time later, Rebecca joined them and Callie told of her confrontation with Caleb—and what she sensed were his growing suspicions of her.

Callie sighed, looking from Rebecca to Sheridan. "My buying Israel today is going to cause Caleb to examine everything I do—and why I do it."

Sherrie nodded. "But it couldn't be helped—we had to buy

him." She explained to Rebecca how they'd been with him when his family was captured in Oberlin.

"He told us today—during the short time we had to speak—that his wife Bethenia and their baby girl were returned to Vicksburg. The owner sold them to the MacIntosh plantation here in Natchez. Israel was caught in Vicksburg after working a short time with the Underground Railroad there. He was returned to the same owner, who then sold him to a slave trader."

"He'll be working with us, then?" Rebecca asked.

Callie nodded. "He had information that we've been trying to get for weeks."

Rebecca sat forward. "He knows our contact here?"

"He told me the name of someone who can help us."

Sheridan looked up sharply.

Callie laughed softly. "It's Dr. Greenleaf Meade!"

"You told me you hired him to see after Stonehaven's Negroes."

Callie nodded, grinning. "I did."

"Before you knew?"

"Right again!"

Sheridan's voice dropped to a whisper. "It's just a matter of time then until we can set up a station here."

Suddenly, muffled footsteps could be heard in the hall. Callie put her fingers to her lips. It couldn't be Diana and Delcie. They'd already lit the candles in the hall sconces.

For a moment no one spoke. Finally the footsteps faded as they moved down the hall. Callie let out a deep breath, then turned again to Rebecca. "We'll need you to carry messages. Israel will drive you."

Rebecca's expression reflected her eagerness to help.

Callie regarded them both. "I see no reason why you and he

can't deliver every one of the hundred invitations to the barbe-cue." She grinned. "Think of the distance you'll cover. From the MacIntoshes to—" She shrugged dramatically. "Why, honeys, to who knows where?"

The following morning after breakfast, Caleb left for the day to inspect the ripening cotton fields. Callie and Sheridan sat at the massive dining room table writing out the invitations. Titus announced a visitor to see Miss St. Clair, Dr. Greenleaf Meade.

"Thank you, Titus," Callie said. She had earlier sent word to the overseer that she wanted to meet with Dr. Meade when he arrived to look after the slaves. "Tell him I'll see him in the garden."

Titus nodded and returned to the foyer with the message. Callie excused herself, telling Sheridan that she would return in a few minutes, and stepped through the French doors and across the porch to the gardens at the rear of the house.

Dr. Meade waited near a trellis of wild roses. He looked up with a smile as Callie approached, her crinolines rustling as she walked, daintily holding up the skirts of her pale blue day dress.

Callie kept her gaze on the man in front of her, assessing him, pleased with his dignified and trustworthy bearing. He didn't seem to have aged in the years since he had worked for her father.

"Miss St. Clair?" he said expectantly.

"Please, call me Callie." She nodded to a small white iron set-tee. "And please sit down. I've got something I need to ask you…" Her voice trailed off as she watched him intently. She hadn't been surprised when Israel had whispered his name to her, identifying him as sympathetic to their cause.

"As a matter of fact," Dr. Meade said, "there's something I need to discuss with you." His eyes didn't leave hers. "I have taken on a temporary assistant to help with my workload—a young doctor who comes to me with the highest recommendation. He's with me today—out at the quarters. But after he's made the rounds a few times, I'll be sending him out on his own."

Callie said that would be acceptable. If Dr. Meade was satisfied with him, she was sure she would be also.

"He'll be stopping by a bit later this morning to introduce himself."

Again Callie agreed that would be fine. Then she moved the conversation back to her original intent.

"I bought a slave yesterday," she said. "His name is Israel, and he's from Vicksburg. Seems he was sold because he's known to be a runaway."

Dr. Meade watched her, his expression mild, interested.

Callie's voice dropped. "Before I go on, Dr. Meade, I must ask you not to repeat what I am about to tell you. Please tell no one unless it will further our cause. You must promise me."

His expression changed almost imperceptibly. "I don't know what you're talking about." Then he shrugged and said with a smile, "but I'm known as a great keeper of confidences, so please, go on."

Callie's gaze fell briefly upon Stonehaven's grounds, then back on the kindly face before her. She had picked the formal gardens in which to speak because of their privacy. They were filled with lacy rose trellises, azaleas, and low-cut Australian cherry hedges.

She went on. "Israel tells me that you are an abolitionist… that you are sympathetic to the Underground movement."

"Then he's told you wrong." Dr. Meade's demeanor changed abruptly. He stood and was about to speak when Callie put out her hand, touched his arm, and implored him to please hear her out.

156

He sat next to her, though the white-lipped expression remained on his face.

"Please," she said again, her hand still on his forearm. "You don't need to say whether you are or aren't until you've heard me out." Then she told him about her years at Oberlin College, her work with Sheridan in the Underground, their near capture and flight from Ohio. "In short," she finished with a bitter laugh, "I'm a fugitive from the law. If I'm found—" She didn't finish.

Dr. Meade took her small hand between the two of his. "And you're telling me this because—?"

"Because I want to set up a station out of Stonehaven. That's partly why I came back. It was pure chance that I found Israel yesterday. But he can help. We need to get his wife and baby to Canada. They almost made it once. At Oberlin they were days away from freedom." Callie felt the return of the same helpless anger she had felt that night. "When the slavers caught them—" She didn't finish.

Dr. Meade patted her hand. "I am who Israel says I am." And he told her of his connections with others who were ready to actively get runaways into the Underground Railroad. Then as if it had just occurred to him, he asked, "Does anyone here know of your previous activities?"

"Rebecca, and of course, Sheridan."

"Does your uncle have any suspicions?"

"No. He thinks I've come to reclaim Stonehaven." She smiled ruefully.

"And have you?" His question surprised her.

"If the plantation did become mine, it wouldn't be for the reasons he might think."

Dr. Meade smiled, satisfied. "I don't need to remind you of the dangers of coming in with us, Callie. You've seen them first-hand. But I wonder if the penalties are as severe if you're caught in the North as they would be in the South."

"I'm sure they're worse here," she agreed.

He nodded thoughtfully. "You'd be hanged—or worse. You'd probably not even make it to trial."

"I know."

"It's still worth the risk?"

"Yes," she said solemnly. "It is."

Dr. Meade stood and looked down at Callie thoughtfully. "I promise you," he said again. "Your secret is safe with me."

Callie nodded.

"And there's something else I need to tell you—" he began.

Just at that moment, Titus opened the French doors. "Your assistant is here, sir. And he says you're needed at the stables. A new driver named Israel is asking to see you."

"Callie, I need to explain—" Dr. Meade began again.

But she wasn't listening. Her eyes were fixed on the figure at the top of the wide porch stairs.

For a moment, Hawk stood as still as a deer in a meadow glen, his eyes locked on hers. Then he walked slowly toward her along the stone-covered pathway through the formal gardens to where she waited.

Hawk stood before her without speaking. His gaze seemed to embrace her with the feel of the wild lands where they'd first met, with those eyes the color of New Mexico's purple skies, and skin the hue of its bronzed mesa sands.

"My assistant, Dr. Jones," the older doctor finally said to Callie. "I believe you've met." Then he quietly slipped away to see about his business with Israel at the stables.

CHAPTER

Eleven

"Callie," Hawk reached for her hands in greeting.

Callie gave him the barest smile, then lowered her gaze, her emotions in turmoil. "Hawk," she finally whispered, lifting her face. "It's good to see you." For the briefest moment neither spoke. She pulled her hands from his grasp, regaining her composure. "So you were wrong—we do meet again."

He nodded. "Yes."

"But not due to the promise I tried to extract from you that night."

His expression was solemn. "No," he said.

"I didn't think so." Callie turned away from him, hoping her deep disappointment didn't show. "You're here because of what happened at Oberlin."

"Yes, Callie." He again reached for her hand, and she turned to see the softness of his expression as their eyes met again. "Juliana is worried. She has no idea whether you're dead or alive. No matter why you left Oberlin so abruptly—you could have at least let her know your whereabouts." His words were chastising, but his tone was gentle.

Callie didn't speak. How could she ever explain her reasons to him?

Hawk pulled a letter from inside his vest and handed it to her.

With trembling fingers, Callie unfolded the pages. The letter was wrinkled and smelled of leather and woodsmoke. It reminded her of the scent of the buckskins Hawk usually wore in New Mexico. Today he stood before her as handsomely dressed as any other Southern doctor in his black suit and gray waistcoat. She missed the buckskins.

Callie read Juliana's desperate words, feeling her sister's raw fear, her dismay at not hearing from Callie for so long.

She fought to keep the tears from coming. Hawk was right: Juliana deserved better than this. No wonder he'd come to tell her.

"I'm sorry—" she began, still looking at the letter, its words now wavy from the moisture in her eyes.

Suddenly, Hawk stood closer. Callie had forgotten how silently he moved. He touched her cheek with his fingers. Then he cupped her chin in his hand, gently lifting it until her gaze was level with his.

He didn't speak; he just stood looking at her. The flood of her emotion was so strong, Callie caught her breath. There was love in his eyes, so deep and pure that it flowed from his soul to hers like a thousand rushing rivers.

She smiled at him, at last recognizing what she'd known from the first day they met, the day she'd tumbled from Darley in the arroyo, yelling at Hawk all the way to the bottom.

She loved him! She loved Hawk!

Callie lifted her hand to touch his, the hand that still cupped her face as if it was too precious to release.

For a moment they stood regarding each other silently, then

Hawk took her hand and led her to the settee.

"Callie—" he began, his voice husky.

"Please," she interrupted, "let me say this first: I've caused you to come thousands of miles out of your way—looking for me on behalf of Juliana instead of heading to the upper Missouri. No one knows better than I that your heart is there. With your people. Not here." She lifted his hand to her cheek. "Please know how sorry I am, Hawk."

"I wanted to come here, Callie." He smiled into her eyes. "I had to see you again. From the moment I found that you'd mysteriously disappeared from Oberlin College, I was desperate to find you."

"You went to Ohio?"

He nodded.

Callie's voice became serious. "How did you find me? We told no one where we were headed."

"We?"

"Yes, my friend Sheridan and I found ourselves in a rather, shall I say, delicate predicament. We left quite suddenly." Callie intended to tell him the entire story, but sounds of shouting interrupted her, carrying to the gardens from the French doors at the side of the house.

Callie looked up, puzzled. An indignant Titus railed on at Liam Sheridan as the handsome Irishman burst through the door.

"Master Sheridan wouldn't wait, Miss Callie," Titus complained loudly.

"It's all right, Titus. I'll take care of it." Callie stood and took a few steps to meet Liam as he hurried down the stone path to the gardens.

Liam greeted her with his usual exuberant chivalry, bending low to kiss her hand. "Ah, 'tis me beautiful Callasandra," he said, caressing her with his gaze. "You grow prettier each time my eyes are blessed to see you. I've sworn from the day I first laid me eyes on you that you're the only one in the world for this Irishman," he said, with a rakish smile. He winked. "Someday I'll be proving it to you."

Callie laughed, passing off his words as lighthearted blarney. She looped her arm through his. "Come, there's someone I want you to meet."

She turned to introduce Hawk, but he was gone.

"Did you see—?" she began, confused, speaking to Liam while she scanned the gardens and lawns.

Liam nodded toward the path leading from the garden to a back gate, and beyond that, the road to the stables. "The young man seemed in a bit of a hurry," he said.

Holding her skirts, Callie ran down the path, but by the time she reached the gate, Hawk was gone. She wasn't about to humiliate herself by running any farther. Her wonder at his leaving turned to dismay, then anger. How dare he simply leave without saying goodbye? How had she thought of him with such affection just a few minutes earlier?

Suddenly she felt betrayed, as if Hawk had toyed with her emotions—just as he'd done in Oberlin—to see how she would react, then left her alone with no explanation. No goodbye.

She returned to the place where Liam stood waiting, a half-smile on his handsome face.

"I'm so glad you're here, Liam. Sherrie and I had planned to send for you later," she said, again linking her arm in his as they walked together back up the stairs and into the house. She was glad for the distraction, she told herself. At least she could put her mind to something besides Hawk Jones.

She tossed her head and laughed into Liam's eyes.

Hawk strode to the stables where he knew Doc Meade waited. His jaw worked in annoyance as he walked. How could he have been such a fool? One look in Callie St. Clair's eyes and he'd melted, just as always. Then he'd been set straight by reality and cold disappointment. He might as well get it through his thick skull: Callie St. Clair was not for him.

He thought of her words, how she said she'd had to leave Oberlin because of a rather "delicate predicament" with her "friend" Sheridan. What kind of a predicament could she have gotten herself into with a cad such as the man he just observed fawning over Callie? It suddenly made sense, her leaving Oberlin in such haste. When President Welland mentioned Callie leaving with a friend, Hawk had assumed the friend was female. How wrong he'd been!

But the sweet image of Callie wouldn't leave his mind, the velvet softness of her skin as he touched her face, the deep green eyes that shimmered with emotion. But no! He willed himself not to think of her beauty, her spirited ways, the gentle music of her voice.

He would help Doc for a few more days, then head for St. Louis. He'd had quite enough of chasing Callie St. Clair around the country. It was time to again think seriously about his calling. Tonight he would write a letter to Juliana, telling her that he'd seen Callie and all was well. Tomorrow he would book passage on the next riverboat north.

He looked up to see Doc heading toward him. The older man swung his arm around Hawk's shoulders as they walked to the carriage.

"You spoke with Miss St. Clair?" he asked casually.

"I did."

"And?"

Hawk took a deep breath. "I thought she'd changed. But I was wrong. She's just like the child I remembered from our days in New Mexico—beautiful, though capricious. She's the most exasperating woman I've ever met."

Doc grinned. "I didn't find her that way at all. She's one of the most serious, level-headed, honest, and giving young women I've encountered in a long time."

Hawk raised an eyebrow, thinking the older man must be joking—or mad.

Dr. Meade slapped him on the back. "You probably bring out the worst in her, son."

Callie and Liam joined Sherrie in the dining room. Wilhelmina was in her office, but Callie didn't trust her to stay there, so she suggested they move to a more private setting.

After a few minutes they settled into the front parlor. Callie closed the door behind them.

"Now," Callie said, her eyes on Liam. "It seems you've got some explaining to do."

"I, for one, am ashamed of me own cousin leadin' me on this way," Sherrie added, frowning. Then she proceeded to tell Liam that she knew about his financial woes. "I also know who it was visitin' you that night," she said.

Without speaking, Liam looked through the parlor window for a moment, seeming to gather his thoughts, then back to the young women. "I should've told you in the beginning." He looked directly at Callie. "The reason I know so much about your uncle's underhanded dealings is because I'm one of his victims."

"Why *didn't* you tell us?" Sherrie asked.

He shrugged, shaking his head. "I wasn't sure I could trust

you." He directed his attention to Callie.

"Why now?" Callie met his tired gaze. "Why do you think you can trust me now?"

He laughed lightly. "Let's just say, the better I get to know you, the better I like you."

Callie squinted at him. "Liking hasn't anything to do with trust."

"Aye, but it does. I'm a businessman who trusts his instincts when it comes to dealing with others."

"Your instincts certainly didn't help you with my uncle," Callie challenged.

Liam stared at her, unblinking. "Touché," he said quietly. "Touché." His vulnerability showed in his manner and in his voice.

Suddenly Callie felt ashamed she'd been hard on him. Of all people, she knew the underhanded ways of her uncle. "You're right, Liam," she said, leaning toward him. "You can trust me. I'm sorry you didn't realize it earlier."

"What will you do, Liam?" Sheridan's voice conveyed her worry.

"I am to meet Caleb at his lawyer's office tomorrow—sign over the deeds to Sheridan Hall and to my business. Everything I own will be gone. It will belong to Caleb Benedict."

Sherrie gasped. "You can't let him, Liam!"

"Can you put him off? Postpone the meeting?" Callie stood as she spoke and moved to the door, listening for anyone who might be eavesdropping.

"No, he's adamant. Said he'll get the law to throw me out of my home and business by midnight tomorrow. I either pay him what I owe—or sign the deeds."

"We've got to find something to stop him." Callie again leaned toward him, her voice low as she spoke. "I've already searched through the books Wilhelmina keeps. I didn't find anything unusual. There's always his desk—he keeps some of his important papers there." She let out a sigh. "I've just been hesitant to go through his personal things."

Sherrie reached over and patted her hand. "If you're not feelin' right about it, Callie, maybe Liam and I should do it. That way, if anything's said about it later—sure, you could claim you knew nothing about it."

Callie nodded slowly, considering the plan.

Liam looked concerned. He suddenly took her hand in his. "Callie, if you're not sure—"

Callie drew in a deep breath. "Caleb Benedict robbed my family, his own relatives, and has ruined countless other lives. I don't know why I'm so concerned about trespassing on his private affairs when he's caused such pain and sorrow by trespassing on others." She met Liam's gaze. "No. Please, let's do it. I'll occupy dear Wilhelmina while the two of you search the library." She checked the mantel clock. "We've not got much time, however. Caleb's due back by four and it's after noon now."

"And what if we don't find anything?" Sherrie asked, as Callie stood and led the way to the door.

Before she opened it, Callie smiled. "Then we might have to pay Caleb's attorney a visit."

"What good would that do? He's not going to give us any information." Liam sounded puzzled.

"Are you thinking what I'm thinking?" Sherrie grinned at her friend.

Callie nodded. "Our visit will not be during office hours." Then the mistress of Stonehaven swung open the parlor doors and ushered her guests into the dining room.

An hour later Callie tapped at Wilhelmina's office door and asked if she could speak with her about the plans for the upcoming barbecue. "I've got quite a complicated list of questions and problems—everything from where to dig the barbecue pits to what music to play for dancing," she said with a guileless smile and seated herself opposite the woman.

Wilhelmina seemed pleased that Callie had sought her advice. She spoke at length about the details.

"How about food recipes?"

Wilhelmina straightened her narrow shoulders. She recommended some of Pleasant's recipes and the servants best suited for carving and serving.

Then she frowned and set a piercing gaze on Callie. "Where are your guests?"

"You mean Liam and Sherrie?" Callie asked innocently.

She nodded. "Of course…you've left them alone all this time?"

"Yes. They're discussing some family issues—in the garden, I believe." Callie hoped that's where they were by now. She smiled sweetly at Wilhelmina and hurried on. "One more thing," she said. "The guest list." And she pulled out the list that Caleb had given her, asking for clarification about this person or that—family and political connections and social standing in Natchez.

After a while the older woman stood, signaling that Callie had overstayed her welcome. Callie stood, graciously thanking Wilhelmina for her assistance, then backed out of the room, hoping Wilhelmina wouldn't follow.

Callie took a deep breath as she passed the open library door and saw that the room was empty. A few minutes later she spotted Liam and Sherrie in the gardens, absorbed in conversation.

She asked Titus to bring them each a lemonade, and then she

made her way across the porch and down the path to meet them.

"Did you find anything?"

"Not about my affairs," Liam said solemnly.

Callie tilted her head. His tone said there was more.

Sherrie spoke up next. "Callie, did you say you'd had Caleb sign some papers recently?"

Callie nodded.

"You signed away any claim to Stonehaven?"

"Yes, though it's temporary. In exchange for my not making any fuss about how my father lost the plantation, Caleb drew up a new will naming me sole beneficiary upon his death."

"What was the date of that will?" Liam asked.

Callie told him.

Liam looked at Callie sympathetically as he took her hand. Gently he said, "Callie, he's already had another drawn up."

She was glad for Liam's understanding, but the knowledge of Caleb's treachery still hurt. And she felt foolish for trusting him at all. "And I'm obviously not in the new will."

Liam squeezed her hand as if trying to soften the blow. "I found it in the same file with the papers you had him sign about your responsibilities here—that's why I thought it connected."

Callie shook her head sadly. She didn't know why the news surprised her. Her uncle had tricked her just as he probably had her father. "Did you find anything else?"

"No." Liam let out a long sigh. He looked far older than his years, a man about to lose everything he'd worked for all his life. She wondered what it was like for her father when he found out Caleb had betrayed him. She felt a rush of emotion for the man who sat beside her. She would fight to help him overcome what her father could not.

"We can't give up," Sherrie said quietly. "Callie, were you serious about—?"

"About breaking into his lawyer's office?" She nodded. "Yes. I'll do it if you'll help me."

Liam sat forward. He still held her hand. Affection shone in his eyes. "I can't let you do that, lass. Here at Stonehaven is one thing. But I can't let you do this for me."

"It's not just for you, Liam. I've got to know what happened all those years ago. And there are others. You told us about them yourself—families ordered off their land, businesses closed." Her voice dropped off. "We've got to do something. We can't just stand by and let this happen to you or anyone else again."

"Let me go then. I'll do it alone."

"No. It would take you too long. The three of us can get through the files that much faster."

Sherrie agreed and they quickly made plans to meet at Sheridan Hall after midnight. A short time later, the two stood to leave. Sherrie excused herself and stepped to the front portico, leaving Liam and Callie alone.

Liam held Callie's gaze with his own. "Callie, what you're doing for me is more than I deserve."

"What do you mean?"

He moved away from Callie, stepping to the window as if to gather his thoughts. Then he turned towards her once again. "When you first arrived and I discovered your plans, I meant to use you to get to your uncle."

"I thought we'd agreed to help each other—"

He interrupted. "Aye, we did." He gazed at her, a self-deprecating half-smile on his ruggedly handsome face, clearly seeking forgiveness. "But I had intended to see to it that I'd benefit far more than you."

Callie lifted her face toward him. "I still don't know what you mean."

"I planned to have you dig through your uncle's private

papers for information to benefit my cause."

Callie still didn't understand what he was leading to. She watched him quizzically.

"Don't you see, lassie?" Liam moved toward her, touching her cheek gently with his fingertips. "That was before I realized that I'd fallen in love with you."

"Love?" Callie croaked, backing away from him. "Love?"

"Aye, lassie. Love." He smiled broadly. "I know this comes as a surprise. And you don't need to be giving me an answer now. I'll give you all the time you need."

"Answer?" Callie was too stunned to utter more than one word.

"Yes, darling. I mentioned it earlier."

"Mentioned what earlier?"

He laughed softly. "I said that from the day I first laid me eyes on you, you were the only one in the world for me." He caught both her hands in his, lifted them to his lips, and kissed her fingertips. "Callie, I'm asking you to marry me."

"Oh, Liam," Callie said, pulling away from him. "You can't possibly...I can't begin to—"

"Darling, as I just said—don't answer me now. I'll give you all the time you need."

Then before Callie could answer, Liam turned and made his way to the front portico to say goodbye to Sherrie.

Liam's vehicle pulled away just as Callie joined her friend. In the distance, Caleb, on a sleek chestnut mare, and his overseer, riding beside him on a gray, made their way toward Stonehaven. They slowed and looked quizzically at Liam's carriage as it passed them, nearly running them off the road.

Moments later they reined their horses to a halt before the portico where Callie and Sheridan waited.

After tipping their hats to the young women, Caleb called up to them. "Who was that?" he demanded, looking toward the dust caused by the departing carriage.

"Me own cousin Liam, sir," Sherrie responded sweetly.

"What was he doing here?" The horse snorted and shook its head, dancing sideways on the drive below the portico.

"He came to visit me." Sherrie winked at Caleb, then looked over at Callie with a teasing smile. "Though I'm thinkin' it was really someone else he came to see."

Caleb scowled. After a moment, he and the overseer nudged their horses into motion for the ride to the stables.

The household lamps and candles were extinguished by nine-thirty. By then Callie and Sheridan had said goodnight to Caleb and retired to their rooms. Callie pulled on dark trousers and an old shirt from her days in Oberlin. She tucked her hair into an old felt field hat. Sherrie dressed herself in the same manner. Rebecca showed her dimple when she saw them, then her expression turned serious.

"I'll be prayin' for you and Miss Sherrie," she said, "that God will keep you safe."

Callie gave her a quick hug, aware of her small, thin frame. "Thank you, Becca. But I think he's counting on us to take care of ourselves."

For the briefest moment Callie thought about the illegalities of their actions. If God *was* personally concerned about her, how would he feel about such activities? Callie swallowed hard, suddenly feeling uncomfortable. But then she reminded herself that she'd always had an unspoken pact with him: She'd go her way and he'd go his. Someday it might be different, but for now she could take care of herself. She jutted out her chin and at the same time glanced at Rebecca.

The girl's dark eyes seemed to look right through to Callie's soul. Embarrassed, Callie turned away.

Rebecca said again, "You'll be in my prayers."

Callie didn't answer, just kept her chin high as she opened the door.

"Don't go worryin' about us," Sherrie said, touching Rebecca's shoulder. "We'll be back before dawn."

Rebecca nodded, but the concern didn't leave her face.

Hawk couldn't sleep that night. After tossing in bed, he rose and stepped out onto the balcony and felt a refreshing breeze from the river.

A full moon had risen, its silvery light casting a dawn-like glow across the houses and buildings below. The town was still; even the crickets had quieted and the fireflies had ceased their glittering flights.

He wrestled with his thoughts about Callie and about whether he should go or stay. He wanted to leave. Being close to Callie made his feelings for her all the more painful. Maybe if he headed to the upper Missouri River he could forget her. After all, wasn't that his calling?

Then he wondered if leaving for the Mandan villages was his way of running from his feelings. He thought of the emotion he had seen in Callie's eyes when he touched her face. It was as if her heart had cried out to him with the same emotion that stirred inside him. Surely he hadn't imagined it.

Who, then, was this man Sheridan? When Callie stood to greet him, she'd obviously been glad to see the blackguard. Could they simply be friends? If so, then why had they left Oberlin College in such haste, under such questionable circumstances?

No, he thought, it was better to leave Natchez and all

reminders of Callie St. Clair. That afternoon he'd booked passage on *The Dixie*. It was steaming its way from New Orleans and would dock at Natchez in five days.

But as he looked into the heavens and began to speak to the Lord, his decision to leave didn't feel right. Perhaps his work here wasn't finished after all. And maybe it had nothing to do with Callie. Could it have to do with helping Doc Meade? He thought of the godly man he was beginning to appreciate more every day he spent working alongside him. Doc was as dedicated to helping the Negroes as Hawk was to helping the Mandans.

Hawk left the moonlit balcony and stepped back into his room. There he dropped to his knees beside his bed. With his head bowed, he asked God for wisdom. "Which way should I go, Lord?" He spoke earnestly, as if to a fellow traveler. "You know my heart, my innermost desires. You know the sorrow I feel for my mother's people. You know better than I their limited days. Yet you've brought me to this unfamiliar place I feel compelled to leave, yet cannot." He turned his head toward the open balcony doors and looked out at the moonlit skies. "Lord, what shall I do?"

Still troubled, Hawk reached for his Bible on the small walnut bedstand beside him. He lit a candle, and holding the book close to the light, opened it. He had left his marker in the book of Genesis, at the twenty-eighth chapter. His eyes fell on verse sixteen, *Surely the Lord is in this place; and I knew it not.*

Feeling the heat of tears forming behind his eyes, Hawk touched the words with his fingers, *Surely the Lord is in this place.* God was with him! He was in him; he was in this room! The moonlight paled in comparison to the warmth and light that flooded his soul.

Suddenly it didn't seem to matter whether he left Natchez or stayed. His God was with him and would lead him just as he promised he would. What was the verse in Psalms his mother used to quote? *Lead me to the Rock that is higher than I.*

That was his answer! The Rock. He remembered when he was a child on a trapping expedition with his father and they were unsure which way to go, they would seek the highest point in the region, an outcropping of sandstone or a rock. When they had climbed to its summit, their path became clear because they stood on a rock far higher than themselves.

He bowed his head in thanksgiving. "I come to the Rock; I come to you, Father," he said simply.

For the first time in days, Hawk fell into a deep and peaceful sleep as soon as he put out the candle and covered himself with the light quilt.

A short time later, when the river breeze had stilled and the moon had slipped behind a thin cloud, Hawk awoke with a start. The French doors were open, and he sensed, more than heard, activity in the street below.

Silently he rose from his bed and crept through the doorway to the balcony. He flattened himself against the side wall so he wouldn't be seen when the full moon reappeared.

He could barely make out the three figures that moved along the street. They were on foot, eerily silent, moving steadily toward town. Ruffians up to no good, he thought, otherwise why would they be out at this time of night? He wondered if he should confront them or send for the authorities.

The cloud moved on to the east, leaving the moon to cast its silver light on the street below. Now Hawk could see the figures as they crept toward a building on the corner. One man began working with a side window. Another helped, and in a few minutes the sash had been jimmied upward.

One by one the trio climbed into the building. A curtain was drawn, and a moment later Hawk could see the flicker of a lighted candle.

Was this a robbery? He couldn't remember what kind of business it was, but he did know it wasn't a bank or a shop.

He thought about confronting the trio, but he would be at a disadvantage, not only because they outnumbered him, but he couldn't get into the building except through the same window—they'd see him before he saw them.

He pondered a few minutes and decided he would hide nearby, follow the ruffians home, then report their activities to the business owner the following morning. Pulling on his buckskins and moccasins, Hawk moved silently through Doc's hallway, down the stairs and out the front door. He crossed the street and headed to the corner building.

For an hour he hid behind a pile of wooden crates and pallets at the building's rear. Finally, hearing excited whispers, he peered around the corner.

The men were crawling across the sill. The one remaining inside handed a long flat book to the others. After they were all in the street, the last one out pulled down the window and refastened the sash. Then, moving soundlessly along the side of the street, they headed back in the direction they'd come earlier.

Hawk followed them, the silence of his moccasins keeping his presence unnoticed.

The bandits moved more quickly now. Hawk's strides lengthened to keep up with them, then he stopped abruptly. One of the thieves suddenly twisted his ankle. As he stooped to rub it, his shapeless felt hat rolled into the street.

When the moon suddenly passed from behind another cloud, Hawk squinted in disbelief. If he didn't know better, he might think the cascading flame-colored hair tumbling from beneath the hat belonged to Callie St. Clair.

But no, it couldn't be!

The larger figure of the trio stooped and helped the redhaired bandit stand. Someone whose build looked suspiciously like that of the man he'd met earlier—the man named Sheridan—supported the smaller bandit gently with one arm, helping "him" once again jam the hat onto his head. Then the group continued down the street, the one figure limping noticeably.

Hawk didn't have the heart to follow them any farther. He didn't want to discover he was right.

He turned back to Doc Meade's house, his footsteps slower now as he pondered what he'd just witnessed.

CHAPTER

Twelve

❦

Callie, hanging onto Liam's arm, stepped painfully down the street to Sheridan Hall. Sheridan walked beside her, all of them moving slowly because of Callie's ankle.

After a few minutes they reached Liam's home and slipped in a side door, groping their way in the dark to the front parlor.

Liam lit a lamp and pulled a grouping of chairs close together, placing the lamp on a table nearby. He spread open the ledger and let out a long sigh. "I think we've got what we need." They had already determined that the accounts held vital information about Caleb's activities over the past several years.

"We've got the proof—but we'll need witnesses to back it up." Callie looked from Liam to Sherrie. They nodded in agreement.

"And we don't have much time," Sherrie added.

Liam shook his head. "Much time? We don't have *any* time. Caleb takes over my property this afternoon. *If* I can get witnesses to testify against him—*if* I could get an honest judge to take a look at what we've got—I might have a chance to win this battle." He rubbed his eyes, seemingly lost in thought, then looked up. "If we could just find a way to buy the time it would take."

"I didn't see any other records of your transactions with him—did you?" Callie asked.

"In his office?" Sherrie frowned. "No."

Liam shook his head.

"Look at this." She traced her finger down the list of accounts received. "Here's a list of all your payments, then the date they stopped coming in."

Liam nodded, leaning closer.

"Without this account, he has no proof of what you paid or didn't pay. It's simply your word against his."

"I don't think that would stand up in court." He looked skeptical.

Sherrie touched his arm. "But Liam, even if it did go to court, we'd be buying the time you need."

Liam suddenly grinned. "I think you've got a better business head than I do, lass." The brogue had crept back into his voice.

Callie was still poring over the ledger. "Look at this! If you trace his activity back to when you started being unable to pay, he's got big payments going out at about the same time—to plantations such as the MacIntoshes, the Taylors. Here's one paid to the Jameses. And another! Look at this!" Her voice rose in excitement. "Were these your customers?" She looked up at Liam, smiling at the twinkle coming back into his eyes.

"Aye, he was payin' plantation owners not to ship their cotton through my company. I always suspected—but now we've got proof!" Liam threw his head back, smiling at the ceiling. "Lassies. I think we've done it!"

"*If* they'll testify that's what he was paying them for." Callie sighed, realizing the magnitude of the work ahead.

"But it's a beginning. And it's more than I thought I had to go on twenty-four hours ago!"

"I don't want to take the twinkle again from your eye,

cousin," Sherrie began, her voice solemn. "But have you thought about your meeting with Caleb tomorrow?"

He smiled ruefully, his gaze moving to Callie, though he addressed Sherrie's question. "It's been uppermost in my mind, of course, child. But then, so have a number of other important issues."

Sherrie didn't question his meaning. Callie assumed her friend knew of Liam's proposal. "I mean, what do you plan to do—or say—when he discovers his ledger is missing? It seems to me he'll be thinking you're the obvious one who took it."

"He doesn't have proof," Callie interjected. "We left everything in the office exactly as we found it. If he asks Liam if he has it, Liam can honestly say no."

Liam frowned and looked again to Sherrie.

Then Callie smiled. "Because I'll have it in my possession. Sherrie and I will take it with us to Stonehaven. I want to have more time to examine it, anyway. See if there are any records referring to my father."

Liam nodded. "First let me make a copy of the names I need. I'll get started contacting them tomorrow."

"Make that 'today.'" Sherrie looked at the clock. "We'd better head back, Callie, if we plan to be there before dawn."

Callie nodded, suddenly fighting a fatigue that threatened to overcome her. Liam rapidly noted the names and account numbers he needed, placed the ledger in a satchel, and called for Israel, who waited with the horses in the stable behind the house.

When Callie stood and tried to walk to the door, she gasped in pain. Liam swept her into his arms and gently carried her to her horse, helping her into the saddle. His wide smile told of his delight in doing so. "Aye, you'll need to be taking care of this," he said, nodding toward her ankle. "See to it, will you, dear?" His eyes met his cousin's.

179

Sherrie nodded and said she would.

He looked back to Callie. "And you'd better be thinking of a way to explain your lame gait to Caleb at breakfast tomorrow." Then he grinned. "But it seems that you're as full of the Irish as the best of us, lass. I'm sure you'll think of something!"

The satchel tied securely to the saddlebag of Callie's horse, Israel, Sheridan, and Callie raced through the night. They arrived at Stonehaven well before the household had awakened.

The young women crept to their rooms with Callie wincing at every step. They had just changed into their nightclothes when the first rooster crowed in the predawn darkness. Within minutes, others had joined the morning mêlée.

A new day at Stonehaven had begun.

"Good morning, Uncle Caleb," Callie said brightly as she followed Sheridan into the dining room. She bent to kiss him on the cheek.

Caleb looked up pleasantly, then watched her as she moved to her place at the table.

Callie gritted her teeth behind her smile, trying to cover her limp. Earlier she had pulled on a deep blue plaid dress, hoping it would brighten both her outlook and the pallor she'd noticed in the looking glass. The long skirts also covered her bandaged ankle.

Caleb didn't seem to detect anything unusual. He hurried through his griddle cakes and sugared peaches and cream, and then while Callie and Sheridan lingered over coffee, excused himself, telling them he had business in Natchez and would return by suppertime.

After Delilah had cleared the table, Callie and Sheridan pulled up their chairs to prepare the invitations. By midday

Callie sent for Rebecca and Israel and handed them a map that Wilhelmina had made, showing the location of neighboring plantations and a few town houses, including Dr. and Mrs. Greenleaf Meade.

Soon Israel was popping the whip above the back of the horse, and the carriage pulled away, carrying Rebecca in her finest yellow dress, the stack of invitations by her side. Sheridan retired to her room to nap, and Callie called together the house staff to make plans for the barbecue. First she spoke with Delilah, Titus, and Pleasant about the food, the number of cooks, and the placement of the tables and chairs.

Later, because of her ankle, Callie canceled her tour of the grounds with Titus. She instead invited him to sit with her at her desk to discuss the placement of the roasting pits and the platform for dancing.

As late afternoon shadows fell across the house, Callie started up the stairs to her bedroom. Her ankle throbbed in pain, and she was near exhaustion from lack of sleep.

"Miss Callie, someone's here to see you," Delilah announced. "I directed him to the parlor, chil'."

Callie nodded and, forcing a smile over clinched teeth, turned from the stairs, limped across the polished wood of the entry floor, and opened the parlor door.

Now, near dusk, the room was quite dark. The tall figure near the window turned.

It was Hawk.

His buckskins made her heart sink; he was always dressed this way when he was about to leave her.

"You've injured yourself." He watched her intently, his expression sad as she moved toward him.

She laughed lightly with a delicate wave of dismissal. "It's nothing."

He didn't smile.

"I was just in too much of a hurry." She limped toward a high-backed chair and settled into it, grateful to take the weight from her ankle.

"Do you mind if I examine it?" Then in response to her startled expression, he added, "I am a doctor, Callie."

She nodded and, as he pulled up a hassock in front of her, she lifted the aching limb. He gently held her foot in his hands, unwrapping the crude bandage she'd attempted that morning. She winced at his touch.

"I don't think anything is broken," he said. "It's a little difficult to tell because of the swelling." He let his gaze fall softly on hers.

Callie nodded, suddenly lost in his tender expression.

He straightened the strips of cloth and rewrapped the ankle. "It will take longer to heal if you don't care for it," he said quietly. Callie wondered at the sadness she saw in him.

When he'd finished, he gently set her foot on the hassock. Then standing abruptly, he walked quickly to the window. Outside the mockingbirds and jays scolded. The field slaves could be heard working and talking in the distance.

Finally, she spoke. "Hawk? Why have you come?"

He turned to her. "I'm leaving, Callie. I've booked passage on *The Dixie*."

After what he'd done yesterday, leaving her standing alone without a goodbye, without explanation, his news didn't surprise her. She obviously meant nothing to him. The knowledge of it cut her to the core. She felt tears spring to her eyes, tears of exhaustion, frustration, anger. Why did Hawk have this effect on her? All she could think of was to get away from him, away from the reminder of the love she'd misread in his eyes yesterday.

She stood and smoothed her long skirts around her. Lifting

her chin, she said in a cold tone, "I understand. You searched for me on my sister's behalf. You found what you came for, Hawk. Your job is completed." She saw the hurt in his clear blue eyes, but because of her own pain she couldn't stop. "I hope Juliana pays you well for your time."

He didn't speak. His jaw flexed in silent anger.

Whirling, Callie tried for a proud and graceful exit. But her ankle gave way beneath her. Gasping, she sank to the floor.

In a heartbeat, Hawk was beside her, gathering her into his arms. For a moment neither of them moved, then he helped her to a chair.

She waited for him to speak. But he just stood with a sorrow in his eyes that went deeper than words. Then he was gone.

Callie slowly made her way up the stairs to her room, pondering with each painful step at the grief that filled her heart. Was it just yesterday that she had discovered she loved Hawk? It seemed much longer. After all, for years, he had never been far from her thoughts.

Now he was going away. She hadn't even asked where. If it was to the upper Missouri River, she would likely never see him again.

She sighed as she reached the top of the stairs, feeling more alone than she had ever felt in her life and fighting to keep the tears that brimmed in her eyes from spilling down her cheeks.

The uneasy calm at Stonehaven changed abruptly when Caleb rode in. He dismounted, shouted to Titus for a stableboy, strode into the house, and slammed the library door.

Callie had fallen into a light sleep, filled with whirling dreams of Mandan villages and meadows covered with spring wildflowers. She'd seen Hawk on his horse, his face on the mane, hair flying, bronzed skin gleaming in the sun, eyes the color of heaven. Riding like the wind through village and meadow, away from cities and towns, riding to the places he belonged. Riding away from her.

When the library door slammed, Callie woke with a start. She heard Caleb's shout for Wilhelmina to join him, servants' voices, scurrying feet, then finally the distinctive sound of Wilhelmina's prim footsteps moving across the foyer as she entered the library and closed the door.

Caleb poured himself a brandy, tossed it down his throat, then poured another. There was a ringing in his ears and his heart pounded erratically, just as it had during his meeting with Brown, his attorney, and Liam Sheridan.

He gasped for a deep breath, leaned against the back of his chair, and mopped his face with his handkerchief. He sat for a moment with his eyes closed. When he looked up at Wilhelmina, she was coolly observing him, sitting patiently across from him on the other side of the desk.

"What happened?" she finally asked.

"He tricked us. That conniving Irishman's tricked us."

Wilhelmina waited for him to go on.

Caleb mopped at his brow. Before he'd finished, the perspiration had beaded again on his forehead and upper lip. "The ledger is missing. I told Brown a long time ago that he needed to lock it in a safer place." Caleb slowly shook his head. "But after all these years, he let down. Quit being careful. Left it out where anyone could find it. And they did." His voice started to rise again.

"And you think Liam Sheridan broke in and took it."

"I don't think. I know."

"You can prove it?"

"No. I can't."

"You have other records?"

"Of course. I've got all the important paperwork—deeds, notes of loans. There's no problem with that. I've got Liam's signature on everything that counts."

"Then why are you so concerned about the ledger?"

He looked at her, surprised that she could be so thickheaded. "For one thing, I'll have to take him to court to prove he's in arrears in his payment schedule. It holds up my plans for taking over his properties."

Wilhelmina didn't look impressed with the news. "But you'll get them eventually?"

Caleb pulled out his handkerchief again, removed his spectacles, and wiped the sweat from his nose. Then he downed another swig of brandy. "Yes, yes, of course. No judge around here would take his word over mine."

"Then why are you worried?"

He laughed bitterly. "Because I'm ruined if anyone examines the records. They have details of every transaction I've made over the past ten years."

She didn't answer for a few minutes, letting the news soak in. Finally she said, "I'm sure you have a plan."

He took another drink, then lowered his voice. "First of all, you must understand that I'm certain my niece is in on this."

"I'm not surprised."

"She has as much to gain from this as does Liam Sheridan."

Wilhelmina nodded. "Go on."

"There's nothing we can do right now to stop either one of them from examining the books and taking their case to the authorities. But..." He paused, staring across the desk at

Wilhelmina. "It will take them some time to do that, figure out my methods, figure out who was involved, take the evidence to a judge."

Wilhelmina cocked her head, squinting. "But you still have a plan to stop them?"

He nodded slowly. "Oh, yes, I do." Finally his lip twitched into a half smile. "But we've got to move fast. Tell me what you've found out about the new slave."

It was Wilhelmina's turn to smile. "I made inquiries," she said importantly. "I found out Israel was sold to the auction company by the Winchesters in Vicksburg. Beyond that, the trading company wouldn't give out any information."

Caleb raised an eyebrow. "Any record of him being a runaway?"

"They didn't say."

He was thoughtful a minute, holding his spectacles in one hand, tapping them on the desk.

"You could pay the Winchesters a visit," Wilhelmina suggested.

Caleb nodded slowly. "I would think the sooner the better."

"Tomorrow?"

He smiled. "Yes, I'll leave at dawn." He looked at her sternly. "Tell no one where I'm heading."

"That goes without saying."

For a few minutes they spoke of the two-day steamer trip, possible accommodations, and other details. Then Wilhelmina asked what he expected to find when he talked with the Winchesters.

"I don't really know," he replied. "But I strongly suspect Callie had a much stronger motive for buying Israel than simply needing a new driver. I'm even wondering if she followed him here...." His voice dropped.

"Surely you don't mean—" Wilhelmina's thin, pale cheeks colored.

Caleb looked at her sharply, then laughed, a quick snorting sound. "Oh, no. I don't mean that she had interest in him in *that* way. Of course, I don't mean that." He sighed harshly. "It's something else entirely. I've learned that students at Oberlin College are active in the Underground Railroad."

A knowing smile crossed the woman's face. She nodded slowly, as if finally making sense of something that had puzzled her for a long time. "That's it," she said. "That's the key you've been looking for."

Caleb went on. "I've got to find out where this Israel has been." He took another mouthful of brandy, savored it, then swallowed loudly. "Where he's planning to go—" His eyes met Wilhelmina's, and he added wickedly, "and just who's planning to help him get there."

After supper, Callie and Sheridan climbed the stairs to Callie's room. They settled onto the window seat to discuss the day's events. A few minutes later, a light knock sounded at the door.

Rebecca nodded with a shy smile as Callie invited her to enter and sit with them.

"Miss Callie," she said, "Doc Meade's sent you this." She pulled a crumpled paper from her pocket and handed it to Callie.

Callie unfolded it, read the brief message, then looked up at the other two young women. "The first meeting of the Underground is tomorrow night," she said. "We meet with the others at nine o'clock."

Sheridan raised an eyebrow.

"Don't worry," Callie teased, knowing that Sherrie still fretted over the previous night's hair-raising ride. "It's a much tamer journey than last night's. We'll meet in a deserted sharecropper's house near the river. I know the place well."

Rebecca watched Callie expectantly.

Callie patted her hand. "And all of us will go, Becca. We're in this together."

They spent the remainder of the evening discussing ways they could leave the house either with a surreptitious explanation or without being detected. By the time they went to bed, they still hadn't decided the best way to slip out.

The next morning, however, when Caleb announced his sudden trip to Vicksburg, Callie's eyes briefly met Sheridan's. It seemed the problem had been solved for them.

Thirteen

❧

Callie stood at her bedroom window, holding back the curtain, gazing across Stonehaven's fields toward the river. The sounds of distant thunder made her shiver. If the building clouds were any indication of the coming storm's intensity, the journey ahead would be treacherous.

Lightning split the darkening sky. Another clap of thunder crashed, this time closer. Then brighter flashes struck and thunderous rumbling shook the house.

Large round drops kicked up the scent of dust. Within minutes, the rain came faster, hitting the ground in slanting gray sheets, turning the dust into lakes of mud.

Only a few hours remained until she would step into the carriage with Sherrie and Rebecca. But the weather didn't matter, she thought grimly. Nothing would keep her from that old sharecropper's cabin. Absolutely nothing.

Nashtara, she whispered to herself, glad for the sound of it on her lips. She lifted her head in pride. The name had been given to her by those in the Underground at Oberlin. *Nashtara,* the leader no one suspected because of her guileless smile and Southern, genteel ways.

It would be good to step once more into her role. What better way to forget the recent turmoil of emotions Hawk had caused?

Yes, she thought, as another clap of thunder rattled the house, *it's time I get on with my reasons for returning to Stonehaven.*

After supper, Wilhelmina, nervous from the still-raging storm, bade the household a solemn goodnight and retired to her bedroom at the rear of the house.

Minutes later, Israel drove the carriage around to the portico, and the three young women—Sheridan, Rebecca, and Callie—stepped into the dark buggy. Israel clicked his tongue to the horse and the rig lurched into the rainy night. He lit the lantern far out of sight of the plantation.

The vehicle bumped and sloshed through the steady rain. From time to time, jagged cracks of lightning lit the eastern sky, and a distant drumbeat of thunder echoed.

The road narrowed as they neared the river. Rebecca clutched Callie's hand when the carriage pitched violently then ground to a halt. But Israel's soft voice calmed the horses, and soon they were again rattling along the muddy road.

A quarter moon slipped from behind the clouds just as the carriage rounded the last corner before arriving at its destination. Israel halted the horses close to a decaying barn near the share-cropper's deserted house. Inside, the faint glow of candlelight could be seen through rain-covered windows. The scent of wood smoke filled the air.

Clutching their hooded capes, the women made their way through the puddled water and mud to the front of the house. As they stepped through the door, Callie noticed at least twenty people crowded into the small room. Old Mr. Higgins, editor of the Natchez Enterprise, stood and greeted her with a hug. "I knew your father," he said, his ruddy face beaming. "He'd be proud to know you're here."

Callie warmed at his words. Richard St. Clair had never spoken openly of abolition, though she had suspected his sympathies.

She recognized three slaves from Stonehaven and one from The Elms, a plantation just south of Natchez. A shopkeeper, sitting near the back of the room, nodded in greeting; he had sold Callie and Sheridan their fabrics and notions a few weeks earlier. His rotund, pleasant-looking wife sat beside him.

Callie, Sheridan, and Rebecca took their seats in the front of the room, where a milk stool, two stumps, and a farm chair had been set aside.

Moments later, a tall, thin Negro woman with expressive black eyes stood to greet them. "Nashtara!" she cried joyously, as they hugged. "And Sherrie! It's good to see you both."

"Sadie!" Callie eye's widened in surprise. "I didn't know you'd be here!"

Sadie's gaze took in both young women, a wide grin lighting her face. "It's a miracle that *you're* here. I've worried about you since Oberlin—I had no idea where you'd gone." She shook her head slowly at Callie and Sherrie. "You've been in our prayers."

"How did things turn out?" Sadie had been in place as station master at the next stop north of Oberlin that night, waiting to take those passing through to Canada. "We haven't been in contact with anyone in the Underground since we left."

"Jake Smyth was captured. He talked—told everything he knew about the two of you and the missing slave—Israel, was it?"

Callie touched Sadie's hand. "Israel's here tonight, Sadie." She nodded his direction. "He could've made it to freedom, but he

191

came back for his family. After he was captured, he was returned to his owner, who sold him to—" Callie smiled gently, "—to me."

Sadie threw back her head and chuckled. "I won't even ask how that came about."

"Tell us about Jake." Sherrie's brows knitted into a frown. "What happened to him after the raid?"

"The boy was terrified of their threats—told them everything. About you both. About Israel being the leader of the escapin' slaves. About you, Callie, being Nashtara. After that night, every bounty hunter, every slaver in the county was on the lookout. I don't know how you got through without being discovered."

She paused, her face sad. "Young Jake killed himself not long after. Hated himself for what he'd done—to you—to us all."

"Aye, what a shame." Sherrie whispered. "The poor lad. Callie and I worried he'd be too weak." Tears filled her eyes. "But I'm so sorry to hear it."

Before Sadie took her place in the front of the room, Callie introduced her to Rebecca, explaining her role at Stonehaven and as a messenger for the Underground.

Sadie squeezed the girl's hand, nodding with understanding. "Yes, this will work fine," she said with a pleased glance at Callie. "Just fine."

Soon, Sadie called the meeting to order. "My name is Sadie Johnson," she said. "I'm a free woman. And my only reason for livin' is to get other folks to freedom." Her dark eyes looked out over the crowd. "And if that's not your burnin' desire—then you are in the wrong place."

Callie watched her friend with affection and admiration.

Sadie's gray-streaked hair was slicked back into a small bun at the nape of her neck, emphasizing her high cheekbones and aristocratic chin.

There was not a sound among the listeners as Sadie spoke, only the crackling of the fire, the mesmerizing timbre of her voice. She told how she had escaped to the North some twenty years before, had been taken in and educated by an abolitionist family. They'd even seen to her college education.

"I looked around at the free Negroes in the North," Sadie continued, "—some two hundred thousand. Some were educated. I saw preachers and teachers." She looked out over the group, her black eyes flashing. "It isn't fair. Our brothers and sisters in the South have the right to the same opportunities." She paused, letting her gaze rest on the Negroes in her audience. Her voice dropped to a whisper. Her eyes glistened with emotion. "It's your gift. And I'm here to help you find the way to that road to freedom. To opportunity."

To Callie, Sadie possessed an inner fire that shone as brightly through her dark eyes as the flames in the fireplace behind her. She spoke of Harriet Tubman, the escaped slave who risked her life again and again for the Railroad, leading people from slavery to freedom in Canada. She told of Frederick Douglass, the self-educated former slave, sought after as a writer and lecturer for the abolitionist movement in the North.

"You are like them," she said, her eyes searching the group before her, "or you wouldn't be here. You can help hundreds of people—men, women, little children, and babies—find their way to a better life, a life of promise and hope. You've got the fire. You've got the spirit. I can see it in your eyes."

Throughout the evening, newcomers entered and sat in the rear of the room. Chair legs scooted, feet shuffled, but Callie, caught up in Sadie's delivery, didn't turn to look.

Sadie's voice grew stronger as she continued. "God has

brought us to this place at this time. It isn't an accident that each of us is here. We're here with a purpose. We're here with a single mind—that is, to help our brothers and sisters find freedom.

"We're committed to that above all else. We're ready to give our lives—if that's what's required of us. Jesus Christ himself said there is no greater gift than to give your life for another."

She paused. "Unless each of you is committed to doing just that, then I suggest you leave now. You don't belong among us." Her eyes probed the faces of those before her. "For that is what this is all about." Again she paused, the fire in her eyes bright. "Weakness leads to failure. Lives will be lost—yours *and* those we're tryin' to lead from this place."

Sadie's gaze rested briefly on Sheridan, then Callie, as she spoke. "I want to introduce some folks to you—folks who know what I'm talking about. Their commitment is more than lip service." She smiled broadly. "Nashtara and Sheridan, I know first-hand about your dedication to the cause. I've seen you in action. I've stood beside you in the North waitin' for the train to arrive. I've watched you nurse the injured, stay with the dyin' when we ourselves needed to escape. I've seen you outsmart the smartest, toughest posses." Chuckling, she went on. "Till then, the poor gents didn't know how deceiving looks could be."

She paused, then looked to Callie. "Would you please join me?" Callie made her way to the fireplace. Turning, she looked out at the upturned faces.

Her breath caught.

Sitting at the back of the room next to Dr. Meade, Hawk, dressed in buckskins, gazed up at her. At the instant their eyes met, Callie noticed in his expression a sudden understanding, a knowing. She looked away, unable to bear her feelings at the sight of him.

She forced her attention back to Sadie.

"I have chosen this woman to lead you." Sadie's black eyes

were intense in her seriousness. She examined the faces of those gathered in the room, as if measuring their reaction, perhaps their disagreement with her choice. None was evident, and she continued. "From her position at Stonehaven she can direct the activities, assisted by Sheridan, Israel, and Rebecca. With your help, a station can be formed that will see the safe passage of hundreds—maybe thousands—making their way north."

She smiled again at Callie. "Perhaps, daughter, you have a few words for us."

Callie stepped forward. For a moment she looked from face to face, touched by the earnestness in their expressions. There were nods of approval from some, smiles of welcome from others. They clearly accepted her as their leader.

"One afternoon about two years ago," she began, "when I was a student at Oberlin College, I was out riding on a seldom-traveled trail that led from campus into town. I had stopped to let my mare graze when I heard a scream off in the distance—a sound I will never forget.

"It seemed to come from a thick stand of trees. As I crept closer, the screams continued from somewhere inside the thick underbrush. I was frightened, but curious. I mistakenly thought I would be able to help whoever was in need." She looked down briefly, biting her lip, wondering if she could get through the rest of the story.

Callie raised her head, aware of Hawk's intense gaze. Her eyes met his. In the briefest heartbeat, she felt a jolt inside as powerful and glorious as the lightning had been earlier. It dispelled the darkness of the scene she was about to relate.

Suddenly she wanted Hawk to know about this secret part of her life. She wanted him to understand what drove her to retake Stonehaven, to give her life, if necessary, for the cause of freedom. With new boldness, she spoke on.

"As I crept closer I could hear a woman begging—not for her

own life, but for that of her child. She offered herself. 'Do what you want with me,' she cried. 'Just let my baby live.' Near her a baby whimpered pitifully.

"I pulled back the brush quietly so that no one would hear.

"There in the clearing knelt a Negro woman. Her hands were bound behind her. She was young, maybe just a bit older than Rebecca." Callie glanced at Becca, who watched her with dark solemn eyes. "A slave hunter stood before her, dangling her baby. Two other men stood next to him.

"The man with the baby kept asking where the others were hiding. She cried that she didn't know. And she just kept begging them not to hurt her child.

"The man said he'd kill the baby if she didn't tell. She sobbed, begging for mercy. By now the infant was shrieking in terror.

"Finally, one of the men to the side raised his pistol to the child's head—"

Callie stopped abruptly, choking on the words, her vision blurring with tears. "The man held the baby right in front of that poor mother. And the other man—" Again, Callie couldn't go on. She shook her head slowly, then looked toward Hawk, whose gaze held a deep tenderness. She took a shaky breath. "And the other man," she said, "shot the child in front of its mother's eyes."

A murmuring filled the room and Callie paused until there was again silence. Now her voice was cold, almost mechanical. "Then the men had their way with the woman. She bore the brutal attack in silence. She simply kept her eyes on her dead baby. Afterward they slung her over the back of a horse—to retrieve their reward for her capture.

"The irony was, the woman had told the truth. I learned later that she and her baby had escaped alone. All she wanted was to be free. And for her baby to escape a life of slavery."

Again Callie's gaze rested on Hawk. "I was raised on Stonehaven where slavery was an accepted part of life. My father treated his slaves with respect. They were well clothed, well fed, 'happy,' I always thought. There were no excessive beatings. Many were treated like part of the family. Even after I moved away from the South, I didn't think about their right to freedom. I didn't think about them at all"—she paused—"until the afternoon when a woman lost her beloved child and her precious dignity...just because some human beings see fit to keep others enslaved."

Callie quickly brushed the tears from her cheeks. "That afternoon my world was shaken to its core. I felt helpless—because I was alone. And guilty—because I did nothing to save her. But I decided that day that if I could save the life of just one child, one mother—help them reach freedom—the baby's death, the mother's ravishment, would not have been in vain."

Dr. Meade had not prepared Hawk for seeing Callie at the meeting. Doc had simply asked him to attend, briefly explaining his involvement in the Underground Railroad. Until Callie stood when introduced by Sadie Johnson, Hawk had no idea that she would be there. And when Callie began to speak, suddenly everything about her made sense.

Hawk had known discrimination. Though blue-eyed and lighter-haired, his high cheekbones and skin color gave away his Mandan ancestry. "Half-breed" and worse had been hurled his direction more times than he cared to remember. He knew what it was like to be spit at, to be thrown from the premises of business places or eateries. Though never enslaved, he knew that many of his people and those of other tribes had been.

So he understood the Negro better than most. Though he had his freedom, he knew what it was to crave education and acceptance. He hadn't expected Callie to understand—no, more than that, to feel to the depths of her soul the plight of others.

Now he watched this new Callie. Her eyes burned with a fervency he'd never seen in them. She laid out the plans for Stonehaven, telling how it was perfectly located for its role as a major "hub" in the Underground in Mississippi and Louisiana. Again Hawk wondered how he could have been so dense as not to have guessed Callie's motives for returning to her childhood home.

Callie laid out the plan for the first train. The scheme took shape, details were solidified, duties assigned. "We'll plan several smaller groups, though, before attempting a major run," she said. "At the end of summer, Stonehaven is planning a barbecue. This gives us time to plan the first major departure."

She introduced Israel and Rebecca. "They are your contacts. During the next few weeks they will be crisscrossing the county, delivering invitations to the barbecue." For the first time since beginning to speak, Callie smiled. "They'll also be delivering a few other messages. If any of you need to contact me or anyone else in the station, get a message to either Rebecca or Israel. They'll know what to do."

Finally the meeting drew to a close. Hawk stepped outside, spoke briefly with Doc Meade and some of his friends as they left, then waited for Callie.

The rain had stopped and the stars had turned the sky into a brilliant canopy of fiery pinpoints. Hawk leaned his back against the house near the door.

Finally she appeared, swinging her cape around her shoulders as she stepped from the house. Hawk moved toward her. "Callie?"

She looked up, a tentative smile playing at her lips. She didn't seem surprised that he had waited for her.

He took her hand. "I had no idea..." his voice faltered.

198

"I know, Hawk," she whispered. "You don't have to explain."

"Everything makes sense now—about why you left Oberlin…why everyone there was protecting you. I wish I had known earlier." He paused. "What you witnessed, Callie—that happened before I saw you at Oberlin. Why didn't you tell me? If you had, I wouldn't have left. At least, not then."

Callie's eyes widened. "I was about to tell you that night. But you left so abruptly."

"I know. I was confused."

She tilted her head. "And now?"

"All I know is that I have feelings for you, Callie." His voice was low. He cupped her chin, tilting her face toward his, drinking in the look of her. "I can't ignore them any longer."

Callie nodded, her unblinking gaze meeting his. Her eyes shone in the starlight. In them, he saw love. Or was it simply a reflection of his feelings for her?

"I would have sent for you, Hawk, if I'd had any idea that you would've come. If you had given me any hope that night—"

"Oh, darling. Please forgive me. When I watched you dance at Oberlin I saw only the belle who was born for a life of finery and ease. I didn't look down on you for it. I just thought it was what you deserved—that it was what you were created to be: the mistress of a great house like Stonehaven."

A frown creased Callie's brow. She didn't speak.

"I knew I was falling in love with you."

"Love?" Her voice, now a soft whisper, trembled with the word.

"Yes. Oh, yes! Love, Callie! I discovered that night that I loved you—and probably had from the moment you ran me off the trail in New Mexico."

"Why didn't you tell me?"

For a moment Hawk didn't speak. "I didn't want to ask you

to give up Stonehaven for a muddy rock hut somewhere in the wilds of the upper Missouri. What could I offer you?"

"You didn't know me well."

"I know I was wrong, Callie."

She laughed softly; it was a gentle, forgiving tone. "You always seem to be leaving before we have a chance to resolve whatever question—spoken or unspoken—is between us." She sighed, shaking her head slowly, though still smiling. "Now, tell me why you left me standing in the garden the other day. I was ready to fall into your arms." Again, her eyes shone.

"Oh, that was a mistake. A misunderstanding."

She tilted her head. "I don't understand."

He chuckled lightly. "You had just told me that you'd left Oberlin with Sheridan...under 'delicate circumstances.' I didn't know you meant your friend here." He gestured toward the barn where Sherrie and Rebecca waited while Israel hitched the team. "If you remember, Titus announced that you had a visitor just then. His name was also Sheridan."

"You thought I'd left Oberlin with a man?" Her face fell. "That I'd left because I was in some sort of 'delicate' circumstances?" She stepped backward.

He nodded, wanting her to see the irony.

But instead, she looked angry. Hawk still faced her, dismay filling him. Callie was slipping away from him. He could feel it. He reached for her but she withdrew her hand.

When she spoke, her words were clipped, as brittle as ice on a winter pond. "It's one thing to be thought frivolous—as I know you've thought of me in the past. But it is quite another..." She took a deep breath and looked up at the stars, blinking back her tears. Then her eyes again met his, and he could see the hurt his words had caused. "It's quite another," she finally said again, "if you think I'm capable of being in 'delicate circumstances' with another man."

"Callie." Hawk's voice was a hoarse whisper. He reached to take hold of her hand, to try to explain. "Callie…"

But she had turned away from him and was carefully picking her way across the puddles to the barn. She nodded at Israel and he helped her into the carriage. Within moments the vehicle pulled onto the muddy road and soon disappeared into the darkness.

Hawk listened until he could no longer hear the squeaking and rattling of the buggy as it bumped along the mud-rutted road. Then, shoulders slumped, he turned to join Doc who was saddling his mare in the barn.

Lost in thought, Callie fell silent on the road back to Stonehaven.

Sheridan and Rebecca talked about the meeting and how well it had gone. Rebecca spoke at great length about Sadie Johnson, filled with awe at meeting the Underground leader and listening to her speak.

"Think of it," Rebecca said. "She was a slave, yet she went to college. I would like to do what she did, be like her."

"Maybe you can, Becca," Sheridan encouraged. "Once you've arrived in the North."

"Sometimes I don't think I'll ever get there." Rebecca looked sad. "Maybe it's too big a dream for someone like me."

Sheridan reached across the seat and patted her hand. "Don't be talkin' that way. Sure now, no dream is too big. And look yourself, what you're doin'. Because of you—others will be knowin' freedom. They'll be dreamers, makin' their own dreams come true. All on account of you." Her brogue was soft.

Rebecca didn't speak, just seemed to be considering Sheridan's words.

"Sure, you're already doin' what Sadie Johnson said—helpin' others find hope and promise."

Rebecca nodded, then whispered, half to herself, "Dyin' for someone else...the best present you could give them. Jesus said so." She squinted at Sheridan. "And Sadie Johnson said it too."

Sheridan nodded. "Aye. She did now."

"I don't think I could do it..."

"'Tis very likely none of us think we could until it's time."

"Time?" Rebecca's eyes were bright, even in the dim light of the carriage.

"Aye. Time to decide if we could give our lives to save another's."

"Like Jesus." She fell silent for a few minutes as the buggy rattled along through the night. "It'd take a lot of love to do that."

No one spoke. Each of the young women was lost in her own thoughts.

Callie listened halfheartedly to the conversation, but her mind kept returning to Hawk and his words. She thought about how he had looked standing there in the starlight, his eyes filled with love. He'd explained why he left her alone in the garden. But the explanation was worse than not knowing.

Callie gazed into the black night. She thought of Hawk, her heart aching with the knowledge of what might have been. His riverboat would soon leave, and with it the last slender hope that her love for him would ever be more than an empty dream.

Resting her head against the leather seat, Callie closed her eyes and thought of the future. She would forget Hawk. She would devote her emotions and energies to the task before her.

She lifted her chin and stared again into the darkness.

Fourteen

❧

Caleb Benedict settled back into the rich brocade settee, brandy in hand. In the high-backed chair across from him, Winchester, a tall, distinguished-looking man with graying hair, leaned forward, intent on what Caleb was saying.

"So, I've come for your help, Winchester. It seems I've run into dead ends elsewhere." His lip pulled into a twisted smile. "And it's time to find out exactly what my niece is planning in that pretty little head of hers."

Winchester laughed. "I think I can help you out, Senator. You say she's been to Oberlin College?"

Raising an eyebrow, Caleb nodded.

"You're not going to have to uncover too many rocks to find the key to the mystery. Oberlin is the hotbed of abolitionist activity in Ohio."

Caleb sat forward. "You don't say…"

"Ah, yes. And the college is at its center."

"Of course." Taking a swig of brandy, Caleb slowly grinned. "And where was your Israel captured?"

"Actually he was taken a few miles upriver from here. But he was heading to Vicksburg."

"If he'd escaped, why did he come back?"

"His woman and child were captured in the North—then sent back to me. I actually caught the two of them together here when he came back for her and their baby."

"Let me guess. His family was captured near Oberlin." Caleb settled back into his chair again, nodding slowly. "Of course—he was getting the three of them north. My niece somehow came across him. Maybe offered to help."

"Your niece may have been more involved than that, Senator."

"What do you mean?"

"The Underground Railroad." Winchester stood and walked to his desk, rifled through some paper, then sat again opposite Caleb and handed him a piece of paper. "This letter arrived from Ohio a week ago."

Caleb pulled out his spectacles, rubbed them with his hand-kerchief, and set them on his nose. He scanned the crude letter from an anonymous writer in Ohio. The person wrote that he knew the whereabouts of the slave Israel. For a price, he would lead Winchester to the ringleader of the Underground Railroad there—someone named Nashtara. The slave had last been seen in this leader's presence. Caleb looked up at Winchester, slowly nodding his head. "The Underground Railroad," he whispered, a smile creeping across his face. Then he clamped his lips together, still nodding. "Ah, yes. It makes perfect sense," he said, taking another swig of brandy.

"If you ask me, your niece is more involved than you've given her credit for. Perhaps she still is?" Winchester cocked his head, his small eyes on Caleb. "Not a fitting circumstance for a former Southern Senator, I'd say."

Caleb ignored the inference, then asked why Winchester had

sold Israel and the woman. "As a Southern plantation owner," he said pointedly, "I'd have punished him within an inch of his life—made an example of him. That way the others know better than to try it themselves."

"As a Southern gentleman, I don't believe in that kind of punishment, sir. The fact is, I was surprised that Israel and his woman tried to escape in the first place. I take pride in treating my slaves well. They're happy here. I keep them well-fed—even give them gifts at Christmas. Why, my own mammy cared for me the same as she did my father before me."

He stood and poured Caleb another brandy. "I figured the best thing was to sell the family downriver, so to speak. It was only out of concern for the new owner that I felt it would be better to split them up. That way they'd be less trouble—not as likely to run away again."

"Do you know who bought the woman?"

"I sold her to some traders in downtown Vicksburg. Last I heard she went for a pretty penny to the MacIntosh plantation near Natchez. The child was sold with her."

A short time later, Winchester walked Caleb to his hired buggy at the portico, slapped him on the back and said he remembered the good old days when Caleb was U.S. Senator. "I'm truly sorry you retired, sir. If you ever decide to run again—you've sure got my vote."

By the time Caleb boarded the riverboat the following morning, he'd made his plans. First, he'd send a telegram to friends in Washington, asking if Callie was on any lists for known activity in the Underground Railroad. Authorities might have to contact Ohio, but even considering that, Caleb would probably have the information he needed within weeks.

And he'd certainly observe her comings and goings more closely. Not only Callie, but also her two servants—what were their names?—Rebecca and Israel, and that young friend who was probably as involved as his niece was, the Irish woman, Sheridan. No doubt she was as underhanded as her cousin Liam Sheridan.

The lot of them had already begun tampering with his business by stealing his accounting records. He'd see they were punished for that if nothing else.

In his initial anger, Caleb had considered throwing Callie out of his home. But now he'd have her followed while he waited for word from Washington. Neither Callie nor her friends would be able to execute any plan without his knowledge. If luck was his, he'd catch them all in the act.

As the riverboat churned southward, Caleb stared out across the mud-brown waters of the Mississippi. When they docked in a few days, he would stay in town instead of heading for Stonehaven. And he would visit the telegraph office first thing.

He drew a sigh of relief. He had actually begun to fear losing Stonehaven. He'd seriously misjudged Callie's intelligence and cunning. Begrudgingly, he admitted that she was a worthy opponent. But now he knew what he was up against. And that would change the game decisively.

The first morning that Caleb was in Vicksburg, Callie closed the door to her room and pulled the ledger from it's hiding place in the wardrobe floor. Sitting on the edge of her bed, she opened the book. She turned the pages slowly, scanning the accounts until she came to her father's name. Taking a deep breath, she pored over his accounts, beginning with the years before he lost Stonehaven.

She wrote down the names of cotton buyers who received large sums of money from Caleb at about the time her father's fortunes began to turn.

A pattern emerged. She read through the list twice to make sure. Then she knew: Caleb had paid the buyers not to buy from Richard St. Clair! Her father had been forced into greater debt.

Then she noticed that a large sum had been paid to the overseer just before the man left Richard's employ. She made note of the man's name—Zeke Wakefield—and his last known address in New Orleans.

An hour passed, then two. Callie, lost in her findings, was unaware of anything else. When a knock sounded at the door, at first she didn't respond. It sounded again.

Callie blinked. "Who is it?"

"Sherrie."

Stretching her tired back, Callie stepped to the door. "Come in. I've got something to show you."

Callie had written down pages of information. She sighed and looked up at Sheridan, who was still thumbing through the ledger.

"Aye. I'm thinkin' that you've got enough to convict him, Callie. But what are you plannin' to do with it now?"

"We've got to find some of these people to testify about receiving the money."

"But won't they still be fearin' your uncle?"

"He's no longer Senator, no longer in a position to hurt them—if we can just convince them of that." She frowned at the overseer's name on her list. "This one, though, is different. He had nothing to buy from my father. Why would he be paid off, then leave Stonehaven the following week?"

"How close was that to your father's death?"

Callie shook her head. "No, it's not what you're thinking. My father died of natural causes. And the overseer—Zeke Wakefield—left at least a year before his death." She paused, looking out the window at the cotton fields that stretched as far

207

as the eye could see. She remembered the bad crop years just before she and Juliana left Stonehaven. "No," she said. "It was something else."

"We need to speak with Liam again." Sherrie's dark blue eyes were solemn. "Find out if he's been able to locate any witnesses for his own case."

Callie nodded. "I was just thinking the same thing. If he could find Zeke Wakefield—or some of the others—we could take everything to court at the same time."

Sheridan smiled. "When do we leave—for Natchez to see Liam, I mean?"

"How about tomorrow morning?"

Callie smiled. "Aye. Sure, tomorrow it is then."

The early morning sun warmed Callie's face. She leaned on one elbow, looking out the window near her bed, wondering at the chill in her soul on such a glorious day. Then she remembered: Hawk said he was leaving on *The Dixie*. Today.

Could she let him go without saying goodbye?

She swung her legs over the bed's edge, thinking about going to the dock, just to see him once more before he boarded *The Dixie* and stepped out of her life forever.

Callie pulled the brush through her tangled thicket of curls, the image of Hawk's face before her, the memory of the light in his eyes burning into her soul.

Suddenly she smiled. What was there to stop her? She and Sherrie would be at Liam's by midday. Then Callie could leave Sheridan at her cousin's and head straight to the docks to see Hawk.

Callie felt a place inside her suddenly warm as if it was being held to the sunlight after existing too long in the dark. She'd tell

Hawk how she'd always felt about him, how even in New Mexico her heart had soared each time she caught him watching her, and how seeing him again in Natchez had made her certain of her love for him.

She pulled on a fresh floral shirtwaist, fluffed her crinolines, and tied a ribbon in her hair. Yes, she decided, she would explain that she simply wanted Hawk to accept her for who she was—to see the best in her, not the worst.

Of course, Hawk would still leave Natchez; she knew of his calling to upper Missouri River. But when he left, Callie wanted him to know of her love.

For the first time in days, Callie's heart soared. She stepped to her window and sat for a moment on the window seat, looking out at Stonehaven's lands. The sky seemed a richer blue, the soon-to-be-harvested fields a deeper gold, the mockingbird's songs more joyous.

Why hadn't she thought of speaking to Hawk before? Now it all seemed so simple. Juliana always had said that time had a way of helping a person sort out feelings. And that was exactly what the past two days had done for her.

At midday, Callie, holding the ledger safely tucked inside her satchel, stepped out of the Stonehaven carriage with Sherrie in front of Sheridan Hall. Liam, looking much happier than when they'd last seen him, bounded down the stone walk and escorted them into the house.

"Aye, you're prettier each time I lay my Irish eyes upon you," he said, his gaze meeting Callie's.

He led them into the elegant parlor with its polished mahogany doors, sterling silver fixtures, and Irish lace curtains. He nodded for Callie and Sherrie to sit, then he settled into a chair opposite them.

"Tell us about your meeting with Caleb," Sherrie urged.

"Just as we guessed, they can do little, lassies, without the records. 'Tis their word against mine," Liam sighed, his brogue barely discernible in his seriousness. "I'm worried the court date may be set before I'm ready. But at least I've had time to poke my nose into some of Caleb's dealings."

"And?" Callie watched him expectantly.

He grinned, his handsome face filled with hope. "I've found two men who are willin' to testify on my behalf. Seems they were paid by Caleb to stop using my company for shipping their cotton."

"We've just finished going through the ledger. It seems my uncle's had some similar dealings in the years past."

Liam lifted an eyebrow. "Having to do with your father?"

"I think he did the same thing to him—paid buyers not to give Stonehaven their orders."

"I thought you'd find that. People develop patterns. Caleb probably has dealt with most of his businesses this way." Liam exhaled slowly. "Did you find anything else?"

"One more thing." Callie told him about Zeke Wakefield.

The three discussed their next steps. Liam reminded Callie that Caleb, when he was U.S. Senator, influenced most of the judicial appointments in the county. "It might be hard to find an unbiased judge," he said finally.

Then Callie suggested that Liam take the two witnesses and the ledger to New Orleans, look up Zeke Wakefield, and if he could get the overseer to talk, see that the case got to court in Louisiana.

"Ah, me lass," Liam said, with a grin and a return of his Irish charm, "I'm beginning to see that you've got quite a head for business. Are you sure you're not playing the role of a Southern belle as a cover for your real business? Say, taking your uncle's seat in the U.S. Senate? Or starting up a shipping business of your own?"

Callie met Sheridan's eyes. Their exchanged look didn't go unnoticed.

"So I'm right, am I?"

Callie regarded the man silently. It might serve a future purpose for him to know about the Underground. "Go ahead and tell him, Sherrie," Callie said, as she stood. "And while you tell him of our adventures, I've got business in town. I'll be gone only an hour or so."

Sherrie wore a knowing look and smiled at Callie. Then Liam stood and escorted Callie to the foyer. "You're idea is sound," he said, as he opened the front door for her. "We've still got a lot of work ahead of us."

Callie nodded. "I know. But thank you, Liam, for helping us out. I can't leave Stonehaven right now or I would go to New Orleans myself." She looked toward the parlor window. "Sherrie will explain."

Liam nodded and stood watching as the carriage pulled away.

Several minutes later, Israel opened the door and Callie stepped out of the brougham at the Natchez dock. Two riverboats were loading passengers. Another had just pulled in and its passengers were disembarking.

The wharf teemed with activity. Wagons and carts rattled across the dock's wood slats for loading goods or unloading. Dockhands carried baggage—trunks, satchels, and packages—to and from the paddlewheelers. Couples and families with little children milled about, some saying goodbyes, others hurrying to one of the two steamboats preparing to leave.

Callie hurried across the dock to the railing, searching for Hawk. When she didn't see him, still favoring her injured ankle, she hurried down the wharf to the docked *Dixie*. Suddenly the ramp lifted, the departure bell rang, and the riverboat moved slowly away from the dock.

She ran to the railing, frantically examining the faces of the passengers. Dozens stood on the main deck. Some waved to folks standing on the dock, others simply looked away, watching the progress of the steamer as it moved into the deeper waters of the river. Still others milled about on the lofty hurricane deck.

Callie's gaze moved from one face to another, hoping she might at least catch a glimpse of Hawk as the boat pulled away. But there were too many people.

For a long time Callie didn't move. She just watched as the boat slid gracefully to the center of the river, swung north, and finally disappeared around a bend. All she could think was that Hawk had begun his journey away from Natchez. Away from her.

Fifteen

❧

Doc pulled down the window shade, flipped over the "closed" sign, then turned to Hawk, who was drying his hands next to the basin. "Say again?" Doc grinned expectantly.

"I said I've decided to stay—if you'll have me."

"I hoped I'd heard you right!" Doc slapped Hawk on the back. "I couldn't be more delighted, son. I'm glad you're staying on. I won't ask how long. Or why. Just know I'm glad to hear it. Bea will be in heaven when she finds out."

"Thank you, sir. I'm glad to be staying."

Doc nodded. "It wouldn't have anything to do with Callie St. Clair, would it?"

"You said you wouldn't ask."

"That I did, didn't I? Well, sorry. I just couldn't help noticing—"

Hawk raised an eyebrow.

Smiling, Doc when on. "I've piqued your interest, have I?" Then he chuckled. "A person would have to be blind not to see the bolts of lightning between the two of you when you're together."

"Things—feelings between us seem clearer when we're *not* together..." Hawk's voice trailed off. He shook his head. "I've known Callie for several years. But I think it was easier to talk with her when she was a hot-headed, tantrum-throwing, exasperating sixteen-year-old." He paused again. "But I can't leave without seeing her again. I've *got* to see her. To try to explain."

"Explain?" Doc prompted.

Hawk considered the question, then grinned slowly. "That's the part I don't know—what to explain. Or for that matter, how to explain it. Or when I'll have the chance if I ever figure out what it is I'm trying to tell her."

Doc slapped him on the back again as they left the office. "It'll come to you, son, when the time's right. Trust me. You'll know the words..."

After breakfast two days later, Hawk carried his leather bag with surgical instruments to the buggy. After hitching the roan, he stepped into the driver's seat only to be hailed to a stop by Doc Meade.

"I've got some messages I'd like you to deliver on your rounds today," the older man said.

Hawk nodded. It hadn't been the first time.

"You'll be heading out to the MacIntosh place?"

"It's my first stop."

"There's a slave woman there. Her name's Bethenia. She's got a child, a little girl named Cody. Do you remember the slave Israel from the meeting the other night?"

"Yes, he was sitting next to Callie."

"That's the one. Anyway, Bethenia and Cody are kin. They'll be leaving soon on the Railroad—probably with the large group the night of the barbecue."

"Do they know about it—about leaving, I mean?"

Doc shook his head. "No. You'll be the one to tell Bethenia. She may be brought along with the MacIntoshes—many of the slaves will be coming with their masters for festivities of their own. But if not, it will be up to her to get to Stonehaven anyway."

"Where will she go once there? Has the rendezvous been decided yet?"

"It's in an old overseer's house at the edge of the Stonehaven property. I'll draw you a map—but you'll have to memorize it. Tell her where the meeting place will be. It's too risky to give her anything written down."

Hawk nodded in understanding. "You said messages. There's another?"

"Yes. You'll need to stop by Stonehaven's quarters—talk to Israel about seeing Bethenia and Cody. Let him know they've gotten the message." Doc looked hesitant. "There's one more thing, though, about Stonehaven. You can't go near the house. Callie's sent word that she's being watched by her uncle. Seems that she can't make a move without him knowing about it."

"She's all right?"

"Oh, yes." The older man smiled knowingly. "Callie's fine. But we don't want to draw any undue attention by your showing up at the main house. Drive straight to the quarters to see if anyone needs medical attention. Then find Israel. He'll be at the carriage house or in his cabin at the quarters."

As Hawk raised the whip, Doc winked and said, "One more thing."

Hawk cocked an eyebrow.

"You need to come with us, you know—to the Stonehaven barbecue."

"I wasn't invited."

"I believe our invitation was addressed to Bea, myself, and our family. We figure you're family."

Hawk suddenly smiled. "In that case, thank you. I wouldn't miss it."

"I didn't think so."

Hawk snapped the whip lightly, reined the horse onto the road, and headed to the MacIntosh plantation.

During the morning Hawk saw more than twenty patients. He set broken bones, cleaned and bandaged wounds, and pulled a tooth. Mostly he treated field slaves who headed back to the fields as soon as he was finished with them. He pulled the tooth, though, from a white-haired house servant.

When he'd finished, Hawk asked directions to Bethenia's cabin. When he got there, he found her lying on a cot in the corner of her dingy cabin. Near her on the floor, Cody played with a cornhusk doll.

"Bethenia?"

She looked up at him, her eyes strangely blank.

"Bethenia?"

Finally she nodded, acknowledging that was her name.

"May I come in?

She nodded wordlessly again.

Hawk stepped through the doorway. As his eyes adjusted to the dim light, he could see the woman was large with child. Doc obviously hadn't known or he would have mentioned it.

He sat on the edge of the small bed. "I've got a message from your husband."

Her dark eyes brightened. "Israel?" she whispered.

"Yes. He's made arrangements for you and Cody." Hawk glanced at the little girl, probably about three years old, still playing with her doll. "Are you well enough to understand me?"

Bethenia nodded slowly. Her eyes didn't leave his.

"You must bring Cody and come to Stonehaven plantation the night of the barbecue."

"I don't know about any barbecue," she whispered.

He told her of the plans, the night she would need to be there, the time, the place. But even as he spoke Hawk saw this was futile. In her condition, how could she possibly make her way to a plantation miles away? He looked at her carefully. If she was lucky, the baby would come soon and she would be ready to travel by the time of the barbecue. Her swelling ankles and hands told him that complications already had set in.

She turned her head and looked out the room's one small window. "I just wish I could get Cody out," she said, still staring at the sky, her expression hopeless.

Hawk made a decision. "If I come for you, can you be ready?"

She turned from the window. "Israel sent you?" she asked again.

He nodded.

A slow smile crept across her face. "You tell him he'll need to make arrangements for one more on that Railroad. His son will be joining us."

"He doesn't know yet? About the baby?"

She shook her head. "We was sold apart before I knew myself."

Hawk said he would bring a buckboard for her and Cody on the night of the barbecue. Even if she couldn't walk, he promised to see that she somehow got to Stonehaven. They spoke of other details, then Hawk rose to leave.

"By the way," he said, just before he stepped out the door. "How do you know it's a boy?"

She smiled wearily. "My bones are a-tellin' me. It's ornery—

217

like Israel. You tell him for me."

"I'll tell him."

Bethenia's eyes widened in her swollen face. "You tell him I'll be there. Me 'n' Cody and the little one."

It was long past midday when Hawk turned the buggy onto the road to Stonehaven. The sun hung white-hot in a pale sky, and the air lay stagnant against the ground.

The fields were filled with slaves picking cotton, their voices carrying clear across to the winding road. Cicadas buzzed their single-note songs, and here and there a grasshopper added its voice to the cacophony.

Hawk took the road behind the main house that led directly to the slaves' quarters. He intended to see to the slaves first, as he'd done at the MacIntoshes, then set about finding Israel. He knew that Israel's primary role was to drive the brougham, and he hoped the big man hadn't left on a drive with Callie or Sheridan.

When he'd finished setting broken bones and treating lacerations at the cabins, Hawk walked to the carriage house. He looked inside hoping to find Israel, but the brougham was gone, and Israel wasn't in sight. Hawk stood for a moment, trying to decide whether to wait, when he heard the rattle of the carriage's wheels coming down the lane. He thought that Israel would probably halt the carriage in front of the portico, but when the sounds of the horse's hooves and the squeaking and rattling of the brougham drew closer, he knew they were heading right for the carriage house.

Hawk moved back into the shadows just as the grays pulled the carriage through the wide double doors.

Israel jumped from the driver's seat and opened the door for

Sheridan, Callie, and a thin gray-haired woman Hawk hadn't seen before. The woman didn't speak to either Callie or Sheridan, but simply waited for them to join her walking across the wide back lawns and through the gardens to the house. The woman was obviously playing the role of Caleb Benedict's eyes and ears.

At the moment she turned, Hawk caught a glimpse of Callie's face. She seemed sad. Even in the dark of the carriage house, her sprinkle of freckles stood out against her white face. How he wanted to run to her, gather her into his arms! But he couldn't. Callie's stern-faced chaperone would take his actions as scandalous. And Callie herself, judging by her last conversation with him, would probably push him away. God's timing, he reminded himself, would bring the right opportunity: He would have to wait.

As soon as the three women had stepped through the back gate and onto the path leading to the gardens, Hawk announced his presence to Israel.

The big man remembered him from the Underground meeting and nodded a greeting.

"I've been to see Bethenia and Cody."

Israel's broad face softened.

"She asked me to tell you that you're about to have a child. She's sure it's going to be a boy."

The look of pleasure at the news quickly turned to alarm. Israel asked about Bethenia's health, then added, "Will she be able to go? Our leavin's not long away."

"I told her I'd come for her to make sure she gets to the place in time." Hawk didn't tell him about what he'd observed about Bethenia's swelling, her precarious condition.

While Israel unhitched the horses and led them to their stalls, he asked Hawk more questions about Bethenia and Cody. Then the big man thanked him for all he was doing for them and left for the slaves' quarters, deep worry etched in his face.

Just as Hawk turned to leave, he heard the sounds of footsteps approaching on the gravel path outside the carriage house. He stepped into the shadows to remain unseen. He didn't want to endanger Israel by letting his presence be known.

"Israel?" A voice called out from the partially open door. "Israel, I left my parasol in the buggy. Did you find it?" The voice was Callie's!

"He just left." Hawk stepped into the dim light coming from a nearby dusty window.

"Hawk!" Startled, Callie put her fingertips to her mouth. "I…I didn't know anyone—I didn't know you—were here."

Hawk moved toward her.

"Wait—" She held up a hand to keep him from stepping closer. "I saw you leave. I thought you were on *The Dixie.*"

"You went to the docks?"

"Yes." Her voice was quiet. "I wanted to tell you goodbye." Then she seemed to recover composure. "What are you doing here?" she asked again, frowning.

"I had to see you again." This time she didn't stop him from moving closer. "I wanted to tell you how sorry I was for jumping to such an unfair conclusion—the misunderstanding about Sheridan."

Callie suddenly reached up and touched his lips. "Do you remember all those times I said I wouldn't forgive you?"

Hawk smiled. How could he forget?

"Well, I never meant any of them. I have loved you from the moment I set eyes on you, Hawk Jones. There's nothing you could ever do or say that I wouldn't forgive. Even thinking that Liam Sheridan and I"—she blushed—"had something of an 'indelicate' relationship that caused me to flee Oberlin."

Hawk started to speak, but Callie shushed him again with her fingertips. "No," she said, "There's something else I must say—while I have the courage."

"I've never known you not to have the courage to speak your mind, Callie."

She flashed him a smile. "What I want to say is this—I love you, Hawk. I always have and I always will. Whether you are a thousand miles from me—or standing before me, looking at me with those beautiful eyes." She touched his jaw, gently, lovingly. "I want you to know this. You are loved. Totally and completely loved."

"Oh, Callie," Hawk breathed, then pulled her into his arms, tilted her face toward his, and kissed her. Her arms slid around him, and he covered her mouth with his again.

He drew back slightly and looked into Callie's eyes. "Callie, didn't you guess that I've cared deeply for you all these years?" He didn't let her answer. He cupped her face in his hands, holding it gently as he gazed into her emerald eyes. "I love you. Oh, my darling, I love you!" Drawing a ragged breath, he went on. "I still don't know what the future holds—I still can't expect you to drop your life's work—what you feel called to do—to marry me and share my life." He paused, touching her cheek with the backs of his fingers. "I only know that I don't think I can go there without you."

Callie suddenly stepped backward, her expression troubled. "Hawk, you must. Please, don't say that you will give up your dream for me. I won't let you. Oh, darling. Please tell me that you'll go."

Hawk caught her hands in his and held them tightly. "We'll seek God's guidance, Callie."

A nearly imperceptible shadow crossed her face. She swallowed and nodded. "Yes," she breathed. "But Hawk, he's not going to change his mind about what he's called you to do."

Then with tears welling in her eyes, Callie kissed him lightly on the cheek and stepped quickly through the door.

"Callie!" Hawk called, following her to the door. But she continued on the gravel pathway leading to the house. She didn't turn to look when he called after her again.

A few minutes later Hawk tapped the roan on the back with the whip, and the buggy started down the road leading from Stonehaven. His thoughts were filled with Callie. She seemed to be struggling with heartaches and questions that she didn't want to tell him about. She seemed to think that it was enough to love each other from a distance—he following his life's dream, Callie following her's.

Hawk popped the whip above the roan, urging him to move faster through the waning light of the late afternoon. How could Callie profess her love, then suddenly turn her back on him and walk away? She didn't even look back when he called her name.

He felt a rising dismay—even anger—that Callie had shut him out of her thoughts. Setting his lips in a line, he stared into the distance, wondering about this exasperating woman and her way of keeping his life—his heart and his soul—in turmoil.

The sun was settling into a fiery western sky. Fire. Light. Just as moths were drawn to firelight, he was drawn to Callie St. Clair. Maybe it would be better to leave her now—before the pain of separation became too great to bear. If they couldn't—or *wouldn't*—marry, what was left for them? Maybe Callie thought they could love from a distance. But Hawk didn't believe he could.

He gazed west as the sky turned from red-gold to the lonely gray of dusk. It matched the ashen color that had settled into his spirit.

Later that night Caleb Benedict asked Wilhelmina to join him in the library after supper.

As was her custom, Wilhelmina sat across from Caleb at the massive polished desk. He offered her a brandy. When she declined, he poured one for himself.

"I'm sure you're aware," he began, "that I've been making inquiries about Callie's affairs with the Underground Railroad."

Wilhelmina primly crossed her ankles, leaning forward, her small eyes bright. She nodded. "I had guessed that you were."

"I heard from Washington this morning. It seems their investigations turned up nothing concrete. They contacted lawmen in Oberlin. Seems that the one witness they had—a boy by the name of Jake Smyth who'd originally identified Callie as the Underground leader—withdrew his testimony. Hanged himself not long after. He was the only eyewitness. No one else at the college seems to know anything about Callie's activities there."

"So what are you going to do now?"

Caleb took a drink, considering his options. "I know she's involved. I figure she's got something planned here—even though you haven't been able to discover what it is. Her kind never gives up. I'm sure she's doing here exactly what she was doing in Oberlin." He paused, squinting his eyes at Wilhelmina. "We've just got to keep watching, waiting. Sooner or later she'll slip. We need to be ready to act when she does."

As usual, Wilhelmina nodded in agreement. Then she said, "You've had dealings with people of all types. You've been successful in creating the right—shall we say 'consequence'—for them all."

Caleb frowned. He wasn't sure what she was getting at. "Go on," he said.

She smiled primly. "Those you've dealt with are all different.

They've been bankers, shopkeepers, politicians, judges, lawmen—" She looked at him as if he should know what she was leading to. He didn't. She went on. "Yet you've been equally successful in setting up consequences for them all."

He nodded.

"What have you done to overcome their differences and still make the end come out the way you've wanted?"

He frowned again. "I still don't know what you're talking about."

Wilhelmina smoothed her hair, looking pleased with what she was about to say. "Through the years I've watched you. I've seen what you do to outmaneuver your business associates, your opponents."

Caleb was intrigued. "And what is that?"

"It's something that comes to you as naturally as breathing. It's the one thing you haven't done in dealing with your niece."

He waited while Wilhelmina's pinched face broke into a smile. "And?"

"You put yourself in your opponent's place. You become like them, planning each move they will make next in trying to outmaneuver you. You then know their next move, and because you've anticipated it—you move against them first.

"You play a game of human chess, if I may say so. And you always win, Caleb. Always."

Caleb could see the admiration in her small bright eyes.

"But you think I haven't done that with Callie?"

"I *know* you haven't. You've been soft with her. Softer than I've ever seen you with your other opponents."

He suddenly laughed, recognizing that she was right. "And you recommend—?"

"—that you place yourself in your niece's dainty little shoes. Figure out what her next move will be. She paused, her eyes now glowing. "Callasandra's been the leader of an Underground Railroad station in Ohio. She returns to her childhood home in the South. Isn't it ironic that she would come here to simply visit her uncle?"

"I've already figured that much out."

She ignored him and moved on. "This former station master is not going to be content simply working for another group—if there is one in Natchez. She's come home to the biggest, grandest plantation in Mississippi to—"

"—to start another station," Caleb interrupted, leaning forward.

Wilhelmina quickly nodded, repeating, "—to start the biggest, grandest Underground Railroad station in Mississippi."

Caleb let out a deep sigh. "You're right, dear lady. You're right."

"And do you want to know her next move?"

"You've got that figured out as well?"

She nodded. "Of course. You would have too if you'd stopped to think about it."

"Go on." Caleb was beginning to enjoy this.

"To successfully carry out something of the magnitude she has planned, there needs to be a cover. A cover of activity—lots of hustle and bustle, people coming and going, lots of messages sent under cover of—shall we say, as an example—invitations delivered to neighboring plantations, acceptances sent back to Stonehaven. Shall I go on?"

Caleb pulled off his spectacles, cleaned them, then replaced them on his nose. "I've always prided myself for my insight, my intuition. But this time, Wilhelmina, you've put me to shame." He smiled. "You're a genius. I don't know how I missed it."

Wilhelmina's thin, white cheeks colored with pleasure. "I learned it from you, Caleb."

"Now," he said, pouring himself another drink. "Let's get specific."

The two of them talked into the night, speaking of the barbecue, putting themselves in Callie's place, figuring and refiguring the actions she had planned for that night.

As Wilhelmina finally stood to make her way to the door, Caleb said, "There's one more thing."

She looked at him quizzically.

"We'll need to deliver one more invitation."

"To whom?"

"The sheriff. He'll be pleased to hear that he'll be making a few arrests the night of the barbecue. We might also want to tell him to ready the Natchez jail." Caleb chuckled as Wilhelmina crossed the foyer and made her way up the wide stairs to her room.

CHAPTER

Sixteen

Callie saddled Winterstar, a magnificent bay mare and favorite mount since her arrival at Stonehaven. As she swung into the saddle, then reined the horse from the stables, she quickly scanned the nearby lawns and fields. Caleb and Wilhelmina had been none too discreet in having Callie followed nearly each time she left the house.

Sighing, she smiled to herself. No one was in sight. Callie had purposely risen before the household was awake. Around her, dew still sparkled in the pale dawn light, and the birds had just begun their early morning chatter.

Callie nudged the bay into a gallop and rode from the stables without looking back. With the wind in her hair, the rising sun on her back, Callie felt joy and freedom—pure abandon—as she rode. As usual, she closed her eyes, relishing the movement of horse and wind.

She kicked the mare again, urging her to move faster. They approached a wood-slat fence, and Winterstar gracefully cleared the obstacle with inches to spare. Grinning at the feel of exhilaration, Callie reined her in line with a wider stone wall. Up and over they flew, Callie's cheek resting on the mare's neck, her hair flying backward as if part of the mane.

227

Winterstar's hooves pounded the earth, and Callie could feel the powerful animal's rippling muscles beneath her with each graceful stride. She reined the bay toward a stand of willows beyond the cottonfields. Within minutes she slowed the animal to a halt near a small creek, letting her bend to drink.

Callie slipped from the saddle and stood, patting Winterstar's sturdy neck. The air was fragrant with wild mint, growing in clumps near the creek bank. Flowering myrtle provided a carpet of lavender and green. Though the day would later turn hot and humid, now the breeze was cool and the air light with a musky scent.

Winterstar's ears perked slightly as if aware of another presence in the stand.

Callie scrutinized the nearby brush. She saw nothing and turned back to rubbing the mare's coat. The horse lifted her head and looked toward the willows. Her ears again flicked forward as if to better catch the sounds.

Still hearing only the twittering of sparrows, Callie patted the mare again then walked her from the water's edge, wrapped the reins around a nearby branch, and stepped toward the willows just beyond the creek.

She moved quietly forward, then stopped to listen. Still nothing. Letting out a sigh, she decided that Winterstar must have heard a porcupine or a bobcat.

Callie turned back to Winterstar. Then she heard a different sound. It stood out from the chattering calls of the meadowlarks, doves, and mockingbirds. It was a whimper. A child's muffled crying.

Holding her breath, Callie again crept into the undergrowth near the willows, through the tall grasses, vines, and fragrant myrtle. She pulled back a willow branch and squinted into a shadowed clearing. Two pairs of black eyes stared back at her.

"It's all right," she whispered. "Please don't be afraid."

She crawled into the clearing. A Negro woman, holding a boy of about five years, scrambled backwards away from her. "Please," Callie pleaded. "Don't leave."

The woman stopped moving, her dark face watchful. "Don' come any closer," she whispered, her voice low and threatening.

Callie halted a short distance from the two. "I want to help you," she said quietly. "Please, believe me." She glanced at the boy. He'd been injured. Seriously injured. Cocking her head sympathetically, she tried again. "Your child needs care. I can get someone to come here. A doctor."

The woman shook her head. "No," she said, holding her chin high. "We don' need your help, missy. Jes' leave us be."

"What happened to him?" Callie nodded to the child.

The woman's expression softened as she looked into the face of the child. "We was chased. Shot at, my man shot an' kill'd. Zak, my chil' here, was shot too."

Callie crept closer. This time, the mother didn't stop her. She touched the little boy's leg. Yellow fluid oozed from a red, angry wound in his calf. Below the wound the flesh had turned dull gray. Without care, the child would soon die. Even with treatment, he'd probably lose his foot, maybe the limb.

"He needs a doctor." Callie looked into the mother's tortured eyes.

The woman nodded slowly.

"You're runaways?"

She nodded again, her eyes downcast.

"I can help you go north. But you've got to trust me." The woman lifted her head, her dark gaze meeting Callie's. For the first time, there was a glimmer of hope. Callie went on. "What is your name?"

"Dacey."

"Dacey, I'm going to ask you to stay here until I come back. I

229

am going to get you some food and some bandages for the child. I'm also going to send for a doctor. Will you wait?"

Dacey watched Callie solemnly, nodding slowly.

"Then as soon as Zak can travel, I'm going to get you on a wagon heading north."

Again there was hope in Dacey's black eyes. "We'll wait."

Callie remounted Winterstar and headed back to Stonehaven. She found Israel in the carriage house and explained that she needed him to take Rebecca into town, then she slipped into the main house without notice. Breakfast wouldn't be served for another hour, and she had time to pack a satchel filled with food and bandages. Then, finding Rebecca in her room, Callie quickly explained about Dacey and Zak and told her the location of their hiding place.

"You've got to take the carriage into Natchez, find Hawk, then lead him to the place. Do you think you can find it?"

"Yes, Miss Callie." Rebecca gave her an encouraging smile, then bounded down the stairs, heading for the carriage house.

After breakfast with Caleb and Wilhelmina, Callie pulled on her riding habit. She knew it was unlikely that she could ride from the plantation without being seen, so she decided to openly leave for a ride, as if on a whim. Luckily, Caleb at his desk and Wilhelmina, firmly ensconced in her office, barely glanced up when she left for the stables.

Minutes later she remounted Winterstar and nudged her heels into the bay's flanks. They galloped through the fields, the satchel tied firmly to the back of the saddle.

"I'm back," Callie whispered, announcing her presence to Dacey before entering the clearing.

"I'm still here, chil'," came the soft reply. "Jes' as I said."

Callie crept toward the child who now lay sleeping on a dirty cloth beside his mother. She felt his forehead. The little boy was hot with fever, though he shook with chills. Callie pulled a small blanket from the satchel and covered his small body.

Then she opened a cloth napkin and handed Dacey two biscuits, a ripe peach, and some slices of salt pork. While the woman ate ravenously, Callie returned to the nearby creek to fetch water in a pitcher that she'd brought from the washstand in her room.

It was midday when Callie heard the sound of Doc Meade's horse and buggy, followed by Rebecca's soft voice. "Miss Callie? You here?"

Callie smiled at Dacey, reassuring her that the newcomers would not harm her or the child.

"In here, Becca!" she called. She pulled some willow branches back and peered out toward the creek. Rebecca waved, then clambered down from the buggy seat while Hawk tethered the horse to a low-hanging branch.

Rebecca scrambled through the brush to the place where the child lay.

Callie stepped toward Hawk, whose back was to her. Then, just as he lifted the black leather doctor's bag from the buggy, he turned. It was the first time she'd seen him since the afternoon in the carriage house.

His eyes met hers. "Callie," he said with a nod. There was something guarded about his expression.

"I'm glad you're here," she said. There was no time to wonder about his cool attitude.

They walked to the place where the child lay. Hawk knelt and touched the boy's face. "Bring me some water," he said, without looking up.

Rebecca ran to refill the pitcher.

231

Hawk glanced to Callie, who now had knelt on the other side of the child. "I'll need your help."

She nodded without speaking.

"It won't be easy."

"I know that."

"I figured you did." Then Hawk explained the procedure. He needed to cut out the ball, he said, that was still lodged in the boy's small calf. "I'll need you to hold him still while I cut." Hawk calmly regarded her. "He may scream out." He transferred his attention to the child. Callie was struck by the utter compassion in his face. Then he looked again into her eyes. "But I pray he won't feel it—that he'll stay unconscious."

Callie touched Hawk's forearm. "I'm not squeamish about these things, Hawk. Just tell me what to do."

Rebecca returned with the pitcher. She set it down near Callie, then knelt beside the child. Placing her small hand on Zak's forehead, she bowed her head and softly whispered a prayer.

Hawk, in a response that seemed to Callie as natural as breathing, prayed with her, lifting his face to the heavens. "Father, we bring Zak before your throne, asking for mercy and healing. Touch his body and restore him to health." Hawk paused a moment. His expression told Callie that he was in silent communion with someone he loved deeply. Then he bowed his head and spoke again, his voice soft. "My hands are your instrument, Lord. Guide them, use them to your glory. May they bring your healing touch to this, your child."

With his scalpel, Hawk made a six-inch incision from just below the knee to slightly above his ankle. The child whimpered and twitched, but didn't open his eyes. Callie held his body firmly. Dacey cried softly, and Rebecca sat with her, whispering words of comfort.

Hawk cleaned the white, putrid pus from the wound. Callie helped him swab water onto the place, rinsing and cleaning. Throughout the ordeal the child lay deathly still.

"Hold the incision open, Callie," Hawk directed.

Callie nodded and placed her hands near his, letting him guide them into the needed place. She parted the cut in the child's flesh while Hawk probed for the ball.

"I can't find it," he murmured. "But there's no sign of exit. It's got to be here."

Blood filled the incision again, and Callie instinctively cleaned the wound with more water.

Hawk flashed her a brief smile. "You're a natural," he said, then began his probe again. The child cried for his mamma in his sleep.

"There, there, baby," Callie whispered. She stroked his head. The child's eyes remained closed and he seemed to settle again into unconsciousness.

Hawk nodded at her again, his fingers still probing the wound. "Hold him, Callie. I think I've found it."

With all her strength, Callie held the boy, her right forearm across his chest, her left hand holding his ankle below the incision. "I'm ready," she whispered.

As Hawk grasped the ball, the child moaned. His little body twitched under Callie's grasp.

"It's lodged in the bone." Hawk reached for his knife and after a moment of gentle prying, he lifted the small metal ball from the wound. "We've got it," he said, giving Callie a smile of triumph.

Hawk's hands were covered with the child's blood as he showed Callie the round metal bullet. But she saw only his hands, the gentle and strong fingers of the physician. He had called them God's instrument in his prayer. She gazed at them in wonder as if for the first time. Then Callie lifted her eyes to his. "Well done, doctor," she murmured.

Hawk carefully sutured the wound as Callie grasped the child's calf, holding the incision together. When they were finished, Hawk wrapped the leg. By now the child was shivering violently, and his fever had climbed dangerously. Callie sent Rebecca for more water, and Hawk instructed Dacey to sponge off Zak's face with cool water every few minutes until the fever broke.

Later, as Callie prepared to leave for Stonehaven, she and Hawk rinsed their hands in the creek. Rebecca sat with Dacey in the clearing, ministering to the still-sleeping child.

"Callie, many women couldn't do what you just did."

She grinned. "Meaning...the weaker sex can't handle adversity?"

He chuckled. "I should have said, 'many people' couldn't have handled the blood, pus, stench—even seeing a child in such pain."

"It seems you've underestimated me in a lot of ways, Hawk." She looked at him evenly.

"I know."

They stood facing each other by the creek. The fragrance of mint and myrtle hung in the afternoon air, replacing the odor of blood and decay. Hawk reached for her hand, lifted it to his lips, holding her gaze. She pulled back her hand.

"Callie, about the other afternoon in the carriage house..."

Callie drew in a deep breath. He was waiting for her to explain, but she didn't know if she had the courage to do it. The pain of her own realization was too fresh, too deep. She was ready to sacrifice anything—her love for him included—to see that he remained fixed in his determination to go to the Mandan people. But the thought of his leaving cut her heart more deeply than any incision, and there could be no sutures for such a wound.

She wouldn't let him give up his dream for her. She lifted her face to his, feeling his gaze on her.

"Hawk, you need to leave." She knew her words were cold. They sounded clipped, even to her.

"To go back to Doc's?"

"No. I mean away from here. You must go."

The hurt in his eyes turned to cold anger. "What are you try-ing to do here, Callie? First you tell me you love me. Then you tell me to leave. I look into your eyes and I see your soul reaching out to me. Then you say *go!* Just like that, as if no feelings exist— or ever existed—between us." He stared at her, his blue eyes flashing. He ran his fingers briskly through his hair.

Then he suddenly moved closer to her, cupped her chin in his hands and gazed into her eyes. "Tell me you don't love me, Callie," he whispered hoarsely. "Tell me right now that you don't love me...and I'll go. I swear, I'll go and never return."

Callie's lower lip trembled and her tears welled, threatening to spill down her cheeks. But she couldn't speak the words. She could play surreptitious roles at Stonehaven—just as she did in Oberlin—but she couldn't be dishonest about this. She couldn't deny her love, deep and abiding, for the man who stood before her.

For a moment that seemed to last an eternity, Hawk held her gaze. Still holding her face in his hands, he kissed her, a lingering kiss that touched her soul with his. Then, without another word, he turned, untethered the horse, and stepped into the buggy.

He gazed at Callie, then lightly popped the whip above the horse and drove the vehicle toward the road. This time he didn't look back.

During the next few weeks, Callie saw Hawk often, though they didn't speak. It seemed that he avoided being alone with her. She led meetings of the Underground at the sharecropper's place by the river, and Hawk, always in attendance, contributed information and planning ideas.

They met twice at the new station, the old overseer's shack at the edge of Stonehaven. The first time Hawk, dressed in his black suit, had just arranged for Dacey and little Zak to be transported to the next station north. When he saw Callie, he simply tipped his hat and rode off, leaving her standing alone in front of the shack.

The next meeting took place one evening after Hawk brought a group of runaways from Natchez in a wagon. Callie rode up on Winterstar just as he climbed up onto the wagon seat, ready to rein the horse forward and head back to town.

"Good to see you, Callie," Hawk said, smiling and again tipping his black hat formally.

Callie didn't answer. Hands on hips, she just stood watching him as he drove the vehicle down the bumpy, rutted road.

A few days later Rebecca stopped Callie in the downstairs foyer just after supper.

She looked around to make sure no one was watching. "Someone's waitin' to see you, Miss Callie," she whispered. "Waitin' in the carriage house. Israel just came to the kitchen to tell me."

Callie walked with Rebecca to the spiral stairs. "Who is it, Becca? It's not safe for me to leave right now—whoever it is should've realized that."

"It's Hawk Jones. Israel says it's important."

Callie nodded. "Tell Israel I'm coming. I need to think of an excuse."

Rebecca's face brightened. "Israel already thought of that. He said to tell you that Winterstar is ailin'. You need to come see."

Callie smiled. "All right then. I'll come out to see about the horse." Instead of going upstairs, she stepped to the library door and tapped lightly.

"Come in," Caleb called out, and Callie opened the door. Wilhelmina sat in the leather chair opposite his desk. Their discomfort at her appearance was obvious; they must have been speaking of her, Callie decided, then just as quickly thought it surely must be her imagination.

"Israel's sent word that Winterstar is ailing," Callie announced. "I'm going to the stables to see about her."

Caleb looked worried.

"I'll send for you if need be," Callie said quickly, before he volunteered to join her. "It's probably nothing—she was fine when I rode her this morning. Israel just knows how I fuss over her." She smiled.

Caleb exchanged glances with Wilhelmina. "Yes," he said to Callie. "You go. But let me know how she is when you return."

Callie nodded, said she would, then quickly exited the room, closing the door behind her.

Moments later she stepped into the dark carriage house.

"Hawk?" she whispered.

"Over here, Callie." His voice came from across the room.

She stepped toward him. The carriage house smelled of leather and hay, a fragrance sweeter than perfume, Callie had always thought. "Where are you?"

Suddenly he was beside her. She had forgotten how quietly he moved. "I'm here," he said. "I don't think we should light a lantern. If you're being looked for in the stables, it's better that you're not found here."

"I agree," she said, simply.

"We've got some problems, Callie. Mr. Higgins, of the *Natchez Enterprise*, told Doc that a telegram came in a few days ago, telling of your work with the Underground."

Callie gasped softly. "It went to my uncle?"

"Yes. In answer to his inquiries."

"So Caleb knows everything."

Hawk took her hands in his. She could just make out his features in the dim light. His face told of his compassion and concern for her. "Yes," Hawk repeated. "It seems he knows everything about your past. What we don't know is how much he knows about what you're doing here."

Callie sighed. "What he doesn't know, he's probably guessed."

"Yes," Hawk said.

"We can't let this stop us! We're so close to our first really big run. What can we do?"

"Maybe it would be better to stop the activity for a while—just until Caleb's suspicions are found to be in 'error.'"

"No." Callie shook her head. "The barbecue is just days away. Runaways are already heading for the station. We have to go through with it." She paused. "Besides, if Caleb really knew any details he'd have already figured out the plan, the station's location, everything. But he hasn't."

"Callie—" Hawk's tone was pleading. "Promise me that you will stay away from the station that night. Let everything else go according to plan." He touched her cheek. "I'll be there—I'll let others know your orders. You can stay here at Stonehaven—see to your party guests. That way, Caleb won't have any reason to believe you're involved, even if anything does go wrong."

"I can't do that, Hawk. How can I ask you—or anyone else—to be willing to give their lives so that others can be free if

I'm not willing to do the same?" She looked into his eyes. "I'll be there beside you, Hawk. No matter what happens, we'll be together."

Hawk pulled her into his arms. They stood together in the darkness holding each other without speaking. Callie could feel his pounding heart. She reached her arms around his neck and held him close.

$\mathcal{S}ever"="teen$

The morning of the barbecue the dawn sky turned from a silver lavender to a deep purple-blue. A few clouds, bright and harmless, drifted lazily through the early autumn heavens. A breeze from the river had recently cooled the land, and as Callie looked out across Stonehaven's fields from her bedroom window, she thought that a more perfect day for a barbecue had never existed.

After an early breakfast, Callie returned to her room to ready herself for the party. First she bathed, luxuriating as long as she dared in the fragrant bubbles. Then she brushed her hair dry in the sunlight streaming through the large bay window. An hour later she asked Rebecca to help arrange her unruly curls, lifting them into a cascading crown.

Rebecca's dimple showed in the looking glass as she wove a thin green ribbon through the hair, then tied it into a bow that fell with Callie's hair nearly to her waist.

"You look pretty as I ever saw you, Miss Callie." Rebecca's dark eyes shone with excitement.

"You'll look the same in a few minutes, Becca—as pretty as you've ever looked."

Rebecca ordered Callie to grab hold of the bedpost. Then she grasped the corset laces and pulled hard. Grinning, she then lifted a lacy chemise over Callie's head. A few minutes later, Callie stepped into her crinolines.

Short of breath from the corset, Callie sat on the edge of her bed for a moment, fanning herself and grumbling about the stiff garment. "At least if I went to the upper Missouri, I'd not have to go through this," she muttered.

Rebecca, pulling the green organza gown from Callie's wardrobe, looked around at her quizzically. "Where you goin'?"

Callie chuckled. "I'm just talking to myself, Becca. Dreaming about wearing buckskins instead of crinolines."

"Now that'd be somethin'," Rebecca said, shaking her head. "That'd be somethin' to behold."

Rebecca lifted the pale green gown so that Callie could slip it over her head. Then she fastened the dozens of tiny covered buttons at the back and fluffed the soft gigot sleeves. Next she tied a dark ribbon at Callie's waist so that its ends floated daintily to the bottom of the full skirt.

"That's much nicer th'n buckskins could ever be, Miss Callie," Rebecca said, standing back to admire her handiwork.

Callie helped Rebecca don a new white organdy dress with a lace-trimmed chemisette. Underneath it, her white crinoline made the soft material fall in graceful folds from Rebecca's tiny waist. She slipped her feet into white leather lace-up shoes—a gift from Sheridan. Delighted, Rebecca twirled in front of the looking glass.

"One more touch," Callie said with a grin. From her wardrobe she pulled a wide crimson ribbon and tied it in a sash around the girl's waist.

Rebecca whirled and danced around the room, a wide smile covering her face. How different she was than the child on the auction block. Her eager mind and quick wit amazed Callie. Rebecca had already learned to read—even verses from a childhood Bible Callie had found in her wardrobe.

And she was learning to write. She kept a list of words she had mastered. Mostly they were from the Holy Bible, words such as *Jesus, love, peace, joy*. Once though, Callie had asked her about another word she'd seen on Rebecca's list. The word was gift.

Rebecca had smiled a secret smile and said that it was to remind her of something Sadie Johnson had said.

"Becca," Callie said suddenly. "Did you ever think any more about taking a last name?" Callie had asked her several weeks ago when she noticed the girl struggling to write "Rebecca" and realized she'd never been given a surname.

Rebecca stopped dancing. "Yes, ma'am. I did."

"What did you decide?"

"Johnson, Miss Callie. After Miss Sadie Johnson."

"Then Johnson it is, Becca. From this moment on you're Miss Rebecca Johnson."

Rebecca's face came alive with joy. "It sounds...dig... digni—" she struggled with the word.

"Dignified," Callie finished for her. "It's a name of dignity, Rebecca Johnson, for a young woman of dignity."

Tears filled Rebecca's eyes. "No one's ever said that to me before, Miss Callie."

Impulsively, Callie hugged her. "Don't ever forget that it's true, Becca. And don't ever let anyone tell you otherwise."

"Dignity is somethin' wonderful," Rebecca said quietly.

An hour later, Callie stood with her uncle in the front portico. A smoky haze hung over Stonehaven's vast acreage. The smell of hickory and roasting lamb, pork, and veal wafted on the faint breeze. The barbecue pits had been burning since before dawn, and now the glowing embers sizzled and hissed as juices dripped from the slow-turning meats above them. Even behind the stables, separate barbecue pits had been dug for roasting meats to feed Stonehaven's field slaves and house servants.

Wagons and carriages from plantations throughout the county formed a line along the road leading to Stonehaven. One by one they pulled up, and guests stepped out.

Caleb, ever the country gentleman and dignified ex-senator, stood at Callie's side, shaking hands and introducing his niece. Callie smiled and nodded in her role as Stonehaven's mistress.

Still on the portico with her uncle, Callie looked out across the lawns. The squeals of playing children, both black and white, carried across the lawns. Milling about, the guests visited in groups, some enjoying the shade of the wide porch, others under the lacy shade of the oaks and magnolias. Others strolled through the formal gardens, talking and laughing.

And still the wagons, broughams, and buggies lined up with guests waiting to disembark. Callie stayed beside Caleb until it seemed that all the guests had arrived.

"Callie!" Sheridan hurried toward her and gave her a quick hug. She was a vision in lavender organza and lace. The color set off her dark blue eyes and gleaming black hair. Sherrie looked Callie up and down in admiration. "Aye! If cousin Liam could only see you now!"

"Have you heard from him?"

"Not since he arrived in New Orleans. Last telegram said he'd not found the overseer—what was his name?"

"Zeke Wakefield."

"Aye. But he was diligently lookin', he was."

Callie put her arm around Sherrie's waist and the two of them strolled together through the gardens.

Sheridan suddenly stopped, looking around at the long rows of tables that graced the lawns and gardens. "Though we planned it all on paper, 'tis different to see it before me eyes, Callie."

"A lot of this was your idea, Sherrie—the flowers, the candles."

"Aye, so it was. But I never dreamed it would look like this." Her gaze swept the lawns, a smile of amazement on her face. "'Tis a fairy land, Callie." The tables were covered with Stonehaven's finest linen cloths, china, and silverware. In the center of each table, on Sherrie's instruction, Delilah and some of the others had placed basket arrangements of tiger lilies, sweet-peas, and ivy. Candles, already flickering, rose like miniature sentinels from their centers.

As Callie mingled among the guests, she watched for Hawk, hoping his carriage might have arrived after she stepped from the portico. But she saw only Caleb's friends and Stonehaven's neighbors standing in small groups, mostly discussing the possibility of war or arguing about the balance of slave states and free. The young women exchanged glances.

"Politics!" Sherrie said, rolling her eyes. "It seems they could forget at least for a day."

"Maybe they can't, Sherrie—just as we can't."

Sheridan nodded, her face solemn. "Aye," she said softly. "Though what we're not forgettin' for one day has more to do with our fellow man than with politics."

By four o'clock the roasted meats were cooked to perfection and Caleb announced dinner. There were sighs of delight as the guests approached the tables.

Callie, lifting her skirts daintily, stepped among the tables, smiling and speaking to the guests and directing the servants as they set down the platters of meat and bowls of slaw and candied beans. As she moved some biscuits to make room for a long flat dish of peach cobbler, she again glanced around the crowd, hoping to spot Hawk. He was nowhere to be seen.

Disappointed, she went back to handing out some sugared nuggets of fried bread to some nearby children.

At that moment, Hawk, dressed in a dark suit and carrying a slouch hat, stepped from the carriage, then held open the door for Doc and Bea Meade to exit. The three were met by Titus who directed them around the side to the verandah, where they would see the tables set for the guests.

Hawk scanned the faces of the guests, looking for Callie. He finally saw her moving gracefully toward him, completely unaware of his presence. Her flushed cheeks added a pretty pink to her ivory skin. The green of the gown seemed to float from her waist to her ankles, bringing out the emerald in her eyes, even from a distance.

His breath caught as she drew nearer. He waited, expecting her to look up and see him. But in a heartbeat she turned away. A moment later she stepped to a table farther away, bent over Sheridan's shoulder and whispered something, and the two walked back up the stairs and into the house.

For the rest of the afternoon he waited for a chance to speak with Callie alone. A few times he saw her from a distance, but she was always busy with the servants or guests.

Toward evening a group of three violinists, a harpist, and a flute player stepped onto the dance platform and began to play lively music. Stephen Foster's songs were the favorites, and the guests sang and clapped, *Old Folks at Home, Oh! Susanna, Camptown Races,* and *My Old Kentucky Home.*

At dusk a breeze kicked up, causing the servants to bring hurricane glasses for the candles. Then as darkness fell, lamps and covered candles were placed in holders along the dance floor railing.

The music turned to dancing rhythms—waltzes, the cotillion, and the double shuffle. The dance floor filled with couples.

A toe-tapping, lively number caught Callie's fancy and she found herself swaying to the music, caught up in the magic of the sounds. About halfway through the song, she felt someone watching her. She turned.

"May I have this dance?" Hawk asked, his eyes never leaving hers.

For a moment, Callie couldn't speak. She just nodded, and he took her arm and led her to the dance floor.

The harpist struck an arpeggio. He was joined by the flute and the violins in the first waltz of the evening. Hawk pulled Callie into position and began moving to the music.

Callie looked up at him. Hawk didn't say anything, he just held her gaze and moved around the dance floor.

"I was hoping you were here," Callie said.

"I wouldn't have missed seeing you—especially looking like this." His gaze seemed to take her in completely, his frank admiration clear. "You're stunning, Callie," he whispered, drawing her closer, then sweeping around the floor to the music.

Callie found it hard to concentrate on anything but Hawk's face, his eyes, his words. The music swelled, and they gave up speaking for now to move as one through the crowd of dancers. She closed her eyes, letting herself sink into the beauty of the music, the feel of her hand in Hawk's, of his arm around her waist. She never wanted this moment to end. Suddenly she looked up and found him watching her.

"You're beautiful when you close your eyes, you know." He smiled tenderly.

"That's not what you thought when I ran your horse off the trail."

Hawk grinned and for a moment seemed lost in some distant

memory. "The first time I saw you, your eyes were closed. I never told you that the emotion I saw on your face was the same that I feel when riding across the mesa—an expression of total abandon. When I saw it—for that brief moment before our horses reared—your soul touched mine. It was as if I already *knew* you."

Hawk touched her face, lifting her chin lightly. "I knew I loved you at that moment." He suddenly stopped in the middle of the dance floor. All around them dancers continued to swirl. Then he frowned. "Callie, we need to talk—about us, about what's ahead. Can we go someplace private?"

Callie nodded, and he lightly cupped her elbow in his hand and led her from the dance floor.

Moments later they reached the formal gardens, stopping near the trellis of climbing roses. In the distance the music floated on the night air with the sounds of talking and laughing. But where they stood was quiet enough, Callie thought, for Hawk to hear the beating of her heart.

Hawk spoke first. "I can't bear to be apart from you any longer."

She didn't trust herself to speak, so she just nodded, her eyes never leaving his. In the distance the harp and the violin began to play a slow waltz. Closer, the crickets sang and a night bird warbled its mournful tune.

When Hawk took her face in his hands, Callie felt in them both gentleness and strength. Then he kissed her on the lips, softly at first, then with passion and joy. Pulling back slightly, he looked into her eyes and Callie felt she would drown in the love she saw there.

Then Hawk caught her hand in his and held it to his cheek. "I love you, Callie," he whispered.

Callie gazed at him, taking in his strength, and the love in his eyes.

"You are my life," he said huskily. He pulled her close, wrapping her completely in his arms.

Callie rested her cheek against his chest, never wanting to leave his arms. Then she stepped back. In the sea of emotions swirling around her, pulling her under, she had nearly forgotten. Why had she allowed him to speak of love again? What was between them could never be.

"You must leave," she said, feeling as though she would choke on the words.

Hawk gazed at her quizzically. "I want to spend the rest of my life with you. I will never leave you." He reached out to gather her once more in his arms. "I know I threatened to leave once. But that was before I knew you loved me." He paused, shaking his head slowly. "Don't you understand, Callie? I want to marry you."

Callie turned away, unwilling to see his face when she spoke the words she knew she needed to say. But she didn't trust her voice. At least not yet. She took a deep breath.

"Callie?" His hand touched her arm. He gently turned her toward him. "Callie, what's wrong?"

Tears filled her eyes. "I can't, Hawk. I can't marry you."

He stepped back, hurt and shocked, not speaking.

"You will be going to the upper Missouri. It's your calling, your mission."

He watched her intently but didn't interrupt. The music of the violins and harp sounded plaintive, mournful.

"I can't go with you. I can't marry you."

"But Callie—" he began, then his voice broke. He didn't go on.

Callie gazed at Hawk in silence. How could she tell him that his calling was from a God she didn't understand? A God who perhaps she didn't want to understand? It wouldn't be right to pretend that Hawk's calling was hers.

She knew Hawk figured she was as God-fearing as the next person. And perhaps she was by most people's standards. But God was Hawk's friend, closer to him than any earthly brother. Through the years she had seen Hawk talk to him as if they were friends visiting by a nightfire.

Callie didn't begrudge Hawk that relationship. She knew it was real. To Hawk, his God was more important than the food he ate or the air he breathed. This God was the one who had called him into medicine, who was calling him to minister to his mother's people.

For a moment Callie considered her hot temper, her headstrong ways, her weaknesses. She didn't measure up. She knew herself well enough to realize that she probably never would. How could this God ever be the friend of someone like her? How could she explain all this to Hawk?

She looked into his eyes, forcing her voice to be strong, and said simply, "I can't go with you to the Mandan villages, Hawk. It's your calling. Not mine."

The grief in his eyes sliced at her heart. "You want me to stay here? Is that it? You can't leave the South—Stonehaven—after all?"

Callie put her fingertips to his mouth. Oh, how she wanted him to stay! But it wasn't right. He didn't belong here. He never would. Tears spilled down her cheeks. "No," she said quietly. "I don't want you to stay here. I won't *let* you stay here, Hawk."

"Callie—" Hawk's voice was hoarse with agony and dismay. He took her hand in his and held it to his cheek. "Callie—" he said again.

Callie shook her head slowly and backed away from him, crying softly. "I shouldn't have let it go this far. I should have realized. Oh, Hawk. I'm sorry. I'm so sorry. You were right in the beginning—our worlds are too different."

For a moment she couldn't continue, then taking a deep breath, she said quietly, "Please go, Hawk. Now."

He turned away from her, lifting his face upward. All expression of love had disappeared. His magnificent chiseled cheekbones and jaw looked now to be carved from granite, not flesh. She noticed that his eyes seemed to seek guidance from the northern skies—the northern skies of the Mandan.

When he again turned to her, his gaze held no emotion, his voice no hope. "I will leave after I deliver Bethenia to the station tonight."

"Yes, I believe that's best," Callie whispered, her voice trembling. She couldn't bear to look in his eyes again. Without another word she turned and hurried up the path, past the music and the dancing, into the house.

For a long time Hawk didn't leave the place where he'd just held Callie in his arms. He felt a loneliness darker and bleaker than he'd ever experienced.

"Oh, God…" he whispered, looking again into the heavens. But he didn't know how to pray, what to pray. "Father, help me…help us both," he finally managed, his voice breaking. "Show Callie your love and your mercy. She is struggling and I don't know why. Hold her in your arms. Comfort her. Comfort us both."

He paused, looking toward Stonehaven's main house blazing with light and laughter. "Is this your answer, Father? Am I truly to leave this place…to leave Callie?"

Then Hawk headed slowly back to where the harp and the flute had begun playing a bittersweet song of the South.

Eighteen

❦

Lifting her organza skirt and crinolines, Callie hurried up the wide spiral stairs leading to the second-story hallway in the main house. Below her, the foyer's chandelier burned brightly and guests stood in small groups. Laughter and bits of conversations drifted upward, mingling with the faint outside sounds of music and dancing.

Callie spoke a word of greeting as she passed an older woman and her two daughters descending the staircase. After reaching the top landing, she glanced down. She saw Caleb, just stepping into the library. As if feeling her gaze, he looked up.

She caught her breath when their eyes met. Her uncle's expression was cold, suspicious. Callie flashed a wide smile his direction, hoping to diffuse his obvious distrust.

Callie stepped into her room, closed the door, and leaned against it for a moment. Closing her eyes, she fought to push back the fresh pain of her conversation with Hawk.

Oh, how she loved him! She loved him enough to send him away—to the place his heart had sought since childhood. His leaving Natchez would be best for them both. Taking a shaky breath, Callie determined to put the scene from her mind. After all, she told herself, squaring her shoulders and setting her jaw, the duties ahead required her full attention. Hawk would leave tomorrow and they would go on with their lives. But tonight the lives of the runaways lay in their hands.

Callie slipped out of her gown, then pulled on her dark shirt and trousers. She splashed cool water on her face and eyes, hoping to pat away all traces of her tears, then plaited her hair into one long braid and stuffed it into the old field hat.

A light tap sounded at the door. Callie extinguished the lamp and said nothing, worried that it might be Wilhelmina or Caleb. After a moment, Sheridan cracked open the door and poked in her head.

"Callie? Are you there?"

She let her breath out in relief at the sound of Sherrie's voice. "Yes, come in."

"Where's Becca?"

"Next door. I'll get her."

Callie opened the door between the adjoining rooms. A single candle lighted the girl's room. Rebecca, dressed in the same manner as Callie and Sheridan, knelt beside her bed in prayer.

Her thin face was turned upward, eyes closed, her small hands clasped gracefully in her lap. She was talking to God as if he were sitting with her. Her soft voice reflected an inner peace—even joy—as if she could be in no better place this moment than in his presence.

Callie stopped short, reminded of Hawk's same joy in God's presence. The pain of their earlier words flooded over her. When she spoke, her voice was sharper than she intended. "Rebecca! It's time to go."

Rebecca looked up at her, smiled sweetly, and said, "I'm ready."

Callie took Rebecca's hand, and Sherrie followed as they

slipped down the back stairs and away from the house, heading for the stables. In the distance they heard the faint strains of music carrying across the grounds and gardens.

A few minutes later Callie slowly opened the door, then crept into the dark and cavernous stables. Sherrie and Becca followed. Callie swung onto Winterstar, then nudged the mare in the flanks. Sherrie and Rebecca mounted their horses and walked them behind Winterstar. Soon, the three mounts were galloping into the brisk night wind.

After they had ridden several miles, the abandoned overseer's house emerged from the darkness. They slid from their horses, Sheridan walked the animals to the nearby wood, tethered them, then stood watch, waiting for the train's conductor. Callie and Rebecca stepped into the house.

"Remember—no candles," she whispered to Rebecca. "We've got to keep it dark."

Soon the first group arrived by wagon: two young men, a woman and her child from Louisiana. An elderly white-haired man shuffled feebly into the house with them. Callie wondered silently whether he was fit for the journey ahead. No matter their age, these travelers needed every bit of strength they could muster. She thought about those who had traveled a thousand miles under appalling conditions only to be caught within hours of freedom. Just like Israel's family in Oberlin.

The conductor drove away as soon as his passengers had made it safely into the station house, his empty wagon rattling back down the road and into the night. A deep quiet fell over the group; they knew their lives depended on their silence.

Ten minutes passed, then the second wagon arrived. This time, four passengers—a man, woman, and two children—exited and hurried into the house. Taking their places with the others, they sat huddled together without speaking.

Callie stood by the window, waiting for Israel and the two

other missing passengers: Bethenia and Cody. She knew Hawk had left for them right after their sad conversation on the terrace.

Israel rode through a stand of trees moments later. "They here yet?" he asked, as he hurried through the door. "Is my Bethenia here?"

"No." Callie touched the big man's arm. "But there's plenty of time. Don't worry."

"There's another wagon comin'. Listen!" Rebecca stood near Callie at the window.

Seconds later, Sheridan, from her hiding place in the woods, lit a candle then quickly extinguished it, signaling that the conductor of the next station north was waiting with fresh horses and wagons.

"Get ready, folks," Callie whispered to the group. "It's almost time to go."

The runaways stood and made their way to the door, then Rebecca spoke up again. "I see Dr. Hawk a-comin'. I see 'em now," she announced. Then her voice dropped. "But Israel, I don't see your Bethenia. Somethin's wrong. Terrible wrong."

Caleb Benedict, Wilhelmina Holt, and the sheriff, a dark burly man named Zebulon Webb, sat together in Caleb's office.

"She's gone all right," Caleb said. "Wilhelmina here searched the premises—found that she'd changed out of her party clothes. There's no doubt she's gone. But it's anyone's guess where."

"Before we get to where, I want you to tell me in detail exactly what you know about her activities." Zebulon leaned back in his chair, his stomach protruding over his wide belt.

"Well, it's not that easy," Caleb began. "We know she was nearly arrested for her activities with the Underground Railroad while she was at Oberlin College."

"Almost?"

Caleb nodded. "Seems she escaped." He went on to relate how the one witness retracted his testimony then killed himself.

"So it's a documented fact." The sheriff sounded skeptical.

"As I said, there are no witnesses. No proof. But it's known."

"She's your own blood—why would you want to see her hang?" Zebulon peered at Caleb. "You do realize she'll swing for this—if we catch her."

"My reasons are my own. Your job is to see that she's caught."

"What if you're wrong?"

"I'm not."

"But what if we don't catch her in the act?" The sheriff sounded disheartened, as if he knew what Caleb's next words would be. He massaged his temples, frowning.

"You arrest her anyway." Caleb's voice was firm. The matter was settled in his mind.

For the first time since the conversation began, Wilhelmina spoke up. "Gentlemen, let's not quibble over the details. I suggest we concentrate on where she is so that we *can* catch her."

"I suppose you know the place?" Caleb narrowed his eyes at the woman.

The gray-haired woman smiled patiently. "We've already discussed this: The stables are too public. The slaves' quarters are a possibility—but some of the abandoned buildings are more likely."

"Is there a family chapel?" The sheriff asked. "That's a favorite for these kinds of activities."

Wilhelmina nodded. "Yes, but it hasn't been used for years."

"All the more reason to use it now." The sheriff sighed. "My men will begin there—fan out, covering the quarters, then move to the outbuildings."

For a few minutes the men spoke of their plans, then Wilhelmina stood and excused herself. After she left the room, Caleb looked hard at Zebulon. "You understand what you are to do?"

The sheriff nodded, though not enthusiastically.

"I don't need to remind you, do I, what the consequences will be for you if my niece is not arrested tonight?" Unblinking, Caleb held the man's gaze.

Zebulon Webb nodded again slowly.

"Good then. We understand one another." He chuckled heartily and slapped Zebulon on the back. "And no one will ever know that I had anything to do with her arrest. Am I right?"

The sheriff indicated that he was, and the two men exited the room together.

Hawk had pulled the old farm wagon as close as he dared to the MacIntosh slaves' quarters. The grounds were quiet; most of the house servants had gone with the family to the barbecue.

Creeping through the darkness, he found Bethenia's shack. He knocked lightly at the door. There was no answer. Hawk knocked again. Silence.

He quietly opened the door and for a moment let his eyes adjust to the dark. Bethenia lay on the bed in the corner, tossing in distress, though silently because Cody was asleep next to her. He hurried to her side.

"Bethenia?"

She looked up at him with large, tortured eyes. He sat on the edge of her bed, taking her hand. Her pulse fluttered weakly, and her tightening abdomen told him that labor had begun. She breathed in short, shallow breaths.

It would be dangerous to move her. But he had no choice.

They had no time to spare. He decided, too, that the suffering woman would need his help long after the ride to the station. He would stay with her—even if it meant traveling with the runaways for a few days.

"Bethenia, it's time to go."

She nodded weakly and looked at the sleeping child curled next to her. Hawk understood the loving glance and touched Cody on the shoulder.

"Cody," he whispered. "Cody, wake up."

The little girl opened her eyes and looked at Hawk in confusion. She stuck her thumb into her mouth and twirled a lock of hair with her other hand.

"You and your mamma need to come with me. We're going to see your daddy. Can you help me move your mamma?"

Cody's solemn eyes assessed him. Finally, Hawk figured that he passed the child's inspection, because she finally nodded and sat up, thumb still in her mouth.

"I'll need to carry your mamma. And when we get outside, you'll need to stay right beside me. Can you do that?" Cody nodded as Hawk gathered Bethenia into his arms.

The trio moved out of the shack, Hawk carrying Bethenia, whose body was surprisingly light, even though she was swollen with child. Cody held onto his pantleg with one hand and continued to suck her other thumb. Slowly they made their way to the wagon. Hawk settled Bethenia onto the soft bed of quilts he'd made in the back of the wagon. Cody wanted to sit with him on the driver's bench and snuggled against him as he reined the horse to a slow walk.

He purposely didn't allow the horse to move fast. Even so, with each bump or rut along the wooded road, Bethenia moaned in pain.

Soon the wagon moved onto smoother ground and Hawk,

conscious of the passing time, flicked his whip above the horse, urging him to move faster. After a few miles, the wagon broke into open field country, passed well behind Stonehaven, then continued on to the overseer's house.

There in the shadowy distance, Hawk spotted the station through the darkness of the night.

As the runaways moved from the station house across the clearing to the waiting conductor and his vehicles, Hawk reined the horse to a halt at the still-open doorway.

Israel ran to the wagon and gathered little Cody into his arms. "Oh, baby, sweet baby," he whispered. Then he looked down at Bethenia. Her eyes were closed, and she lay as still as death. Israel lifted his gaze to Hawk's. "Is she goin' to be all right?"

"Yes, but I'm going to need to stay with her—with you both. I don't think she should be moved. I'll drive this wagon behind the conductor's. I'm going to need someone else to go along to help." His eyes briefly met Callie's. She had stepped from the doorway to the wagon and stood beside Israel.

"I'll send Becca for Sheridan," she said. Rebecca overheard and ran toward the woods to fetch her.

The big man nodded, his tired face etched with worry. Cody, still sucking her thumb, curled in one arm, her head resting against her father's broad shoulder.

Callie turned to Israel. "I've got something for you. I had these prepared some time ago." She handed him the emancipation papers.

He looked down at them then back to Callie. She knew he couldn't read.

"You're a free man, Israel. These are the legal papers proclaiming your freedom. No man will ever own you again."

"Miss Callie—" he began, then his voice broke as he studied the papers in his hand. He grabbed her hand. "God be with you, Miss Callie. God be with you."

Israel turned back to Bethenia. Bending over the wagon, he said softly, "Did you hear that, Bethie? Did you hear it? We're gonna be free." Tears coursed down his cheeks. "Hang on, baby. We're gonna make it," he said softly. Then he climbed to the wagon seat, Cody still resting in his arms.

Sherrie hurried across the clearing, following Rebecca to the wagon. After speaking briefly to Hawk, she climbed into the wagon bed next to Bethenia. "We must be hurrying now," she called out. "The conductor's ready."

Hawk stared at Callie without speaking.

Callie brushed back a stray wisp of hair. "Will I see you again?"

From across the clearing the conductor signaled that it was time to pull out. Suddenly the cacophony of crickets, the owls' mournful cries, the bats' high-pitched squeals, the dry sycamore leaves rattling in the breeze became part of that eternal moment in which Callie awaited Hawk's answer.

He touched her cheek. "Goodbye, Callie."

Lifting Bethenia's weak wrist, Hawk checked her pulse once more, then climbed to the driver's bench and sat next to Israel. He flicked the whip over the horse's back and the wagon lurched forward.

"God be with you, Hawk," Callie whispered. "God be with us all." Then she wondered at herself. It was the first time she'd ever spoken about God as if he cared.

Moments later Callie and Rebecca lit a candle and checked for any belongings left by the runaways, then made their way from the shack to the waiting horses.

Callie stopped abruptly and turned to Rebecca. "I want you to go on the next train."

"Why?" Rebecca's expression saddened. "I didn't do right tonight?"

"Oh, no. Don't misunderstand me." Callie laughed gently. "You were a wonderful help. It's just that I think it's time for you to go to school."

Rebecca's face broke into a wide grin.

"I'll write to Sadie Johnson. See if she can find a place with a family where you could go to school."

Rebecca gave Callie an impulsive hug. She started to speak then tilted her head, listening. "I hear someone coming," she whispered.

Callie listened. For a moment her eyes met Rebecca's. "Horses?" She put her finger to her lips, straining to hear better. "It's a posse."

Rebecca nodded.

Wordlessly, they bounded into the woods toward their own horses.

Callie threw her leg over the saddle. Rebecca scrambled onto hers, slipped, and tried again. She finally mounted as the riders entered the clearing near the overseer's house. The voices of the posse carried to their hiding place.

Callie held up her hand to stop Rebecca from riding out. Any move they made would be heard. Now they could only wait and hope they'd go undetected until the men moved on.

The horse that Sheridan had ridden earlier waited nearby. There was a rustle in a nearby thicket, and a possum waddled from underneath. Startled, the horse whinnied softly.

Callie cast a frantic glance at Rebecca just as her horse snorted and reared. Callie caught her breath, hoping that the horse would calm itself and settle into silence. She patted its neck, hoping her touch would soothe the animal.

The possum scurried by the horse again. The animal whinnied, this time louder, and reared, crashing into the thicket.

By now the posse had moved closer. Their lanterns cast a shadowy glow on the place where Callie and Rebecca waited.

The young women exchanged a knowing look. Callie had already guessed from snatches of their conversation that the men were looking for the runaways. Rebecca grabbed Callie's hand just as the posse burst through the brush.

"Well, now. Lookie what we have here." One of the men growled delightedly.

The lanterns they held up bathed Callie and Rebecca in a harsh glow.

"They're holding hands. Jes! look at that. We got ourselves a n—— lover."

By now the posse, still on horseback, had circled them. Callie decided it would be better not to speak until she saw who was in charge.

"You helping this runaway escape?" A dark-haired man with a protruding stomach asked.

Callie shook her head. "She's not a runaway. She belongs to me."

"Then what're you doin' out here in the woods with her?" someone else called out, his voice the sound of gravel. "Oh, I get it. Yer both helpin' the runaways."

"Who's in charge here?" Callie finally asked.

One of the posse moved his horse nearer. He ignored her question. "Mind telling me just what brings you out here this time of night?"

"Sheriff," she began, keeping her voice steady, "my name is Callie St. Clair. I'm from Stonehaven. I'm sure if you contact my uncle he'll confirm—"

The sheriff interrupted. "That you're aiding and abetting runaways?" He spat into the dirt, then laughed. "I'm sure he'd do that, missy. I'm sure he would."

"I told you this girl isn't a runaway." She looked at the man in front of her. "Please believe me. If you'll just contact Caleb Benedict he'll tell you that I'm mistress of Stonehaven."

Several of the men guffawed at her words. "And I'm the king of England," said one.

Another moved his horse closer and assessed Callie, looking her up and down. "These are the clothes of a plantation mistress, all right," he said, fingering the cloth of her old shirt. Then he reached for her felt hat, chuckling as the plaited hair fell to Callie's shoulders. He held the long braid into the lantern light. "This is almost long enough for a noose," he said, laughing at his own joke. Some of the others sniggered.

"Now, boys, don't get it in mind that we're doing any hanging. We're gonna wrap this up nice and legal-like in town. We're gonna let the judge decide this. The hangin', if there is one, will take place in the town square."

"You have no evidence against me—" Callie began again. Her horse moved sideways.

"I say we caught you redhanded, missy." He cast an appraising glance at Rebecca. "Either you were trying to help the n—escape or you both were helping others get away. That's all the evidence you need in these parts. It's my word against yours." His eyes met hers. They glittered in the lantern light. "And who do you think he'll believe?"

Before Callie could answer, the sheriff looked at one of his deputies. "Tie 'em up."

The man who'd taunted her earlier rode forward and tied Callie's wrists to her saddlehorn. Next he tied Rebecca's hands in the same manner. Then taking their reins, the posse led the young women into the bleak and dark night toward Natchez.

Nineteen

It was near dawn when Titus led Sheriff Webb into Stonehaven's library. Caleb looked up wearily from his desk and raised his eyebrows without speaking.

"We found her."

"Where?"

"Out at the old overseer's place—one of the last places we looked."

"Any runaways with her?"

"If you mean, did we catch her in the act, the answer's no, we didn't. We don't even know if any slaves are missing."

"I'm sure you'll find that out eventually." Caleb sighed. "But how about making the charges stick?"

"She was with a Negress named Rebecca. Said the girl belongs to her."

The older man nodded. "Actually, Rebecca's been freed. My niece drew up the papers herself. Wilhelmina found the papers in the girl's room."

"Then Callie wasn't helping the black girl escape. They were both working with the Underground Railroad." The sheriff paused. "I figured it was one or the other."

Caleb's lip curled downward. "Yes, it seems you're right."

"A free black who's convicted of a crime returns to slavery."

"A black—free or slave—helping in the Underground is hanged," Caleb countered.

Zebulon Webb nodded slowly. "They'll both hang if you go through with this. Are you sure—"

"I'm aware of the consequences. It's a sad fate that Callasandra has brought upon herself. A blight on the whole family." Caleb's eyes narrowed. "I want this finished as quickly as possible. How soon can a judge rule?"

"This is the weekend. It'll have to wait till Monday. They'll both be held in the Natchez jail until then."

"Then it's settled. I don't want to know anything more about this affair. It's never to be mentioned again in my presence. Is that understood?"

Zebulon nodded, and when Caleb said nothing more, the sheriff quietly left the room, closing the door behind him.

Callie was taken to a small cell near the back of the jail.

"Let me see your hands." The jailer yanked her arms forward and sliced the ropes that bound them. Then backing out of the dark cell, he left Callie alone.

She rubbed her chafed wrists as she sat on the single cot in the room. Beside the small bed, a dirty washtable stood with a pitcher of water and a smudged towel hanging at its side. A chamber pot had been pushed into the opposite corner. The room's only window let in dawn's ashen light, spilling a ghostly glow across the floor.

A few minutes later, Rebecca was shoved into the cell next to Callie's. The jailer sliced the ropes that bound her, slammed the barred door, and locked it noisily.

"Becca, are you all right?"

"Yes." But Rebecca's voice was soft, frightened.

After a few minutes, Callie heard Rebecca crying. Her heart went out to the girl. But she didn't blame her; Callie was scared, too. She knew that if no one came forward in their defense, they would both hang.

Who could help them? Liam was in New Orleans, Sheridan and Hawk were on their way to the next Underground station and beyond—if Bethenia needed them. And Caleb? Earlier she'd thought that simply getting word to him would get her out of this fix. But now that she'd had time to think it through, she felt certain that her uncle had set up the arrest. He had much to gain by getting her out of the way: She stood between him and clear ownership of Stonehaven. No other motive mattered.

"Becca?"

"Yes?" She was still sniffling.

"Becca, we've got to think of a plan. We've got to get out somehow."

"How?"

Callie laughed softly. "I don't know. But we'll think of something."

They talked over their ideas. Nothing seemed plausible. Finally, both of them exhausted, they fell into silence. A short time later, Callie slipped into a light and troubled sleep.

At sunup a breakfast of thin cornmeal mush arrived on a dirty tray. Callie and Rebecca began to talk again. They felt surprisingly refreshed after a few hours of sleep.

"Callie...God's with us, you know," Rebecca said simply. She settled daintily to the floor, sitting cross-legged and facing Callie.

"I know, Becca. I've been thinking the same thing."

"He's here."

"One time in New Mexico my sister and I were held captive. I remember Juliana praying that God would be with us. I'll never forget the way I felt afterward. It was as if there was a third person with us in that small room."

For a moment neither one spoke, then Callie said, "I've heard you pray, Becca. It sounds like you know God very well."

"I don't think anyone knows him like that. He's too—" she struggled with the word, then finally added, "—big. He's too big." She fell quiet for a moment. "But I know who he is to me."

"Who?"

Rebecca sat forward, holding onto the bars. "Why're you asking me about all this?"

Callie leaned against the bars for a moment and closed her eyes. Why was she asking? Was it because she'd seen the same peace in this young Negro girl, a former slave, as she had seen in Hawk? The same joy that she'd seen in Juliana and Parker and Sun and Jeremiah?

Her thoughts turned to Juliana and how her life had changed one morning in a New Mexico mountain meadow.

Juliana had thought Parker had died in an Indian uprising. At the darkest point of her grief, Juliana had cried out to Christ, and he'd been there. Her sister said that when she found him, she'd discovered that Jesus had been there all along. He'd been waiting simply for her to recognize him.

She opened her eyes. "I just want to know who he is to you," she said to Rebecca.

"My mamma started tellin' me 'bout Jesus when I was a baby. Ev'ry flower, ev'ry smile, she said, was made by him. Once when my daddy was beat and near died from it, he said Jesus'd been beat too." Rebecca's eyes widened. "It wasn't right—for him or my daddy—but somehow just knowin' it made it bearable.

"I asked Mamma why Jesus had been beaten. If he was God—I said—why didn't he stop it? And mamma said that he

266

could've if he wanted. But he allowed it on purpose. It was 'cause he was carryin' all the bad things all the people ever did. He was beat and killed for them."

Rebecca paused, her dark eyes large with passion. "Do you know why?"

Callie shook her head.

"Because of love."

"His love for the world?"

"Yes, but that feels too big," Rebecca said wisely.

Callie agreed.

Rebecca went on. "My mamma tol' me if I was the only person in the world, Jesus would've been whipped and killed for me. *Just* for me."

For a moment neither spoke. Then Rebecca said, "Sadie Johnson says there's nothin' better than givin' up your life for someone else."

"Yes." The thought frightened Callie.

"You're doing it."

She looked at Rebecca quizzically.

"You're givin' up your life so's Israel and Bethenia and baby Cody'll be free."

Callie hadn't actually considered that she might hang for her deeds. She shuddered, trying not to dwell on the possibility.

"Becca?"

"Yes."

"I've seen you talking to God like he's your friend. Yet you said he's too big to understand. How can that be?"

Rebecca seemed lost in her thoughts for a minute. Then she said, "I figure if somebody loves me enough to die for me, it doesn't matter how big he is. He's my friend." The girl reached through the bars and squeezed Callie's hand.

Late Monday afternoon, Sheriff Webb came in to speak to Callie. "You'll be going before the judge tomorrow," he said.

For the first time since her arrest Callie felt a glimmer of hope. A judge would see the lack of evidence against her. "I want to see a lawyer."

"We've appointed one for you."

Callie was incensed. "I want my own." She gave him the name of Liam's friend.

"And you have funds to retain him?"

She knew by now that Caleb Benedict wouldn't lift a finger to help her. Without him, she had no financial resources. "Well, no. I don't. But that won't make any difference—"

"It's clear to me that you need a court-appointed lawyer." The sheriff's clipped manner told Callie that she'd lost the argument.

"What about Rebecca?"

He turned, giving the girl an indifferent glance. "She doesn't get a trial."

"Why not?"

"She's not entitled."

"Why not? She's a free black."

"Is she now?" The sheriff's tone was sarcastic.

"Yes. I can prove it—if you'll just contact the lawyer whose name I gave you—"

"Doesn't make any difference. A Negro, free or slave, caught helping in the Underground hangs until dead. It's a good lesson for the rest."

Rebecca gasped and stepped back into the darkness of her cell.

"You can't mean that. Look at her. She's barely more than a child."

The sheriff shrugged. "That's the law. But I wouldn't get too up in arms over it, missy. You'll probably swing together." He chuckled as he walked away from them.

"Callie?" Rebecca called softly, as soon as he was gone. "I'm scared."

"I know. I am, too." After a moment she added, her voice threatening to break, "Becca, can you talk to your God for us? We need him."

"He's yours, too, Callie," Rebecca said simply. She reached through the bars for Callie's hands. "Precious Jesus, help us," she prayed. "Help us."

Around midnight a ruckus in the streets near the jail woke Callie.

"In there, the n—— lover's in there." People milled about beneath her window, shouting, jeering. She could see the sky through the bars. It had turned from black to an angry, dark red.

One other time in her life she had seen the same sight: during the uprising in Fort La Sal, New Mexico. Instinctively, Callie knew this glow was caused by fire…by a torch-carrying mob!

The voices grew louder, more boisterous. "Let's hang her! Hang 'em both!" Bumps and thuds sounded on the outside wall.

Moving toward Rebecca, Callie bit her lip, trying not to cry. She hugged the trembling girl though the bars.

"Dear Jesus, help me be ready," Rebecca prayed.

The clamor grew closer, louder. By now Callie could hear words like "lynching" and "gallows" chanted louder and faster.

Rebecca listened for a moment, then cried out, a small scared sound. "I'm not very brave, Callie."

"Don't say you're not, Becca. You're one of the bravest people I know. You could've left tonight with the others. But you stayed, knowing the danger. You stayed to help others get out. That takes courage. Don't ever believe it doesn't."

The crowd gathered on the street in front of the jailhouse. Callie could hear the sheriff's voice. He seemed to be reasoning with them. She heard him talking about the judge and the coming trial. He called for calm, saying what they had planned would serve no purpose. He finished by saying, "You'll get what you want anyway."

Then someone yelled out, "Why wait, then? Save the cost of court. Let's do it now!"

The mob responded as one in a loud, coarse voice. "Hang 'em. Hang 'em both!"

The voices moved closer. Smoke began to fill the cells. "Hey, girlies," a loud voice yelled, "wait'll you feel that rope around yer necks!" Gutteral laughter rolled through the crowd.

Callie glanced at Rebecca. The girl was on her knees beside her bed, praying. Frail, sweet Rebecca. Why would anyone want to hurt her? She hoped Rebecca's God was listening.

Suddenly the heavy door between the cells and the front of the jailhouse burst open. Three men in masks pushed through. Others followed. Most were in masks. *Cowards!* Callie thought. *Can't even show their identity to each other or us!*

Callie watched as they stormed down the hallway to Rebecca's cell, poked the key in her door, and opened it. The girl lifted her face with dignity and stepped from her cell. The man with the keys grabbed her. Rebecca didn't even cry out as he lifted her sideways like a sack of potatoes on his hip. But Callie saw the fear in her face: The child's lip trembled and tears welled in her eyes.

The same man stopped to open Callie's cell.

Callie gasped and backed to the corner.

He pulled the key from the lock. Callie's hand went to her mouth; she tried to squeeze further into the corner.

Suddenly, Rebecca squirmed from his grasp. Moving with the agility of a wood sprite, she slipped through the cell opening.

She slammed the door closed and wrapped her wiry arms through the opening, clinging to the metal bars, trying to keep the mob at bay.

"To git to her, you gonna have to kill me first," she said, her voice pitifully small.

The man with the key tried to pry her arms from the bars. She clung with tenacity that defied his strength.

"Strong little nit," the man declared with a coarse snicker. "Who wants to be the first to break her hold, send her flying?" He laughed again. "We hit 'er hard enough—we'll send 'er clear to the gallows."

"Becca, let go," Callie whispered hoarsely. "It's no use. Let go!" But she couldn't bring herself to move forward to help the girl. "Please, let go," she cried.

But still Rebecca clung to the bars. Tears streamed down her face. "Go away!" she demanded.

Someone guffawed. Others joined in the mocking laughter.

"As if this skinny runt could keep us from doing what we came here to do," someone snickered.

"Let me take care of it." A big man with a bandanna over his face came forward. "Here, missy, you want this?" He stuck a pistol in her face.

Rebecca closed her eyes but she didn't let go of the bars.

"Leave her alone!" Callie ran to Rebecca's side. The child couldn't hold the mob at bay with her skinny arms. *Doesn't she know that?* "You want me, not her," Callie shouted. "She did nothing."

Someone shoved hard against the cell door. At the same instant, the gun blasted. The door swung open, and the men rushed in.

Callie crept backwards into the corner, a chill of fear skittering down her spine. *Where is Rebecca?* Her gaze darted around the cell, finally spotting the girl's body crumpled on the floor.

"This-un's dead," someone said, sounding disappointed. But Callie barely heard the words. More of the jeering, laughing vermin crowded into her cell.

"Becca…Becca!" She cried, trying to push through the mob to the place where Rebecca lay. "Oh, sweet Becca," she whispered, "God help her!"

A big man suddenly yanked Callie from her feet. She screamed and kicked as he lifted her like a trophy, then slung her across his shoulder. "I'll take 'er to the gallows," he growled. The mob cheered.

The man sprinted out the heavy door and through the jailhouse to the street, Callie bouncing on his shoulder as he ran. A smaller man ran next to him, fist in the air, cheering him on. Behind them, the crowd jostled, yelling for the man to slow down.

Someone called out, "This lynchin'll be over by the time we all make it to the gallows!"

Callie beat her fists furiously on her captor's back. They weren't far from the livery. If she could free herself, run into its shadows, hide, find a horse…. She hit at the man again. Harder. And again.

"Put me down," she screamed, squirming and kicking her legs. "Put me down. Now!" But his iron-hard arms held her fast. "Let me go!"

"Callie," the man muttered softly as he ran. "Please, be still. This is hard enough as it is."

"Hawk?" she half-sobbed, half-whispered, unable to believe she'd just heard his voice.

"And Sherrie," he breathed.

Sheridan, dressed in a mask and men's clothing, touched Callie's hand. "Aye! 'Tis me," she whispered.

They rounded the corner and neared the gallows.

"Look at 'im go!" someone called from close behind. "Never seen anyone so quick with such a load!"

"Hey! Wait fer us!" a coarse voice called out.

Callie smelled the acrid smoke from the torches and heard the frenzied excitement in their voices. They were out for blood. Her blood.

Suddenly, in the shadows ahead, Callie could see four waiting horses, one with a masked rider in the saddle holding the reins of the others.

"Get ready to ride…the minute…I put you down," Hawk panted.

The crowd, still in hot pursuit, called out for Hawk to turn toward the gallows.

"Hey, mister—where're you off to?" someone yelled. "Yer goin' outta yer way!"

"You showin' off or what?" another voice cried. Loud guffaws of laughter followed, as if Hawk were playing a joke on them.

"Here it comes, Callie," Hawk murmured breathlessly. "Get ready!"

A moment later, Callie slid into the saddle. The angry voices of the lynching mob cried out in surprise.

Callie turned to Hawk, who was hefting himself onto his mount. "We must go back." Her horse pranced nervously. "We've got to see to Rebecca."

"We can't."

She set her jaw stubbornly and reined the horse around to return to the jail.

In an instant, Hawk was beside her, his face grim. "No,

Callie!" Grabbing the bridle, he turned her horse. "We don't have a choice." The animal whinnied and reared. Hawk slapped the horse's rump. It lurched forward into a wild gallop. "Now, go! Ride!" he shouted, starting after her.

Callie swung around in the saddle to look at Hawk. "We can't leave Becca!" Fresh tears flowed down her cheeks. "They'll hang her...Please, Hawk. We've got to go back!"

Sherrie, now astride her horse, pulled up beside Callie. "She's already dead, Callie," she called across to Callie, her voice sorrowful. "'Twill do her no good to turn around."

"How can you be sure?" Callie bit her lip. "There wasn't time for you to check. We've got to go back." She reined her horse hard to the left, again causing the animal to neigh and rear.

Hawk, now riding beside Callie, reached over and grabbed her animal's reins. "You're endangering us all." His voice was gruff. "You must keep going." He kicked his horse and, still leading Callie's mount, galloped through the night.

Twenty

❧

H awk snapped his horse's reins, nudging the animal to move faster through the night. The others followed, hooves pounding.

Enraged yells and curses spewed from the mob as they trailed the riders for a distance on foot. By the time the men scrambled to saddle and mount their horses, Hawk, Callie, Sheridan, and the fourth rider had left them miles behind.

Hawk reined his horse to a longer stride, guiding the group west toward the river. A half hour later, he drove his mount into the shallow edge-waters of the Mississippi, wheeled the animal, then headed south. Callie reined into the same turn, aware of the splashing of hooves and horseflesh behind her as Sherrie and the last rider followed.

She turned to watch, identifying the rider, now unmasked, who had held their horses during the escape: It was Liam Sheridan.

He caught her gaze and shot her an encouraging smile with a nod.

Callie transferred her attention to Hawk as he moved his horse into a zigzag pattern, still galloping at breakneck speed. He turned his horse one direction, leaving obvious prints, then doubled back, heading into the river to erase them, then once again headed along the muddy bank.

Finally, Hawk directed them north, leading the horses into the water. They swam for several miles upstream, then he signaled them to make for land. The four horses, whinnying and splashing, emerged from the water. Callie, a half-length behind Hawk, clung to her horse's neck; she urged the animal up the muddy bank toward a brush-hidden trail.

The group rode hard for three long hours. By now dawn was spreading a gray light across the river and nearby foliage. Hawk held up his hand to halt, and Callie eased her hold on the horse's reins.

"We'll rest here for a short time," Hawk said, "then move on."

Callie slid from the saddle to the ground.

In a heartbeat, Sherrie was beside her. "Callie," she whispered, gathering her friend into her arms for a quick hug. "I've been so worried—"

"I'm all right. It's just—" Callie's voice broke. "—it's Becca. She tried to save me.... If only—"

Liam stepped to Callie's side, touching her arm. Callie turned.

"Oh, sweet lassie," he whispered, taking her hands, his handsome face filled with sorrow and compassion. "What they could've done to you..." His blue eyes narrowed at the thought. His grasp tightened. "But now you're safe. Oh, blessed day! You're safe."

Callie lifted her gaze to Hawk. He stood near his horse, rubbing down the animal's neck and foreleg. He regarded her solemnly but said nothing. Soon he signaled that it was time to move on.

By now the rising sun had washed the gray from the skies.

Here and there a meadowlark sang. The early morning sunlight painted a dappled yellow on nearby trees and turned the sky from lavender to pink to vivid blue.

Callie inhaled deeply, feeling safe for the first time since her arrest. She swung into the saddle and reined her horse onto the trail. She nudged the animal to move closer to Hawk, sitting tall on his mount. Sherrie and Liam followed immediately behind.

An hour later, Hawk again held up his hand to halt the small band. Callie's horse whinnied nervously.

"There's a deserted chapel beyond the willows. Doc Meade suggested the place. Seems the plantation burned several years ago, but the family's chapel was left untouched. It's run-down but usable for our purposes."

Callie kept her attention fixed on Hawk. "I'll need to stay here?" she asked, though she already knew the answer.

He nodded. "Yes. Alone." He studied her silently for a moment. "It's better for you that the three of us aren't discovered missing," he finally said. "We need to return to Natchez immediately."

"I understand. How long will I be here?"

"Maybe I can answer that, lassie." Liam rode up beside her, his horse prancing sideways on the trail.

Hawk urged his horse to the lead, and the three other mounts followed, slowly making their way through the thick foliage to the chapel.

Liam kept his horse in step with Callie's. "I've just returned from New Orleans."

During the events of the previous days, Callie had all but forgotten about his mission to find her father's old overseer. "Did you find him?" she whispered.

"Aye, it wasn't easy, lass, but I found Zeke Wakefield living near a bayou a ways from the city. Seems he'd spent more of his days drunk than not since leaving your father's employ."

"Did he admit to any wrongdoing?" Callie lifted her chin, this time holding Liam's gaze.

"Oh, yes. He seemed more than happy to get it off his chest. He's had a hard time living with himself." Liam reined his horse around a small willow, then again pulled beside Callie's mount.

"What did he do"—her voice was soft—"to my father?"

Liam paused. "He said he'd been paid to destroy some of Stonehaven's crops."

Callie briefly halted her horse. "How did he do that? I would've remembered anything that devastating."

Liam nodded, and the two horses again started walking slowly forward. "Ah, yes, child," he continued. "That you would've. That's a fact. But what he did—what Caleb had him do—was far more ingenious."

"What do you mean?"

"He had some of the slaves help him—threatened them within an inch of their lives if they told. Had them destroy the cotton plants at random. Crush them. Dig them under."

Callie nodded. "So it decreased the yield." Seeing that Hawk was nearly out of sight ahead, she nudged the horse's flanks, urging him to move faster.

"Aye." Liam gently urged his horse to keep in step with Callie's.

"How long did this go on?"

"Caleb had them destroying more crops each year for about three years. That destruction—coupled with the loss of buyers who took their business elsewhere—depleted your father's resources."

"And he had borrowed heavily from Caleb."

Liam nodded. "Exactly the same method of control he used over me."

Callie sighed, taking a moment to let it sink in. "And you took this to a New Orleans court."

Liam couldn't contain his smile. "Aye, lassie, that I did."

"And?"

"The ruling was in our favor. The judge even contacted the Governor of Mississippi to begin the investigation here—at the Capitol, not in Natchez. Seems your uncle owns just about every judge and lawman in the immediate vicinity."

Callie and Liam walked their horses over a small rise. Hawk had halted his mount, waiting for the two to join him. Callie could see the chapel in the distance, washed gleaming white by the morning sun.

She took a deep breath, turning her attention again to Liam. "And has it been done? Has a Mississippi judge ruled?"

Hawk, riding beside Callie, joined the conversation. "Liam asked me to go with him to Jackson. We'll be taking witnesses with us—others who've been cheated by your uncle. Extortion is a serious crime."

Sherrie rode up from behind, her horse dancing sideways. "And Callie," she called out, "the court date has been set—your uncle's been ordered to appear—in Jackson."

"What about the charges against me?"

After a moment Hawk spoke. "They have nothing to do with your uncle's other…activities. The best we can hope for is that after your uncle is found guilty, he'll be discredited and the sheriff will drop the charges." He shrugged. "I realize it's not much—"

Callie interrupted him with a short bitter laugh. "So I may get Stonehaven back after all only to be thrown in jail…or perhaps to have to run away from my childhood home."

Hawk regarded her for a moment, a shadow crossing his face. Then he lifted his gaze toward the chapel. "It's time to go," he said quietly, nodding toward the small white building. "Doc

Meade contacted a friend to supply everything you need—food, clean clothing, bedding."

Callie nodded.

A few minutes later, she slid from the saddle at the chapel's entrance. Stopping at the bottom of the stairs, Callie lifted her eyes to the cross on the steeple. The whitewashed brick walls were faded, but the sturdy-looking cross gleamed in the morning sun.

She felt strangely comforted as she stepped into the small building.

"Callie?" Hawk caught up with her near the bare wooden altar at the front of the sanctuary. "Will you be all right here—alone?"

She looked up, meeting his eyes. Smiling softly, she reached up to tuck a wayward wisp of hair into her long braid. "I'll be quite comfortable," she said, looking around the cozy room.

Someone had indeed readied the place. The stained-glass windows had been scrubbed, casting into the room a light the color of a New Mexico sunset. The floor had been swept clean, and a cot with fresh linens welcomed her from a corner near the front altar. A larder of food and a satchel of clean clothing had been neatly placed on the front pew near the small bed. On the three-legged table near the window lay a small bouquet of wild-flowers. Callie smiled at the sweet gesture. "I'll be all right."

"Doc said there's a creek for drinking water."

Callie nodded. "I'll find it."

Liam was standing nearby. "No need, lass," he said eagerly. "I'll both find it and fetch the water." He rummaged for a pail, shouted, "Here it is!" then bounded out the front door. Sherrie announced that she would see if the pasture was fenced adequately for Callie's horse and followed her cousin through the doorway.

Suddenly, Callie was alone with Hawk. He stood close. Too close. Callie swallowed. She wanted to speak of anything but those words they'd uttered the last time they were alone.

"Tell me what happened with Bethenia," she finally said.

Hawk drew in a breath as if he'd read Callie's thoughts. "Bethenia's baby was born in the back of the wagon that night—with Sherrie's help," he said, smiling for the first time. "Bethenia was right—it was a boy. Israel danced with delight." He grinned. "They named him Hawk." He paused, his expression tender. "That was a wonderful thing you did for them, Callie."

She looked at him quizzically.

"Giving Israel his emancipation papers."

Callie nodded slowly. It seemed so long ago.

"His freedom and his baby's birth were the only things he could talk about." Hawk smiled. Callie thought she would melt in his gaze. Her mind skipped back to the first time she saw him smile—in New Mexico when she thought she'd just stepped into a pool of liquid sunlight.

Hawk moved toward her. Callie caught her breath as he cupped her face with his hands. "Callie," he said hoarsely. "Oh, Callie…we must talk. There's so much left to be said."

Just then the door opened. Sunlight streamed into the room.

Liam cleared his throat, hesitated, then walked briskly down the middle aisle. "Aye! 'Tis bad timing on my part. I seem to have interrupted something." He didn't appear sorry.

Blushing, Callie stepped back from Hawk.

But Hawk, ignoring Liam, held Callie's gaze with his.

"I need this time," she finally said, looking into his eyes, willing him to understand. "I just—" she faltered, "I just need to be alone. To think…to pray…to figure out so many things in my life." She surprised herself by saying it.

Hawk nodded slowly. Then moving toward her, he tenderly

lifted her face, gazed once more into her eyes, then kissed her softly on the forehead. He turned to leave.

"Hawk—?" Callie's voice was soft.

He faced her again, regarding her without speaking.

"Thank you," she whispered. "Thank you for coming for me."

Standing nearby, Liam cleared his throat nervously. "I think we ought to be leaving," he said, "and let this lass rest. It's been a long night for us all..." He stepped toward Callie and gave her a gentle embrace. Then he pulled back and winked. "'Tis a smart man who knows when he's lost the battle, lass."

She tilted her head, noticing the twinkle in his blue eyes.

"And I'm that smart man, I am... God be with you, lass." Then he headed quickly down the aisle and out the front door.

After a quick hug from Sherrie at the chapel's entrance, Callie watched the trio mount. Almost before they'd ridden out of sight, she closed the door behind her and collapsed on the small cot, falling into a deep and dreamless sleep. She didn't wake until dusk, rose to eat a cold biscuit, then slept again.

For three days and nights, Callie repeated the routine of sleeping and eating. Once a day she stumbled out to check on the horse. But immediately after seeing to the animal's well-being, Callie slipped under her cover and closed her eyes.

Finally on the fourth day, she woke with the sunrise. Stretching, she walked down the aisle to the chapel's entrance. Pushing open the door, Callie stepped outside and stood for a moment in the sunlight, letting its warmth invade her soul. From the nearby willows, birds sang their morning songs. A mockingbird trilled, then hopped on an oak branch near her, calling out another joyful note.

She stepped onto the path leading toward the river. Finding a flat rock at the water's edge, Callie sat, wrapping her arms around her knees. The sunlight cast a sheen like liquid diamonds on the water. Fish jumped, causing ripples to sparkle and dance.

Callie looked across the swirling waters and for the first time allowed herself to think about Rebecca. How could someone so small and scared have been so brave? How could she have given her life trying to save Callie? And perhaps she did save her life: Perhaps the diversion she caused had gained the time Hawk and Sherrie needed to carry out their rescue.

Then Callie lifted her eyes heavenward. What had Rebecca said about giving up your life for another? That there was no greater gift than to give your life so that another might live?

The fragile girl had faced the lynching mob as a gift of love for Callie, the greatest gift one person could give another.

Callie picked up a pebble and tossed it into the water. Ripples circled outward. She tossed another.

Rebecca said that though he was God and too "big" to understand, if he—through his Son Jesus—gave his life for her, he was her friend. It was as simple and profound as that.

Callie had seen how Rebecca spoke to him. He was her precious friend. She could tell him anything, without fear and with the assurance he was listening, caring as deeply for her as she did for him.

Rebecca had given her life for Callie. So had Jesus.

She looked out over the river waters, watching them, deep and powerful, flow ever southward. Nothing could stop the mighty river from flowing; nothing could stop God's love from flowing into her heart.

Callie thought about what Jesus had done through his death. He had given his life for her just as surely as Rebecca had. If that was true, he was her friend. He would listen as if she were the only one in the world, even if it took forever to tell him what laid deep in her soul.

Callie again lifted her eyes to the heavens.

"Jesus…" her heart cried. A gentle river breeze lifted wisps of hair from her brow. She drew in a soft breath. "Jesus," she whispered again. "I want to belong to you, but I am so unworthy…"

Callie thought about all the times she had too stubbornly sought her own way, often at the expense of others. She recalled how she had pushed God away, ignoring him, refusing to believe he cared about her intimately—because he might interfere with her plans, she admitted grimly. She'd heard once that in human relationships indifference caused greater pain than downright hateful actions.

But she'd been indifferent to God. She'd ignored the almighty God of the universe, the God who'd sent his Son to give his life for her.

Callie breathed in shakily. "I'm so unworthy," she repeated, cut through to her soul with remorse. "Oh, God…I'm so sorry." Tears spilled down her cheeks, and Callie wiped at them with her fingers. "You've been with me all along—you walked alongside Juliana and me when we headed to New Mexico; you protected us from harm in Fort La Sal; you saved me from the fire—from capture—in Oberlin; you brought me to this place and saved me from lynching. Yet I dared to lift my head and say to your face that I did it all!" Callie bowed her head, overcome with sorrow and shame.

"I'm sorry, Father…please forgive me." Her voice sounded small, like that of a child. "I want to belong to you," she said again.

A gentle wind came from across the river waters, rustling the leaves of the nearby willows. Callie drew in a soft breath and let it caress her face.

"Oh, Jesus…I love you," Callie murmured. "I love you!" As she uttered the words she felt something…something much like the wind that had touched her face…something that filled her with joy.

"I need you, Father," she whispered. "I want to give my life to you." She raised her eyes to the heavens. "Give me new life," she breathed to her Lord. "Please live in me."

Callie raised her face to the sunlight, feeling fresh tears on her cheeks. But they no longer flowed from grief. Now they spilled from an overflowing peace that flooded her soul.

In the days that followed, Callie delighted in God's presence. Every morning she rose with the sun, bathed in the cool waters of the nearby brook, then walked to the river, speaking with God. She rejoiced in the fresh wonder of his friendship.

Weeks passed. Callie saw no one except Doc Meade's friend, a round and loving woman, who brought her fresh food from time to time.

Then one evening just before sunset Callie saw the shadow of a lone rider making his way through the foliage on the path leading to the chapel.

Hurrying into the sanctuary, she cracked the door, then standing to one side, peered out.

She caught her breath. It was Hawk riding the Arabian. He was dressed in his buckskins. His traveling clothes. Her heart fell.

As the Arabian brought him closer, Callie opened the door and stepped from her hiding place. She watched him with both delight and sadness: a deep joy because she was looking on his face again...and a nearly unbearable sorrow because he was probably here to tell her goodbye.

Hawk's gaze held hers. Without speaking, he slid from the saddle and wrapped the reins around a nearby post. Then he strode to where Callie stood at the chapel entrance.

He grasped both her hands, his deep blue eyes regarding her solemnly. Finally, he said hoarsely, "I've missed you, Callie. Are you all right?"

Callie could barely speak for the racing of her heart. She nodded. "Yes," she whispered. "I am." She wanted to say more, but she didn't trust her voice.

A brisk breeze from the river suddenly kicked up, lifting stray tendrils of hair from her brow. She shivered. Hawk placed his arm around her shoulders and turned her toward the chapel.

"I've come to tell you something you've waited years to hear, Callie," he said, as they walked through the entrance. "It will take some time to explain it all."

The waning sun slanted through the stained-glass windows, bathing the sanctuary in glorious rainbow colors. Callie and Hawk stepped down the aisle and sat facing each other in a front pew.

Hawk let out his breath slowly. His eyes again met hers, but now she saw his sadness. When he spoke there seemed to be a finality to his words. "It's yours, Callie," he said finally. "Stonehaven belongs to you." Then he added with a rueful smile, "And, of course, to Juliana. The ownership has reverted to the St. Clair family. The two of you comprise the family."

"Oh, Hawk!" she whispered shakily, suddenly overcome with emotion. "It's happened. It's actually happened! But how—?"

"The judge in Jackson convicted Caleb. There were at least twelve witnesses who testified against him." He chuckled. "It seems the friends in high places he once had disappeared into the woodwork once his activities became known." He paused, his expression again solemn. "He'll be in prison for a long time Callie—maybe for the rest of his life."

Hawk smiled sadly. "You owe a great deal to Liam. It was his influence that convinced the witnesses they had a chance of winning back the property—the reputations—that Caleb had robbed from them." He paused. "He cares about you, Callie."

She smiled. "I know." But she didn't want to speak of Liam.

Instead, she asked, "What about the charges against me? When can I go home? "

Hawk smiled. "It seems that with Caleb's arrest, the townspeople are willing to accept that it was he who discredited you with false charges. Even the sheriff's been run out of town."

For a long moment Callie didn't speak. Then her eyes searched Hawk's. "It's over then. It's finally over."

"Yes, Callie, it is. And it's time for you to go home. Stonehaven awaits her mistress."

"You've come to accompany me?"

"No. I've come to say goodbye, Callie. Liam will be here tomorrow to take you home."

"Liam? Tomorrow?"

Hawk nodded.

"Liam?" she repeated, setting her lips in a stubborn line. She jumped to her feet, turning her back to Hawk.

For a moment she didn't speak. Then suddenly she felt his arms turning her to face him. As always she was surprised at how quietly he moved, especially in moccasins.

She lifted her eyes and met his gaze.

"I don't know what I'll do without you," she whispered hoarsely. "Oh, Hawk...please don't go away."

Hawk touched her cheek with the backs of his fingers, then cupped her chin. He smiled wryly. "As I recall, that's what you wanted, Callie."

"I—I thought it was—" She let the words hang, not knowing how to proceed.

"Callie," Hawk said gently. "You're about to become mistress of Stonehaven." He cocked his head, regarding her intently. "I have no part in that world..."

For a moment he didn't go on, then he let out a long breath.

"You were right to tell me to leave...and now it's time. Weeks ago I came to Natchez to find you—to solve the mystery of your disappearance for Juliana. I've accomplished my mission." He laughed softly. "Here you are, safe and secure. Your new life will soon begin. Nashtara can continue running the Railroad. Lives will be saved—"

"Is that all I am to you," Callie interrupted, "a mission? Finding me was a *mission* on my sister's behalf?"

Hawk inhaled, nodding slowly. "I must say this—it was a mission I'll never forget."

"But nothing more?" she persisted.

"You know it was more, Callie. Or maybe I should say it could have been more."

Callie reached for his hand and held it to her cheek. "Oh, Hawk..." she breathed, then her throat closed and she couldn't go on. The last faint rays of the setting sun had died, and with it, the rosy glow in the little chapel. It matched the gathering darkness in her heart.

"Goodbye, Callie." Hawk pulled his hand away. "I really must go. I've got a long journey ahead."

"To the Mandan villages."

"Yes."

"Then you'd better leave."

He nodded. "Yes, I'd better leave." He regarded her yearningly for another long minute, then turned abruptly and made his way down the aisle toward the chapel's entrance. The door closed behind him.

Callie's heart left with him.

Suddenly, she whispered hoarsely, "Hawk!"

She picked up her skirt and ran down the aisle, nearly blinded by a haze of tears.

"Hawk!" she cried again, as she burst through the doorway.

Hawk, about to mount the Arabian, turned, reins in hand.

"Hawk!" Tears coursed down her cheeks. "Please, don't go!"

Hawk dropped the reins. His eyes searched hers.

"Hawk Jones, I love you," Callie sobbed, as she threw herself into his open arms.

Hawk pulled Callie into his arms, feeling their hearts beating in unison. "Callie, my beloved..." he murmured into her hair, that thicket of red curls he'd first seen flying in the wind in New Mexico. He drew back slightly, kissing away her tears, gazing into her shimmering emerald eyes.

She relaxed in his arms and he pulled her closer again. For a moment they stood without speaking.

"I want to go with you," Callie whispered.

Hawk stepped back, not sure he'd heard her correctly.

She gave him a tremulous smile. "I want to go with you to your mother's people."

"Callie—" he hesitated. "Darling, you don't know what you're saying." He shook his head slowly, thinking of the dangers, the hardships. "It's too much of a sacrifice. For someone like you—" His voice dropped. He remembered Callie in her crinolines and gowns, dancing, laughing, enjoying life at Stonehaven.

Callie interrupted his thoughts. "Something wondrous has happened to me, Hawk." She averted her gaze shyly for a moment, then looked again into his eyes. "I met someone who has been with me always, but I had never really known him."

Hawk took Callie's hands in his as she spoke. Her face—that beautiful face with its sprinkling of freckles—glowed with a light he'd not seen there before.

"He found me, Hawk, and took away my darkness, my grief, my pain." Her gaze moved to the cross at the top of the steeple. "Everything is different now. I am different."

Hawk waited for her to continue. She regarded him, her

expression solemn. "A moment ago you mentioned sacrifice."

He nodded.

"When Becca tried to save me—when I saw her stand up to the jeering crowd—her action branded my soul like a fiery iron. It provided a picture of love so deep, so giving, that it will be with me until the day I die." She looked toward the river. "When I thought of Jesus' sacrifice—his death on the cross—suddenly it no longer seemed impersonal—a faraway act in a faraway place.

"It was an act of pure love—done for me as if I were the only person in the world to save. It didn't matter to him how undeserving I was. All that mattered was love, his deep and everlasting love for me."

She drew in a shaky breath, again gazing into his eyes. "Becca told me in the jail cell that there is no greater love than to give your life for another.

"I don't know what God has ahead for us—what dangers or hardships we might find in the upper Missouri—but if this is the work he's called us to do, it's worth every sacrifice, even our lives."

Hawk's heart leapt inside him. "Oh, Callie…" he breathed. How he had longed to hear these words! Then he chuckled, "But there's something I need to ask you." He drew her closer, tilting her face toward his.

She looked at him quizzically.

"Will you marry me?"

Callie laughed softly. "I thought you'd never ask."

Hawk gathered her to him and kissed her on the lips. His mouth lingered on hers, warm and passionate. Callie could feel her heart pounding almost in unison with his.

Then he drew back and looked into her eyes. "You still didn't answer my question, Callie." But instead of giving her a chance to answer, he touched her face then kissed her eyelids, her cheeks, her chin.

Callie melted into his arms, thinking only of his love.

Hawk stopped kissing her and she looked up at him. He smiled into her eyes, one brow raised. "You didn't answer my question."

"Actually, I have three answers," she said, her voice soft and earnest. "I'll marry you. Oh, yes, my darling, I will marry you!" She laughed lightly and, pulling his face gently toward her, kissed him on the lips.

Then she added, her voice joyfully exuberant, "And I will go with you to the Mandan villages…or to the ends of the earth, if you should ask."

Homeward

Homeward

❧

Stonehaven Plantation
Spring 1855

On her wedding day, Callie stood with her sister Juliana on Stonehaven's wide verandah. They looked out over the plantation's terraced gardens and newly planted fields, shimmering pale green in the spring sunlight.

Callie turned to Juliana, admiring her sister's aristocratic beauty. "Do you remember how you once told me to memorize the look of all this?" She didn't give Juliana a chance to answer. "I remember your exact words. You said to take in every crooked oak...the moonlight dancing on the magnolia leaves...the sounds of the crickets and mockingbirds with their night songs. You told me to fill my heart with it all. You said that we'd never be back."

Juliana laughed softly. "I was paying more attention to my own sorrow than to your grit. I should've known that you'd figure out a way to come back to Stonehaven. You were only sixteen—but filled with stubborn determination."

"I'm just sorry I ended up being right about Caleb. I had suspected him for years, but I wanted to be proven wrong."

"I know, Callie. But he did bring it all on himself."

"He's a broken man, Juliana. You wouldn't recognize him.

He's in a filthy place. It would break your heart. I guess I wanted to spare you that. "

"But you went to see him....I wish I'd been here in time to go with you."

Callie nodded. "I told him for both of us that he's forgiven for what he did to Father."

"How about for what he did to you, Callie? He almost caused you to be hanged. He wanted you dead." Juliana's voice was quiet, sad.

"That was harder. But God was with me, reminding me that Jesus forgave those who crucified him." She smiled sadly. "I didn't even make it to the gallows." Then she gazed at Juliana, knowing her sister understood. "I just wanted to tell him that he's loved no matter what he's done. Loved and forgiven."

Juliana squeezed her hand. "Did you tell him our plans for Stonehaven?"

Callie nodded. "Yes." She raised her eyes to the sign above the doorway: *The Rebecca Johnson School of Higher Learning and Medical Research.*

Callie and Juliana had signed the final papers the previous week, selling Stonehaven's vast acreage to three neighboring plantations. The house itself would remain under the sisters' and their husbands' ownership.

With the proceeds from the sale an endowment had been set up for a medical research facility run by Dr. Meade. Scientists and medical doctors from around the world would be invited to come to Stonehaven and study diseases afflicting the poor, diseases such as rickets, scurvy, cholera, consumption. Hawk's contacts at Harvard would bring the very finest physicians and researchers to the new facility.

Suddenly, from the terraced gardens, the sweet sounds of harp, flute, and violin drifted to the place Callie and Juliana stood.

Juliana hugged her sister, gazing into her eyes. "I'm so proud of you, Callie—giving your life to help Hawk minister to Sun's people." Tears shimmered in her eyes, and she gave Callie another quick squeeze before stepping down the wide verandah stairs to the rose garden.

Callie took a deep breath and straightened her lace and satin skirt, daintily fluffing the crinolines underneath. Then she pulled the soft white veil over her face and glanced backward to see if it was billowing out properly behind her.

She took her place at the top of the verandah stairs. The music rose, and with it, Callie's heart soared. She drew in a deep breath, gazing across the lawns to the lilacs, the roses, the azaleas…the ivy-lined gazebo at the end of the path where Hawk stood waiting.

She took her first dainty steps down the stairs and the guests stood and turned toward the bride. On one side Morning Sun and Jeremiah watched with loving gazes; on the other, a tearful Juliana and Parker stood with their tiny daughter Morgan and their son Richard. Sheridan, sitting next to Liam, smiled tenderly as Callie moved past.

At the end of the stone pathway, Hawk lifted his face as Callie approached. Then he stepped forward and grasped both her hands. His eyes, the color of New Mexico skies, never left hers.

I'm home, Callie breathed to herself. *At last, I'm home.*

Dear Reader:

My characters—even the most ornery—have a way of taking up residence in my heart as they come to life. At times they delight me with their behavior; other times they exasperate me by dictating their own actions, completely ignoring their creator. But just as a mother cares unabashedly for her children, I love them through the final pages of each book...and beyond.

Sometimes I wonder if my Creator considers me in the same way. One of my favorite verses is Zephaniah 3:17: "He will take great delight in you...he will rejoice over you with singing." What a comforting thought, especially in light of those times when he must agonize over my stubborn willfulness. And what a relief to know that his heart is a full of forgiveness, grace, and love as a mother's is for her child (Isaiah 66:13).

A new cast of characters is already moving into my heart as I work on *Everlasting*, in which Sheridan O'Brian travels West in search of her missing twin, Shamus. (He's disappeared after staking out a claim to a California gold mine called Everlasting Diggin's.) While following her brother's trail, Sheridan's life turns upside down when she encounters the dashing, mysterious Marcus Jade, who's not at all who he says he is.

My husband and I soon will visit California's gold country to do research for the book. I'm excited about the locale; I grew up in the Sierra Nevada mountains—not far from where Sheridan, Marcus, and Shamus's story will unfold.

Watch for *Everlasting* at your Christian bookstore in the spring of 1996. Also, if you would like to receive my semiannual newsletter—telling about my books in progress, research trips, and writing and publishing tidbits—please write to me at the address on the next page.

I'll love hearing from you.

Blessings always,

Amanda MacLean

Amanda MacLean
c/o Palisades
P.O. Box 1720
Sisters, Oregon 97759

Palisades...Pure Romance

Refuge, Lisa Tawn Bergren
Torchlight, Lisa Tawn Bergren
Treasure, Lisa Tawn Bergren
Secrets, Robin Jones Gunn
Sierra, Shari MacDonald
Westward, Amanda MacLean
Glory, Marilyn Kok
Love Song, Sharon Gillenwater
Cherish, Constance Colson
Whispers, Robin Jones Gunn
Angel Valley, Peggy Darty
Stonehaven, Amanda MacLean
Antiques, Sharon Gillenwater (September)
A Christmas Joy, Darty, Gillenwater, MacLean (October)

Titles and dates are subject to change.

THE PALISADES LINE

Treasure, Lisa Tawn Bergren
ISBN 0-88070-725-9
She arrived on the Caribbean island of Robert's Foe armed with a lifelong dream—to find her ancestor's sunken ship—and yet the only man who can help her stands stubbornly in her way. Can Christina and Mitch find their way to the ship *and* to each other?

Secrets, Robin Jones Gunn
ISBN 0-88070-721-6
Seeking a new life as an English teacher in a peaceful Oregon town, Jessica tries desperately to hide the details of her identity from the community...until she falls in love. Will the past keep Jessica and Kyle apart forever?

Sierra, Shari MacDonald
ISBN 0-88070-726-7
When spirited photographer Celia Randall travels to eastern California for a short-term assignment, she quickly is drawn to—and locks horns with—editor Marcus Stratton. Will lingering heartaches destroy Celia's chance at true love? Or can she find hope and healing high in the *Sierra*?

Westward, Amanda MacLean
ISBN 0-88070-751-8
Running from a desperate fate in the South toward an unknown future in the West, plantation-born artist Juliana St. Clair finds herself torn between two men, one an undercover agent with a heart of gold, the other a man with evil intentions and a smooth facade. Witness Juliana's dangerous travels toward faith and love as she follows God's lead in this powerful historical novel.

Glory, Marilyn Kok
ISBN 0-88070-754-2
To Mariel Forrest, the teaching position in Taiwan provided more than a simple escape from grief; it also offered an opportunity to deal with her feelings toward the God she once loved, but ultimately blamed for the deaths of her family. Once there, Mariel dares to ask the timeless question: "If God is good, why do we suffer?" What follows is an inspiring story of love, healing, and renewed confidence in God's goodness.

Love Song, Sharon Gillenwater
ISBN 0-88070-747-X
When famous country singer Andrea Carson returns to her hometown to recuperate from a life-threatening illness, she seeks nothing more than a respite from

the demands of stardom that have sapped her creativity and ability to perform. It's Andi's old high school friend Wade Jamison who helps her to realize that she needs inner healing as well. As Andi's strength grows, so do her feelings for the rancher who has captured her heart. But can their relationship withstand the demands of her career? Or will their romance be as fleeting as a beautiful *Love Song*?

Cherish, Constance Colson
ISBN 0-88070-802-6
Recovering from the heartbreak of a failed engagement, Rose Anson seeks refuge at a resort on Singing Pines Island, where she plans to spend a peaceful summer studying and painting the spectacular scenery of international Lake of the Woods. But when a flamboyant Canadian and a big-hearted American compete for her love, the young artist must face her past—and her future. What follows is a search for the source and meaning of true love: a journey that begins in the heart and concludes in the soul.

Whispers, Robin Jones Gunn
ISBN 0-88070-755-0
Teri Moreno went to Maui eager to rekindle a romance. But when circumstances turn out to be quite different than she expects, she finds herself spending a great deal of time with a handsome, old high school crush who now works at a local resort. But the situation becomes more complicated when Teri meets Gordon, a clumsy, endearing Australian with a wild past, and both men begin to pursue her. Will Teri respond to God's gentle urgings toward true love? The answer lies in her response to the gentle *Whispers* in her heart.

Angel Valley, Peggy Darty
ISBN 0-88070-778-X
When teacher Laurel Hollingsworth accepts a summer tutoring position for a wealthy socialite family, she faces an enormous challenge in her young student, Anna Lisa Wentworth. However, the real challenge is ahead of her: hanging on to her heart when older brother Matthew Wentworth comes to visit. Soon Laurel and Matthew find that they share a faith in God...and powerful feelings for one another. Can Laurel and Matthew find time to explore their relationship while she helps the emotionally troubled Anna Lisa and fights to defend her love for the beautiful *Angel Valley*?

Stonehaven, Amanda MacLean
ISBN 0-88070-757-7
Picking up in the years following *Westward*, *Stonehaven* follows Callie St. Clair back to the South where she has returned to reclaim her ancestral home. As she works to win back the plantation, the beautiful and dauntless Callie turns it into a station on the Underground Railroad. Covering her actions by playing the role

of a Southern belle, Callie risks losing Hawk, the only man she has ever loved. Readers will find themselves quickly drawn into this fast-paced novel of treachery, intrigue, spiritual discovery, and unexpected love.

Antiques, Sharon Gillenwater (September)
ISBN 0-88070-801-8
Deeply wounded by the infidelity of his wife, widower Grant Adams swore off all women—until meeting charming antiques dealer Dawn Carson. Although he is drawn to her, Grant struggles to trust again. Dawn finds herself overwhelmingly attracted to the darkly brooding cowboy, but won't marry a non-believer. As Grant learns more about her faith, he is touched by its impact on her life and finally accepts Christ, and together they work through Grant's inability to trust.

A Christmas Joy, MacLean, Darty, Gillenwater (October)
ISBN 0-88070-780-1 (same length as other Palisades books)
Snow falls, hearts change, and love prevails! In this compilation, three experienced Palisades authors spin three separate novelettes centering around the Christmas season and message:
By Amanda MacLean: A Christmas pageant coordinator in a remote mountain village of Northern California meets a spirited concert pianist.
By Peggy Darty: A college skiclub reunion brings together model Heather Grant and an old flame. Will they gain a new understanding?
By Sharon Gillenwater: A chance meeting in an airport that neither of them could forget...and a Christmas reunion.

PALISADES BACKLIST

Refuge, Lisa Tawn Bergren
ISBN 0-88070-621-X
Part One: A Montana rancher and a San Francisco marketing exec—only one incredible summer and God could bring such diverse lives together. *Part Two:* Lost and alone, Emily Walker needs and wants a new home, a sense of family. Can one man lead her to the greatest Father she could ever want and a life full of love?

Torchlight, Lisa Tawn Bergren
ISBN 0-88070-806-9
When beautiful heiress Julia Rierdon returns to Maine to remodel her family's estate, she finds herself torn between the man she plans to marry and unexpected feelings for a mysterious wanderer who threatens to steal her heart.